STUDIES IN THE DEAD SEA Sc

M000251532

Peter W. Flint, Martin G. Abegg Jr., and Florentino García Martínez,
General Editors

The Dead Sea Scrolls have been the object of intense interest in recent years, not least because of the release of previously unpublished texts from Qumran Cave 4 since the fall of 1991. With the wealth of new documents that have come to light, the field of Qumran studies has undergone a renaissance. Scholars have begun to question the established conclusions of the last generation; some widely held beliefs have withstood scrutiny, but others have required revision or even dismissal. New proposals and competing hypotheses, many of them of an uncritical and sensational nature, vie for attention. Idiosyncratic and misleading views of the Scrolls still abound, especially in the popular press, while the results of solid scholarship have yet to make their full impact. At the same time, the scholarly task of establishing reliable critical editions of the texts is nearing completion. The opportunity is ripe, therefore, for directing renewed attention to the task of analysis and interpretation.

STUDIES IN THE DEAD SEA SCROLLS AND RELATED LITERATURE is a series designed to address this need. In particular, the series aims to make the latest and best Dead Sea Scrolls scholarship accessible to scholars, students, and the thinking public. The volumes that are projected — both monographs and collected essays — will seek to clarify how the Scrolls revise and help shape our understanding of the formation of the Bible and the historical development of Judaism and Christianity. Various offerings in the series will explore the reciprocally illuminating relationships of several disciplines related to the Scrolls, including the canon and text of the Hebrew Bible, the richly varied forms of Second Temple Judaism, and the New Testament. While the Dead Sea Scrolls constitute the main focus, several of these studies will also include perspectives on the Old and New Testaments and other ancient writings — hence the title of the series. It is hoped that these volumes will contribute to a deeper appreciation of the world of early Judaism and Christianity and of their continuing legacy today.

PETER W. FLINT
MARTIN G. ABEGG JR.
FLORENTINO GARCÍA MARTÍNEZ

SERIES OF STUDIES ON THE ANCIENT PERIOD
OF YAD BEN-ZVI PRESS

THE DAVID AND JEMIMA JESELSOHN LIBRARY

THE DEAD SEA SCROLLS
and the
HASMONEAN STATE

Hanan Eshel

WILLIAM B. EERDMANS PUBLISHING COMPANY

GRAND RAPIDS, MICHIGAN / CAMBRIDGE, U.K.

YAD BEN-ZVI PRESS

JERUSALEM, ISRAEL

Published jointly 2008 by
Wm. B. Eerdmans Publishing Co.
2140 Oak Industrial Drive N.E., Grand Rapids, Michigan 49505 /
P.O. Box 163, Cambridge CB3 9PU U.K.
and by
Yad Ben-Zvi Press
P.O. Box 7660, Jerusalem, 91076, Israel

Printed in the United States of America

13 12 11 10 09 08   7 6 5 4 3 2 1

Library of Congress Cataloging-in-Publication Data

Eshel, Hanan.
[Megilot Kumran veha-medinah ha-Hashmona'it. English]
The Dead Sea scrolls and the Hasmonean state / Hanan Eshel.
p.   cm.   — (Studies in the Dead Sea scrolls and related literature)
Includes bibliographical references and index.
ISBN 978-0-8028-6285-3 (pbk. : alk. paper)
1. Dead Sea scrolls. 2. Maccabees — History — Sources.   I. Title.
BM487.E83513 2008
296.1′55 — dc22
2008021422

Designed and typeset by Keterpress Enterprises, Jerusalem

Contents

Preface

In 1987, I attended a conference organized by Yad Izhak Ben-Zvi, the University of Haifa, and Tel Aviv University in commemoration of the 40th anniversary of the discovery of the first Dead Sea Scrolls. At this conference, Professor Carol Newsom of Emory University lectured about a scroll from Cave 4 that contained an actualizing interpretation (a pesher) of Joshua's curse on whomever would rebuild Jericho: "At the cost of his firstborn he shall lay its foundation, and at the cost of his youngest he shall set up its gates" (Josh 6:26). The pesher asserted that the curse had fallen upon the "Man of Belial" who had rebuilt Jericho and appointed his two sons to succeed him. At the conference, I informed Prof. Newsome that her observations could be corroborated by evidence from archaeological excavations conducted in Jericho by Prof. Ehud Netzer who had recently uncovered an agricultural estate and palace complex built by John Hyrcanus, who ruled over Judaea between 134 and 104 B.C.E. I also pointed out that according to Josephus, Hyrcanus' two sons who had succeeded him died within less than a year. Prof. Newsom thanked me for the information, but went on to say that she had no archaeological training. Although I tried to convince her that such archaeological data is within anyone's reach, she persisted in maintaining that she did not have the necessary skills to deal with it critically. After the conference, I called Prof. Ehud Netzer and with much excitement told him about the scroll, Josephus' account, and how it all fit in perfectly with his archaeological findings. I suggested writing an article together with him, demonstrating how his excavations at Jericho illuminated the pesher's application of Joshua's curse on John Hyrcanus and the death of his two sons. Prof. Netzer, however, protested that he had no background in the Dead Sea Scrolls. In the end, I wrote the article myself.

This story illustrates that Dead Sea Scroll scholars are generally uninformed about current archaeological findings, and archaeologists tend to be unaware of the contents of the scrolls. Consequently there is room for both sides to inform each other's field. In time, I learned that the situation is even more complicated, as I describe in the introduction. It is not just that Qumran scholars are unaware of archaeological finds, but they further avoid dealing with the historical kernels imbedded in the scrolls. On the other hand, historians frequently fail to take the scrolls into consideration. The present book is an effort to integrate the disciplines of archaeology, history, and Qumran studies, demonstrating how the Qumran scrolls can contribute to our understanding of the Hasmonean Period.

This book was written over an extended period of time. I began writing it in 1998 when I was a visiting lecturer in Late Second Temple Judaism at Harvard Divinity School, although most of it was written in Jerusalem. I wish to thank my students at Bar Ilan University and at Harvard with whom I first shared my thoughts about the historical data I felt could be gleaned from the scrolls. Also deserving thanks are the librarians of the Judaica Reading Room at the Jewish National Library on the Givat Ram campus of the Hebrew University in Jerusalem, who make it the most conducive place in the world for academic research in the field of Jewish Studies. I would also like to express my gratitude to many others who assisted me over the years as I wrote this book. First and foremost are my own mentors, Prof. Daniel R. Schwartz and the late Professor David Flusser, with whom I discussed most of what I have written here. Even though they did not always agree with me, they nevertheless willingly shared their thoughts with me and encouraged me to publish my own ideas.

In 1999, Dr. David and Jemima Jeselsohn decided to establish The David and Jemima Jeselsohn epigraphic Center of Jewish History at Bar Ilan University, and invited me to serve as Chair of the center. With time, Jemima and David have become dear friends, and today it is hard to imagine how I would have been able to invest so much time and effort in academic research without their help. I take this opportunity to express my sincere thanks to them.

Dr. Esti Eshel is my partner and companion in many ways, including her dedication to Dead Sea Scrolls research. Without her constant encouragement and unwavering support, I would not have been able to finish this book. Anyone who reads chapters one and five will realize how much she has contributed to this research. I am convinced that by our joint effort we have accomplished more than the sum of what we could have done had we worked independently. I pray that our collaboration will last many more years.

The Hebrew version of this book was published by Yad Izhak Ben-Zvi in 2004. I would like to thank its director Dr. Zvi Zameret for having followed the book's progress and encouraging me to publish it under their auspices, as well as Yohai Goell, of the Yad Ben-Zvi Press, who labored with much skill and dedication to bring the English version to completion. I am greatly indebted to the staff of the pre-press department of Keterpress Enterprises in Jerusalem for their meticulous efforts towards publication. I express my grateful thanks to the publishers of the copyrighted translations from which I have quoted for permission to do so.

In 2005, David Louvish began translating the book into English. After completing the first three chapters, he suffered a stroke and was unfortunately unable to finish the task (I take this opportunity to wish him a complete recovery.) The last six chapters were therefore translated by Aryeh Amihay. Thereafter, Merle Brenner, my friend from the University of Michigan, volunteered her time to read the manuscript and improve its style. Finally, my student Dr. Brian Schultz took upon himself the job of checking for consistency of style in the footnotes as well as bringing the project to its end. To all I express my deepest thanks.

This book is dedicated to Esti Eshel, who by her optimism is responsible for its completion and publication.

Hanan Eshel

Diacritical Marks, Sigla, and Abbreviations

Abbreviations of journals, reference works, and other secondary sources generally conform to the "Instructions for Contributors" in the *Membership Directory and Handbook* of the Society of Biblical Literature (1994) 223–40. For abbreviations of Qumran sigla, see J. A. Fitzmyer, *The Dead Sea Scrolls: Major Publications and Tools for Study*, rev. ed. (SBLRBS 20; Atlanta: Scholars Press, 1990) 1–8.

Diacritical Marks and Sigla

[Daniel]	The bracketed word is no longer extant but has been restored.
Da[niel]	The bracketed part of the word has been restored.
[דני]אל	As above.
Da^{n}iel	A supralinear letter has inserted by the copyist or another scribe.
to (his) throne	The parenthetical word has been added to improve the English translation.
[ ] or [...]	There is a space between fragments or the surface of the leather is missing.
]...[	Letters (in this case three) with ink traces remaining, that cannot be identified.
" "	A quotation of a biblical verse in the Pesharim.
< >	Letters or words that were erased in antiquity.
frg. 10 ii 4–5	Fragment 10, column 2, lines 4–5.

Abbreviations

AB	Anchor Bible
Ant.	Josephus, *Jewish Antiquities*
BA	*Biblical Archaeologist*
BAIAS	*Bulletin of the Anglo-Israel Archaeological Society*
BAR	*Biblical Archaeology Review*
BASOR	*Bulletin of the American Schools of Oriental Research*
BETL	Bibliotheca ephemeridum theologicarum lovaniensium
BHS	Biblia Hebraica Stuttgartensia
BIS	Biblical Interpretation Series
BZAW	Beihefte zur *Zeitschrift für die Alttestamentliche Wissenschaft*
CBQ	*Catholic Biblical Quarterly*
CD	Cairo Damascus Document
DJD	*Discoveries in the Judaean Desert*
DSD	*Dead Sea Discoveries*
HTR	*Harvard Theological Review*
HUCA	*Hebrew Union College Annual*
ICC	International Critical Commentary
IEJ	*Israel Exploration Journal*
INJ	*Israel Numismatic Journal*
JAOS	*Journal of the American Oriental Society*
JBL	*Journal of Biblical Literature*
JJS	*Journal of Jewish Studies*
JQR	*Jewish Quarterly Review*
JSOT	*Journal for the Study of the Old Testament*
JSOTSup	*Journal for the Study of the Old Testament,* Supplement
JSP	*Journal for the Study of the Pseudepigrapha*
JSPSup	*Journal for the Study of the Pseudepigrapha,* Supplement
JSJ	*Journal for the Study of Judaism in the Persian, Hellenistic and Roman Periods*
JSS	*Journal of Semitic Studies*
J.W.	Josephus, *Jewish War*
MMT	מקצת מעשי התורה
OTL	Old Testament Library
OTS	*Oudtestamentische Studiën*
PEQ	*Palestine Exploration Quarterly*
RB	*Revue Biblique*

RQ	*Revue de Qumran*
SBLRBS	Society of Biblical Literature Resources for Biblical Studies
SCI	*Scripta Classica Israelica*
STDJ	Studies on the Texts of the Desert of Judah
VT	*Vetus Testamentum*
VTSup	*Vetus Testamentum*, Supplement
ZAW	*Zeitschrift für die Alttestamentliche Wissenschaft*

Introduction

The discovery of the Dead Sea scrolls marked the beginning of a new era in the scholarship of the Second Temple period. In this book I have attempted to summarize the contribution of the scrolls to the understanding of the political history of the Hasmonean state. Some 900 scrolls were found in 11 different caves around Qumran between 1947 and 1956. Twenty of these scrolls were preserved in reasonable condition, while most were represented only by small fragments which survived the hazards of time and insects. Most of the fragments were found in Cave 4, situated west of Khirbet Qumran, which contained more than 16,000 fragments belonging to some 600 scrolls. The scrolls primarily include religious texts, such as manuscripts of the Hebrew Bible, Greek and Aramaic translations of the Hebrew Bible, traditions about biblical figures, commentaries on biblical texts, and collections of laws and prayers.[1] These texts carry great significance for the reconstruction of the religious history of Judaea during the Second Temple period, but it is hard to extract information from them on the political history of the period. In the sixty years that have passed since the first scrolls were discovered, hundreds of books and thousands of articles have been written to address the various aspects of the most important archaeological discovery in the Land of Israel,[2] but no book has been written focusing on the

---

1   See A. S. van der Woude, "Fifty Years of Qumran Research," in *The Dead Sea Scrolls after Fifty Years*, vol. 1 (ed. P. W. Flint and J. C. VanderKam; Leiden, Boston, and Köln: Brill, 1998) 1–45.

2   According to Yigael Yadin, "The Dead Sea Scrolls are undoubtedly the most important discovery found in Israel in the field of the Bible, and the history of Judaism and Christianity" (*The Message of the Scrolls* [New York: Crossroad, 1962] 30). The bibliography of publications relating to

1

contribution of the Dead Sea scrolls to the understanding of the political history of the Hasmonean State during the Second Temple period.

A considerable number of the Dead Sea scrolls were composed by authors who belonged to a religious sect that believed they were living in the eschaton, the eve of the Day of the Lord.[3] These authors composed contemporizing commentaries on biblical texts which are called pesharim. These pesharim were written from a point of view that salvation was near, and included exegesis of biblical texts from the Prophets and the Psalms by sectarian authors, who construed the words of the prophets to refer to the Second Temple period. The authors sought to prove that since the prophets' words were fulfilled in their times, the description of the eschaton in those biblical texts would also soon be fulfilled. The authors of Qumran concealed their precise intent, perhaps because they feared harm if their views were known, or because they wanted only the members of the sect to be able to understand their works. Therefore, the pesharim do not mention names of historical figures who had an impact on the sect's history. Rather than using clear identifiers, the authors of the pesharim referred to these figures by pseudonyms or aliases. Thus, the authors did not state the given name of the priest who led the sect and who instructed his followers on the interpretation of the words of the prophets, but referred to him as the Teacher of Righteousness. They also did not mention the name of the priest who persecuted him (the Teacher of Righteousness) and who tried to kill him on the Day of Atonement but designated him as the Wicked Priest. Other political leaders of Judaea were referred to as the Man of Belial and the Lion of Wrath. The followers of the Teacher of Righteousness were named Judah, the Pharisees were called Ephraim or the "Seekers After Smooth Things," and the Sadducees were Manasseh.[4] The leader of the Pharisees who debated with the

---

the scrolls since their discovery to 2000 has been compiled in four volumes: W. S. LaSor, *Bibliography of the Dead Sea Scrolls 1948–1957* (Pasadena: Fuller Theological Seminary, 1958); B. Jongeling, *A Classified Bibliography of the Finds in the Desert of Judah 1958–1969* (Leiden: Brill, 1971); F. García-Martínez and D. W. Parry, *A Bibliography of the Finds in the Desert of Judah 1970–1995* (STDJ 19; Leiden, New York, and Köln: Brill, 1996); A. Pinnick, *The Orion Center Bibliography of the Dead Sea Scrolls 1995–2000* (Leiden, Boston, and Köln: Brill, 2001).

3   On the distinction between sectarian texts and texts brought to Qumran from elsewhere, see D. Dimant, "The Qumran Manuscripts: Contents and Significance," in *Time to Prepare the Way in the Wilderness* (ed. D. Dimant and L. H. Schiffman; STDJ 16; Leiden, New York, and Köln: Brill, 1995) 23–58.

4   On the usage of these terms, see J. D. Amoussine, "Éphraïm et Manassé dans le Péshèr de Nahum (4 Q p Nahum)," *RQ* 4 (1963) 389–96; A. Dupont-Sommer, "Le Commentaire de Nahum découvert près de la Mer Morte (4Q p Nah): Traduction et notes," *Semitica* 13 (1963) 55–88;

Teacher of Righteousness was named the Man of Lies.[5] Precisely because the authors of the pesharim succeeded so admirably in writing their commentaries while creating ambiguity about the names of the historical figures, scholars have been debating the identification of some of these men for the past sixty years.[6] Those pseudonyms were documented separately from the pesharim in the Damascus Document which incorporates historical details regarding the history of the sect.

Although approximately 900 scrolls were found in Qumran, but as a consequence of the authors' avoidance of proper names in their writings, only ten scrolls mention a known historical figure by name.[7] These scrolls identify the following Jewish leaders: Onias (probably one of the High Priests who served in the Jerusalem Temple prior to the Hasmonean Revolt),[8] Jonathan and Simeon (probably the sons of Mattathias), John (probably John Hyrcanus I), King Jonathan (who should be identified as Alexander Jannaeus), Salamzion, and Hyrcanus. The scrolls also mention Antiochus and Demetrius (both were Seleucid kings), Ptolemy (who might be one of the Ptolemaic rulers), and Aemilius, a Roman general whose full name was Marcus Aemilius Scaurus and who was appointed by Pompey as the governor of Syria in 63 B.C.E. The scrolls note a certain Potlais, probably a Jewish officer who commanded a military unit in Judaea between 57 to 53 B.C.E. In this book I will discuss in detail the scrolls which mention these dozen figures.[9] Their activity spans over a hundred

---

Y. Yadin, "Pesher Nahum (4Q pNahum) Reconsidered," *IEJ* 21 (1971) 8, n. 2; D. Flusser, "Pharisäer, Sadduzäer und Essener im Pescher Nahum," in *Qumran: Wege der Forschung* (ed. K. E. Grözinger; Darmstadt: Wissenschaftliche Buchgesellschaft, 1981) 121–66.

5   On the "Seekers After Smooth Things" and the "Man of Lie," see J. C. VanderKam, "Those Who Look for Smooth Things: Pharisees and Oral Law," in *Emanuel: Studies in Hebrew Bible, Septuagint and Dead Sea Scrolls in Honor of Emanuel Tov* (ed. S. M. Paul, R. A. Kraft, L. H. Schiffman and W. W. Fields; VTSup 94; Leiden and Boston: Brill, 2003) 465–77 and the bibliography listed there.

6   For a brief survey see J. H. Charlesworth, *The Pesharim and Qumran History* (Grand Rapids and Cambridge: Eerdmans, 2002) 30–37.

7   These ten scrolls are: a scroll labeled "*Pseudo-Daniel*" (4Q245), four *Annalistic Scrolls* (4Q331–333 and 4Q468e), the *Prayer for the Welfare of King Jonathan* (4Q448), the *Pesher on Nahum* (4Q169), a fragment mentioning Ptolemy (4Q578), a text related to the book of Ezekiel which may have a mention of Jonathan (4Q523), and a financial document from the first century C.E. (4Q348). On the financial documents found at Qumran, see n. 9 below.

8   During the third and second centuries B.C.E., four High Priests named Onias served in the Temple in Jerusalem. These priests should be distinguished from Onias who made the rain fall. The latter lived during the first century B.C.E.; he will be discussed in chapter seven.

9   The vast majority of the Dead Sea scrolls are literary compositions, though there are

3

years, from the middle of the second century B.C.E. (Onias and Antiochus) to the mid-first century B.C.E. (Aemilius and Potlais). The basic assumption of this study is that the pseudonyms in the pesharim and in the Damascus Document refer to historical figures of the same period. I will attempt to identify these figures through a reconstruction of the political history of Judaea during the Hasmonean period (170 B.C.E. to 48 B.C.E.).

The book consists of nine chapters. The first eight chapters are arranged in chronological order. They discuss various historical events reflected in the scrolls beginning with the circumstances which led to the outbreak of the Hasmonean revolt in 167 B.C.E. and ending with the assassination of Pompey on the shores of Egypt in 48 B.C.E.. In the ninth chapter, I offer an explanation as to why we do not find in the scrolls any allusions to historical events which occurred after 48 B.C.E. Six chapters of this book are based on historical allusions within the sectarian scrolls, those composed by members of the Qumran sect. The other three chapters discuss historical allusions documented in scrolls which are not sectarian, but were probably brought to Qumran from various places in Judaea.

Our historical knowledge of the Hasmonean state relies on subjective and arguably prejudicial accounts. Second Maccabees is an abridgement of a five-volume composition by Jason of Cyrene on Judas Maccabeus.[10] Jason described the events that took place in Jerusalem and Judaea from 175 B.C.E. to the victory of Judas Maccabeus over Nicanor in 161 B.C.E. It recounts only the period of Judas Maccabeus.[11]

First Maccabees is an account of the events in Judaea between 167–134 B.C.E. and was composed by one of the allies of Simeon, the son of Mattathias. He compiled the history in order to establish the rule of Simeon and his son John Hyrcanus as leaders of Judaea.[12] First Maccabees opens with the description of

---

seven financial documents discovered among them. One of the documents (4Q438) seems to mention a "Joseph son of Cam]ydus," a High Priest who served in 46 and 47 C.E. Since this is an economic document and not a literary composition I will not discuss this document here. For a further discussion of this document, see H. Eshel, "4Q348, 4Q343 and 4Q345: Three Economic Documents from Qumran Cave 4?" *JJS* 52 (2001) 132–35; J. C. VanderKam, *From Joshua to Caiaphas* (Minneapolis: Fortress, 2004) 454–55.

10 On Jason of Cyrene, see J. A. Goldstein, *II Maccabees* (AB; Garden City, NY: Doubleday, 1983) 55–70.

11 On the date of 2 Maccabees, see Goldstein, *II Maccabees*, 71–83; D. R. Schwartz, *The Second Book of Maccabees* (Jerusalem: Ben-Zvi, 2004) 16–19, 289–95 (Hebrew).

12 On the date of 1 Maccabees, see A. Momigliano, "The Date of the First Book of Maccabees," in *L'Italie préromaine et la Rome républicaine: Mélanges offerts à Jacques Heurgon* (ed. A. Balland, M. Gras, and P. Gros; Collections de l'École française de Rome 27; Rome: École française de

the events of 167 B.C.E., the religious decrees and Mattathias' actions. The battles of Judas Maccabeus are detailed at length, while the political achievements of Jonathan are described in brief. A rather long account is dedicated to the election of Simeon, the son of Mattathias, by a "Great Assembly of Jews" to be the High Priest and the leader of the people of Judaea. The book concludes with the assassination of Simeon by Ptolemy his son-in-law, the son of Abubu, in 134 B.C.E. in Jericho. The historical details provided in 1 Maccabees will contribute to the clarification of the events discussed in the first three chapters of this book.

The only accounts of the events in Judaea after 134 B.C.E. are provided by the writings of Josephus. Josephus recorded the history of the Hasmonean state twice: first in his book *The Jewish War against the Romans* (Book I), and second in *Jewish Antiquities* (Books XIII-XIV). *The Jewish War* was made public between 79–81 C.E.[13] While the book was intended to describe the war in Judaea from 66–73/4 C.E., Josephus realized that he could not begin his book without describing the events in Judaea prior to the revolt, so he began *The Jewish War* with an account of the conflicts in Jerusalem which led up to the Hasmonean revolt during the 70's of the second-century B.C.E. Book I of *The Jewish War* and the first part of Book II may be viewed as an introduction that describes the 240 years that preceded the events which Josephus wished to describe in *The Jewish War*.

Josephus stated that he wrote *The Jewish War* in the language of his homeland, referring probably to Aramaic or Hebrew. He described sending *The Jewish War* to people residing in the upper Tigris region (*J.W.*, 1.3), meaning the Jews of Babylon. If we accept this testimony, we must assume that after writing *The Jewish War* in Aramaic or Hebrew, Josephus translated his book into Greek. He wrote that he had assistants to improve the Greek style of the book (*Ag. Ap.*, 1.50).[14] Josephus also wrote that Titus wanted the Romans to learn of the war in Judaea through *The Jewish War* and the emperor gave it his

Rome, 1976) 657–61; B. Bar-Kochva, *Judas Maccabaeus* (Cambridge: Cambridge University Press, 1989) 151–70; S. Schwartz, "Israel and the Nations Roundabout: I Maccabees and the Hasmonean Expansion," *JJS* 42 (1991) 16–38.

13 M. Stern, "Josephus and the Roman Empire as Reflected in *The Jewish War*," in *Josephus, Judaism and Christianity*, (ed. L. H. Feldman and G. Hata; Detroit: Wayne State University, 1987) 71–80, esp. n. 9; C. P. Jones, "Towards a Chronology of Josephus," *SCI* 21 (2002) 113–14. On the possibility that Book VII was composed at a later period, see S. Schwartz, "The Composition and Publication of Josephus's *Bellum Iudaicum* Book 7," *HTR* 79 (1986) 373–86.

14 On Josephus' assistants, see H. St. J. Thackeray, *Josephus: The Man and the Historian* (New York: Jewish Institute of Religion, 1929) 100–24; T. Rajak, *Josephus: The Historian and His Society*, 2nd ed. (Avon: Bookcraft, 2002) 233–36.

signature of approval and commanded its publication (*Life*, 363). *The Jewish War* is a coherent composition written in the best tradition of Greek literature, filled with pathos. It reflects Josephus' view of the war, namely that resulted in a catastrophe for his people.[15] The contradictions in the book are the result of the author's complex situation: while he had previously been a leader of the rebels, at the time of writing the book, he had become a propagandist and a released slave of the emperors who destroyed Jerusalem. Even so, this did not influence the manner in which Josephus described the history of the Hasmoneans in Book I of *The Jewish War*, since these events took place before the Roman rule of the Land of Israel. Consequently, the reliability of the details provided by Josephus in describing the Hasmonean state in Book I of *The Jewish War* are determined more by the quality of the sources to which he had access while writing his book than by his own worldview.[16]

After Josephus completed *The Jewish War*, he turned to writing *Jewish Antiquities*. In this composition, he sought to describe the whole course of human history from the creation of the world up until 66 C.E.[17] Since during the writing of *Jewish Antiquities* he did not have Greek assistants to help him enhance his Greek style, he copied entire paragraphs of Greek sources available to him. For this reason, *Jewish Antiquities* is filled with contradictions.[18] Josephus completed *Jewish Antiquities* in the 13th year of Emperor Domitian, which is 93/94 C.E. (*Ant.*, 20.267).[19] In Book XII of *Jewish Antiquities*, Josephus discussed the Hasmonean revolt and concluded with the death of Judas Maccabeus in 160

---

15 Stern, "Josephus and the Roman Empire," 74–77.

16 See S. J. D. Cohen, *Josephus in Galilee and Rome* (Leiden: Brill, 1979) 44–47; Bar-Kochva, *Judas Maccabaeus*, 186–93.

17 On the question of the intended audience of *Jewish Antiquities*, see S. Mason, "Should Any Wish to Enquire Further (*Ant.* 1.25): The Aim and Audience of Josephus's *Judean Antiquities/ Life*," in *Understanding Josephus* (ed. idem; JSPSup 32; Sheffield: Sheffield Academic Press, 1998) 64–103.

18 On the literary difference between *The Jewish War*, a sophisticated coherent work, and the eclectic character of *Jewish Antiquities*, see D. R. Schwartz, "On Drama and Authenticity in Philo and Josephus", *SCI* 10 (1989/90) 120–29; L. Ullmann and J. J. Price, "Drama and History in Josephus' *Bellum Judaicum*," *SCI* 21 (2002) 109–11 and the bibliography listed in these studies.

19 It is possible that Josephus postponed making *Jewish Antiquities* public until after the death of Agrippa II. We know that *Jewish Antiquities* had earlier editions which were improved later on; see J. Sievers, "Josephus, First Maccabees, Sparta, the Three *Haireseis* – and Cicero," *JSJ* 32 (2001) 241-51. On the difference between the pessimistic worldview Josephus held while writing *The Jewish War* and the worldview reflected in *Jewish Antiquities* see H. Eshel, "Josephus' View on Judaism without the Temple in Light of the Discoveries at Masada and Murabba'at," in *Community without Temple* (ed. B. Ego, A. Lange and P. Pilhofer; Tübingen: Mohr Siebeck, 1999) 229–38.

B.C.E.. In Book XIII, he dealt with the history of the Hasmonean state. Some of the sources used by Josephus to write Books XII and XIII are available to us today. For example, he relied on the *Letter of Aristeas* when he described the translation of the Pentateuch into Greek during the time of Ptolemy II,[20] and on 1 Maccabees when he wrote about the actions of Mattathias, Judas Maccabeus, and Jonathan. A comparison of the account in 1 Maccabees with *Jewish Antiquities* sheds light both on Josephus' dependence on his sources, as well as on changes he made when employing these sources. These changes do not reflect additional historical knowledge, but rather his views of the Hasmonean period.[21]

The main source which Josephus used when writing the history of the Hasmonean state in *The Jewish War* I and *Jewish Antiquities* XIII was a Hellenistic composition of a historian hostile to the Hasmoneans, most particularly to Alexander Jannaeus. Though this composition has not survived, there is no doubt that it can be identified with the work of Nicolaus of Damascus, a friend and counselor of Herod.[22] Nicolaus was adversarial to the Hasmoneans because they fought the Hellenistic cities of Syria and opposed Herod who nonetheless managed to overthrow them after a bitter struggle. Nicolaus wrote his work in good Hellenistic tradition and stressed the dramatic nature of the events. Based on the accounts which Josephus used from Nicolaus' book, it is easy to see that Nicolaus was a supporter of the Hellenistic residents in the Land of Israel rather than of the Jews.[23]

In using Nicolaus' descriptions as the main source on the Hasmonean state in Book XIII of *Antiquities*, Josephus incorporated details he learned from

20 A. Pelletier, "Josephus, the Letter of Aristeas and the Septuagint," in *Josephus, the Bible, and History* (ed. L. H. Feldman and G. Hata; Detroit: Wayne State University Press, 1989) 229–38.

21 I. M. Gafni, "Josephus and I Maccabees," in *Josephus, the Bible, and History* (ed. L. H. Feldman and G. Hata; Detroit: Wayne State University Press, 1989) 116–31; L. H. Feldman, "Josephus' Portrayal of the Hasmoneans Compared with 1 Maccabees," in *Josephus and the History of the Greco-Roman Period* (ed. F. Parente and J. Sievers; Leiden, New York, and Köln: Brill, 1994) 41–68; J. Sievers, *Synopsis of the Greek Sources for the Hasmonean Period: 1-2 Maccabees and Josephus, War 1 and Antiquities 12-14* (Rome: Pontificio Instituto Biblico, 2001).

22 B. Z. Wacholder, *Nicolaus of Damascus* (Berkeley and Los Angeles: University of California Press, 1962) 4–6 and 14–36; E. Schürer, *The History of the Jewish People in the Age of Jesus Christ,* (3 vols.; rev. and ed. by G. Vermes and F. Millar; Edinburgh: T & T Clark, 1973–87) 1.28–32.

23 M. Stern, "Nicolaus of Damascus as a Source of Jewish History in the Herodian and Hasmonean Age," in *Bible and Jewish History* (ed. B. Uffenheimer; Givataim: Peli, 1972) 374–94 (Hebrew); B. Z. Wacholder, "Josephus and Nicolaus of Damascus," *in Josephus, the Bible, and History* (ed. L. H. Feldman, and G. Hata; Detroit: Wayne State University Press, 1989) 147–72.

other Hellenistic historians, such as Strabo and Timagenes for example, as well as details from Jewish sources, some of which are reflected in the rabbinic literature. Consequently, the depiction of the Hasmonean state in *Antiquities.* XIII is filled with contradictions, due to Josephus' reliance on compositions written by various authors with conflicting aims and conceptions of the Hasmoneans.[24] Since Josephus remains the only source which tells the history of the Hasmonean state and his writing includes many contradictions, any new sources which shed light on the history of the Hasmonean state carry profound significance. It for this reason that the historical allusions embedded in the Dead Sea scrolls are so important.

Prior to the discovery of the Dead Sea scrolls we had no historical sources of the Second Temple period written in Aramaic or Hebrew. All the major sources for the study of the Second Temple period were written in Greek, so most historians of the Second Temple period did not train themselves to work with sources in Semitic languages. When the Dead Sea scrolls were discovered, Old Testament scholars who specialized in Hebrew and Aramaic assumed the responsibility for the publication of the scrolls. Even today most of the scholars working on the Dead Sea scrolls are biblical scholars, with limited interest in the history of Judaea during the Second Temple period.

The 18 Continuous Pesharim,[25] which include most of the allusions to the political situation in Judaea during the Hasmonean period, were among the first scrolls to be published at a relatively early stage of Dead Sea scrolls scholarship. Scholarly interest in the historical allusions reflected in the scrolls began in 1950 when the *Pesher on Habakkuk* was published (one of the first seven scrolls found in Cave 1 in 1947), and it flourished in the 1950's and 1960's when the rest of the pesharim were published.[26] While the study of the historical allusions reflected in the scrolls was at the focus of scholarly discussion up to the 1980's, interest has faded for three main reasons. First, several prominent scholars stopped working on the pesharim.[27] Second, the publication of other texts from Cave 4 led most of

24 Schürer, *History of the Jewish People*, 1.48–52; Cohen, *Josephus in Galilee and Rome*, 48–51.

25 The "Continuous Pesharim" are commentaries in which a considerable biblical passage is interpreted according to its order, unlike the "Thematic Pesharim" in which several individual biblical verses are joined together to clarify a certain issue. The 18 Continuous Pesharim were re-edited and discussed by M. P. Horgan, *Pesharim: Qumran Interpretations of Biblical Books* (CBQ Monograph Series 8; Washington, D.C.: Catholic Biblical Association, 1975).

26 See J. A. Fitzmyer, "A Bibliographical Aid to the Study of the Qumran Cave IV Texts 158-186," *CBQ* 31 (1969) 59–71.

27 We shall mention four scholars who made a significant contribution to the study of

the Dead Sea scrolls scholars to focus on other aspects of the scrolls. And third, the shift in historical scholarship to discount sources of such a fragmentary nature that requires a tolerance for ambiguity in the consideration of content, context, and conclusion.[28] Therefore, most historians of the Second Temple period chose not to rely on the scrolls,[29] and the study of the historical allusions reflected in the scrolls, which was one of the most prolific fields of study in the first stage of the scrolls research, has been essentially neglected in recent years.[30] Any vacuum tends to be filled, and as conservative scholars declined to

the Continuous Pesharim and ceased working on these texts. Dennis Pardee wrote an important M.A. thesis on 4QpPs[a] and published an abbreviated version of it (D. Pardee, "A Restudy of the Commentary on Psalms 37 from Qumran Cave 4," *RQ* 8 [1973] 163–94). After the publication of this study, Pardee did not continue to work on the Dead Sea scrolls. Maurya Horgan published her Ph.D. dissertation as a book (*Pesharim: Qumran Interpretations of Biblical Books*) that remains to this day the most important study on these texts. Horgan too did not continue working on the scrolls. In 1984 Joseph Amusin passed away, a Dead Sea scrolls scholar who had taught at Leningrad and had made a highly important contribution towards the understanding of the historical allusions embedded in the Continuous Pesharim. For a summary of his work see J. D. Amusin, "The Reflection of Historical Events of the First Century B.C. in Qumran Commentaries (4Q161; 4Q169; 4Q166)," *HUCA* 48 (1977) 123–52. The delay in the publication of the Cave 4 texts led the Dominican scholar Jerome Murphy-O'Connor, who until then had considerably advanced our understanding of the history of the Qumran sect, to stop studying the scrolls and shift his interest to Pauline Studies. His contributions are summarized in his popular essay, J. Murphy-O'Connor, "The Essenes in Palestine," *BA* 40 (1977) 100–24.

28 For an example of the difficulty that lies in learning history from the Dead Sea scrolls, see D. Dimant, "Egypt and Jerusalem in Light of the Dualistic Doctrine at Qumran (4Q462)," *Meghillot* 1 (2003) 55–58 (Hebrew).

29 To a certain extent, the present study is a response to Phillip Callaway, whose Ph.D. dissertation has been published as a book (*The History of the Qumran Community* [JSPSup 3; Sheffield: Sheffield Academic Press, 1988]). In the name of scientific caution, Callaway dismissed most of the suggestions raised regarding the understanding of the historical allusions in the scrolls. According to him, when confronted with a dispute among scholars regarding the historical background of a text, one cannot determine which suggestion is more plausible than the other, making it impossible to deduce any historical conclusions from such a text. Two books were published on the pesharim in 2002. Timothy Lim's book is an example of such a tendency not to draw any historical conclusions from the scrolls (*Pesharim* [London and New York: Sheffield Academic Press, 2002] 64–78). By contrast, James Charlesworth (*The Pesharim and Qumran*) presented a more balanced approach, but only a small portion of his book deals with the historical aspects of the pesharim.

30 The three Continuous Pesharim which were preserved in a relatively good state are the *Pesher on Habakkuk*, the *Pesher on Nahum* and 4QpPs[a]. Recently, two books on the *Pesher on Nahum* were published, see: G. L. Doudna, *4Q Pesher Nahum: A Critical Edition* (JSPSup 35; Sheffield: Sheffield Academic Press, 2001); S. L. Berrin, *The Pesher Nahum Scroll from Qumran* (STDJ 53; Leiden and Boston: Brill, 2004). Incidentally, the *Pesher on Nahum* is the only pesher from Qumran that mentions historical figures by name. Note that Gregory Doudna also addresses

discuss the historical allusions reflected in the scrolls, a group of scholars trying to study Early Christianity from the Qumran scrolls argued that the pesharim described the life of Jesus and of other leaders of the Early Church.[31] These scholars ignored studies based on paleographic considerations and radiocarbon datings which showed that the scrolls with historical references should be dated to the second and first centuries B.C.E., decades before the consolidation of the Early Church.[32]

It is my view, now that all the Dead Sea scrolls found at Qumran have been published, that there is justification in collecting all the historical allusions reflected in the scrolls and discussing them anew, using them to elucidate and expand our understanding of the historical events which took place in Judaea during the Hasmonean period.

Most of the Dead Sea scrolls have survived only as small fragments, and this is true of the scrolls discussed in this book. Without the accounts of Josephus, it would be impossible to understand most of the historical allusions made in the scrolls. But in order to understand these historical allusions, one should study Josephus' descriptions and assess whether they correspond with what is found in the scrolls. Therefore, there is room for concern that this study could suffer from circular reasoning. Although I have read the scrolls reflectively in the context of Josephus' chronicling, I have sought to maintain a healthy degree of skepticism and analysis in weighing all the available resources.

When examining the historical credibility of the accounts in the writings of Josephus, there is no reason to disregard one's own judgment. Neither can

---

topics which are not directly related to the *Pesher on Nahum*, such as the identity of the Teacher of Righteousness and the Wicked Priest (who are not mentioned in the *Pesher on Nahum*) and the date when the scrolls were hidden in the caves. Unfortunately, many of Doudna's suggestions are implausible. By contrast, Shani Berrin's study is a significant contribution to the understanding of the *Pesher on Nahum*, focusing mainly on the inquiry of the relation between the interpreted verse and the exegesis offered to it.

31 Thus, for example, according to Barbara Thiering who considered the Wicked Priest to be the nickname of Jesus and the Teacher of Righteousness of John the Baptist; see B. E. Thiering, *Redating the Teacher of Righteousness* (Sydney: Theological Explorations, 1979). Robert Eisenman suggested that the Wicked Priest should be identified with Paul and that the Teacher of Righteousness is James; see R. H. Eisenman, *The Dead Sea Scrolls and the First Christians* (Shaftesbury: Dorset and Brisbane, 1996). Michael Wise argued that the Teacher of Righteousness should be identified as a first-century B.C.E. messianic figure, very similar to Jesus; see M. O. Wise, *The First Messiah: Investigating the Savior before Jesus* (San Francisco: Harper, 2000). For similar suggestions, see the discussion and bibliography in Charlesworth, *Pesharim and Qumran History*, 30–36.

32 See M. A. Knibb, "Teacher of Righteousness, " *Encyclopedia of the Dead Sea Scrolls* (2 vols.; ed. L. H. Schiffman and J. C. VanderKam; Oxford: Oxford University Press, 2000) 2.918–21.

there be an equal treatment of all his details, without first trying to determine which sources Josephus relied on. Only after trying to investigate his sources, is one able to consider the credibility of a certain description found in his writings. Even when the scrolls confirm certain details that appear in an account of Josephus, this does not prove that other details, found in the same account, are true. For example, the famous passage in the *Pesher on Nahum* which testifies that Alexander Jannaeus indeed executed Jews who invited Demetrius III to come and conquer Judaea (see chapter six for a discussion of these events), does not prove that Alexander executed exactly 800 people, nor that he massacred their families while he himself was watching. Another example (discussed in chapter three) shows that the people of Qumran interpreted Joshua's curse on the builder of Jericho to refer to John Hyrcanus I, who built the agricultural estate and the Hasmonean palace in Jericho. Josephus recounts that the two sons of John Hyrcanus, Aristobulus and Antigonus, died during 104 B.C.E. Joshua's curse on the builder of Jericho was associated with John Hyrcanus, and this probably supports that the two sons of John Hyrcanus did die within a short interval, but it cannot testify that the dramatic details concerning their death, which Josephus quotes from Nicolaus, are accurate. In other words, even if we are to accept that a passage from the scrolls confirms that the two sons of John Hyrcanus died in 104 B.C.E., we still should not accept the dramatic description of the servant, who was supposed to take out the vessel in which Aristobulus vomited blood, tripped and spilled it at exactly the place where Antigonus had been assassinated. The same is true for the last words which Aristobulus, according to Josephus, supposedly said before he died. Despite these qualifications, it seems that the examples brought in this study show that the scrolls do verify certain details in Josephus' writings about the history of the Hasmonean state.

Among the historians who studied the nine decades of Hasmonean rule of Judaea (152–63 B.C.E.), one finds opposing views regarding the significance of this period. Some considered the Hasmonean state to be a short and unimportant era while others considered this period of Jewish political independence as a critical historical period which determined the course of Jewish history to this day.[33] The present study does not pretend to portray a new historical picture of the Hasmonean period, but only to highlight certain details brought forth in the writings of Josephus that may be verified by the Dead Sea scrolls. The scrolls not only confirm some details, but also testify that we cannot completely dismiss

33 See Daniel Schwartz's preface to Menahem Stern, *Hasmonean Judea in the Hellenistic World: Chapters in Political History* (Jerusalem: Shazar, 1995) 16–20 (Hebrew).

all the negative accounts of the Hasmonean leaders. Though it seems that such descriptions originated in the writings of Nicolaus of Damascus who was hostile to the Hasmoneans, it appears that some of the details he provided were not completely groundless. It seems that the Dead Sea scrolls prove that we ought not to glorify the Hasmonean rulers, but rather regard the Hasmonean period as any other historical period with both its brighter and darker moments, nor ignore the fact that in most cases rulers do not meet the moral challenge posed by their position.[34]

This study is published upon the achievement of the publication of all of the recovered Dead Sea scrolls. Though it does not appear likely that additional scrolls will be found at Qumran, we still hope that with the aid of textual and archaeological findings in the future, whether at Qumran or elsewhere, we will be able to learn further details about the fascinating political history of the Hasmonean state. It is the continuous aim and burden of scholarship to confirm or refute, and fundamentally to refine, the hypotheses I am raising in this book.

34   See D. Flusser, "The Kingdom of Rome in the Eyes of the Hasmoneans and as Seen by the Essenes," *Zion* 48 (1983) 149–76 (Hebrew).

CHAPTER ONE

The Roots of the Hasmonean Revolt: The Reign of Antiochus IV

The historic events in Jerusalem from 169–167 B.C.E. which resulted in the oppressive decrees of Antiochus IV Epiphanes are shrouded in mystery. Our information about these events comes from five sources (1 Maccabees 1; 2 Maccabees 3–7; Dan 7–12; *J. W.* 1.31–35; *Ant.* 12.237–64) and scholars have long been divided as to Antiochus' motives. The texts offer three reasons for the Hasmonean Revolt: (a) the confiscation of the Temple treasures by Antiochus after his return from a military campaign in Egypt; (b) the capture of the city and the massacre of its people by an officer named Appollonius sent by Antiochus; (c) anti-religious edicts. Since there is no other documented case of anti-religious persecution in the Hellenistic period, scholars have proposed numerous explanations for Antiochus' actions.[1] Accordingly, any new historical source that might enhance our understanding of these events is of particular significance.

Antiochus IV undertook two military campaigns to Egypt, one in 170/169 B.C.E., and the other, in 168 B.C.E. During the first campaign he reached

---

1   See V. Tcherikover, "Antiochus Persecution of Judaism," in *Hellenistic Civilization and the Jews* (Philadelphia: Jewish Publication Society, 1959) 175–203; E. Bickerman, "The Maccabean Uprising: An Interpretation," in *The Jewish Expression* (ed. J. Goldin; New Haven and London: Yale University Press, 1976) 66–86; F. Millar, "The Background to the Maccabean Revolution: Reflections on Martin Hengel's *Judaism and Hellenism*," *JJS* 29 (1978) 1–21; J. A. Goldstein, *I Maccabees* (AB; Garden City, NY: Doubleday, 1981) 104–6; E. Gruen, "Hellenism and Persecution: Antiochus IV and the Jews," in *Hellenistic Society and Culture* (ed. P. Green; Hellenistic Culture and Society 9; Berkeley: University of California Press, 1993) 238–64; L. I. Levine, *Jerusalem: Portrait of the City in the Second Temple Period* (Philadelphia: Jewish Publication Society, 2002) 65–86; S. Weitzman, "Plotting Antiochus's Persecution," *JBL* 123 (2004) 219–34.

Memphis, where he crowned himself king of Egypt. He moved on to lay siege to Alexandria, but left after a few months before capturing the city. During the second campaign, he came within four miles of Alexandria, but was stopped there by a Roman delegation headed by Popilius Laenas, forcing him to retreat from Egypt back to Syria.[2] Following these two failures, Antiochus came to Jerusalem. This visit is described differently in the two books of Maccabees. One of the differences between the descriptions of the events leading up to the Hasmonean Revolt in 1 and 2 Maccabees concerns the question as to when Antiochus plundered the Temple treasures. According to 1 Maccabees, he did so after his first Egyptian campaign in 169 B.C.E. (1 Macc 16–25); but 2 Maccabees describes him coming to Jerusalem only after the second campaign in 168 B.C.E. (2 Macc 5:1–21). Most scholars accept the account in 1 Maccabees as being historically accurate.[3]

A small fragment of a scroll, discovered in Cave 4 and labeled 4Q248, is apparently a remnant of an apocalyptic work which offers a precise description of historical events in the early sixties of the second century B.C.E. (170–168 B.C.E.). This historical account was intended to convince the reader that the apocalyptic vision of what was expected to come after those events would also be fulfilled in due time.[4] The Greek king whose activities are described in 4Q248 is Antiochus IV. Since the work lacks the typical terminology of the sectarian scrolls, it was most likely brought to Qumran by a new member rather than written by the sect's scribes. The Tetragrammaton is denoted by five small diagonal lines.[5] The editors of this text have reconstructed the surviving passage of the work in the

2   O. Mørkholm, *Antiochus IV of Syria* (Copenhagen: Gyldalske Boghandel, 1966) 64–101.

3   See, for example, E. Schürer, *The History of the Jewish People in the Age of Jesus Christ* (rev. ed. by G. Vermes and F. Millar; Edinburgh: T. & T. Clark, 1973–87) 1.151–53; V. Tcherikover, "The Hellenistic Movement in Jerusalem and Antiochus' Persecution," in *The Hellenistic Age: Political History of Jewish Palestine from 332 B.C.E. to 67 B.C.E.* (ed. A. Schalit; The World History of the Jewish People 6; London: W. H. Allen, 1972) 132; D. Gera, *Judaea and Mediterranean Politics 219 to 161 B.C.E.* (Leiden, New York, and Köln: Brill, 1998) 153–57.

4   See J. Licht, "Time and Eschatology in Apocalyptic Literature and in Qumran," *JJS* 16 (1966) 177–82; idem, "Biblisches Geschichtsdenken und apokalyptische Spekulation," *Judaica* 46 (1990) 208–40.

5   The scroll was probably copied by one of the scribes of the Qumran sect, who altered two details in the process: he used these five diagonal lines to denote the Tetragrammaton (line 5), and referred to Jerusalem as the "Temple City" (line 7)—a designation documented in other sectarian writings, such as the *Damascus Document* and the *Temple Scroll*.

following manner:[6]

  2   [and he shall rule over] Egypt and Greece, and [against the God of]

  3   [God]s he shall exa[lt himself.] And so they will eat [the flesh of]

  4   their [so]ns and daughters in siege at [Alexandria.]

  5   [And] the Lord shall cau[se] (his) spirit to go through their lands, and he shall r[eturn from Alexandria]

  6   [and] come to Egypt and sell its land, and he shall com[e]

  7   to the Temple City and seize it and al[l its treasures,]

  8   and he shall overthrow lands of (foreign) nations and (then) return to Egyp[t.]

  9   And when the breaking of the power of the ho[ly] people [comes to an end, then

10 shall] all these things [be fulfilled. And] the Children of [Israel] shall repent...

Magen Broshi and Esther Eshel, who published the fragment, believe it to be a remnant of a composition similar to chapter 11 in the biblical Book of Daniel. It lists, very briefly and in chronological order, a series of events associated with Antiochus IV. These events took place in a short period—not more than three years—during the Sixth Syrian War, when Antiochus conducted his two Egyptian campaigns, in 170/169 and 168 B.C.E. The work was most probably written at the time of the events, but before it became clear that the situation in Jerusalem would not improve after Antiochus' second Egyptian campaign.

Broshi and Eshel discuss the events in chronological order. Line 2 seems to have been an introduction to the account of Antiochus' invasion of Egypt; all that remains are the two names Egypt and Greece. The original text may have described Antiochus' plan to occupy Egypt and Greece as noted in 1 Maccabees: "As soon as the kingdom was firmly in Antiochus' hands, he began to think of becoming king over the land of Egypt so as to rule over both empires" (1:16).

Lines 3–4 describe the siege of Alexandria.[7] Antiochus made two attempts to capture the city: first in 170/169 B.C.E., in a siege that lasted a few months; and again in 168 B.C.E., when Roman intervention forced him to retreat. Only the

     6   M. Broshi and E. Eshel, "The Greek King is Antiochus IV (4QHistorical Text= 4Q248)," *JJS* 48 (1997) 120–29; idem, "4QHistorical text A," in *Qumran Cave 4, XXVI: Miscellanea, Part I* (DJD 36; Oxford: Clarendon, 2000) 192–200.

     7   The Hebrew has been reconstructed as *No-amon,* which should be identified with Alexandria; see D. Dimant, *Qumran Cave 4:XII, Parabiblical Texts Part 4* (DJD 30; Oxford: Clarendon, 2001) 157; Eshel and Broshi, "The Greek King," 122.

first attempt involved a real siege of Alexandria. Since Alexandria's fortifications were too extensive to make a complete siege possible, and since its seaways remained open, it is unlikely that the people of the city were starved. The allusion to cannibalism during the siege may be regarded as an exaggeration, a false rumor, or a literary device. Dubious rumors were common during the Sixth Syrian War (as in any war), and the best known was the spurious report of Antiochus' death during his second Egyptian campaign (2 Macc 5:5).

In line 6 we read that Antiochus sold land in Egypt. Jerome, in his commentary on Dan 11:21, reported that Porphyry claimed Antiochus had crowned himself king of Egypt.[8] Epigraphic finds from Egypt have confirmed that Antiochus indeed called himself king of Egypt, and the title enabled him to sell Egyptian lands for cash. It is also known that in the second century B.C.E. there was a considerable demand for private land in Egypt. If so, 4Q248 has provided us with a new historical fact—that Antiochus sold land in Egypt. In turn, this helps us better understand Dan 11:39: "He will distribute land for a price": in all probability, it too is alluding to the sale of land in Judaea, just like the sale of Egyptian land reported in 4Q248. Moreover, it may also cast light on another verse in Daniel 11, "He will return to his land with great wealth" (v. 28). It may now be explained not only on the basis of the archeological record which suggest that Antiochus severely damaged the Egyptian temples during his second invasion, most likely when he looted them, but also by this sale of Egyptian land. That Antiochus left Egypt with considerable spoils after the first campaign can be assumed from Polybius' account of Antiochus' extravagant victory celebrations at Daphne, near Antioch.

Line 7 alludes to the conquest of Jerusalem. The text in 1 Macc 1:20–24 dates the capture of Jerusalem and sack of the Temple to the year 143 of the Seleucid Era, that is, after the first Egyptian campaign (169 B.C.E.). In 2 Macc 5:5–16, however, these events are said to have occurred after the second campaign. Scholarly opinion on the question may be divided into three factions: (a) those who accept the evidence of 1 Maccabees; (b) those who accept that of 2 Maccabees; (c) those who, based on the accounts in Daniel and in Josephus' works, believe that Antiochus came to Jerusalem on two occasions.[9]

---

8   On the importance of Porphyry's work, see P. M. Casey, "Porphyry and the Book of Daniel," *Journal of Theological Studies* 27 (1976) 15–18.

9   Of the considerable literature dealing with this problem, see Schürer, *History*, 1.152–53; M. Stern, *Greek and Latin Authors on Jews and Judaism* (3 vols.; Jerusalem: Israel Academy of Science, 1974–84) 115–16; J. A. Goldstein, *II Maccabees* (AB; Garden City, New York: Doubleday, 1976) 113–23.

If the Qumran fragment is to be believed, he came to Jerusalem between his two Egyptian campaigns. During the second campaign, Antiochus conquered Cyprus and annexed it to his kingdom, and this may be the meaning of the phrase "overthrow lands of foreign nations."

The turning point of the work is line 9, where it is stated that, after the second Egyptian campaign, the trials and tribulations of "the holy people"—probably a reference to the looting of Jerusalem by Antiochus—will "come to an end," after which the Israelites will repent. There is no reference to religious persecution, indicating that the author knew nothing of the stormy events after Antiochus' second Egyptian campaign. At this point the text switches from the description of past events to a prediction of the future. A similar stylistic shift may be discerned in Dan 11:40–45, where the historical account gives way to the prediction of events that had not taken place during the author's time. While the author of Dan 11:21–39 was clearly familiar with the history of Antiochus' reign, the next six verses describe events that never took place.[10] As David Flusser has pointed out, the author of the *War Scroll* was aware that these six verses were an unfulfilled prophecy, but that he nonetheless expected them to eventually come to pass. The first five lines of the *War Scroll* are in fact a paraphrase of these verses in Daniel.[11] Significantly, the Book of Daniel was popular at Qumran—eight copies were found there, three of which include parts of chapter 11.[12]

The last event mentioned in our fragment is Antiochus' second invasion of Egypt (line 8). The above-mentioned turning point is achieved in a sentence which bears much similarity to Dan 12:7: "And when the breaking of the power of the holy people comes to an end, then shall all these things be fulfilled" (lines 9–10). Of the next few words in the line, only the tops of the letters have survived. Milik suggested the reading: "The children [of Israel] shall repent." The author presumably considered the repentance of the Israelites as the climax of the events, predicting that, after the sacking of Jerusalem, the Jews

10 See J. A. Montgomery, *The Book of Daniel* (ICC; Edinburgh: T. & T. Clark, 1927) 470; L. F. Hartman and A. A. di Lella, *The Book of Daniel* (AB; Garden City, NY: Doubleday, 1978) 388–89.

11 D. Flusser, "Apocalyptic Elements in the War Scroll," in *Jerusalem in the Second Temple Period* (Abraham Schalit Memorial Volume; ed. A. Oppenheimer, U. Rappaport, and M. Stern; Jerusalem: Ben-Zvi, 1981) 434–52 (Hebrew).

12 4QDanᵃ (vv. 13–160); 4QDanᶜ (vv. 1–2, 13–17, 25–29), and 6QpapDan (vv. 33–36, 38). On the manuscripts of Daniel found at Qumran see E. Ulrich, "The Text of Daniel in the Qumran Scrolls," in *The Book of Daniel: Composition and Reception* (ed. J. J. Collins and P. W. Flint; VTSup 83; Leiden, Boston, and Köln: Brill, 2001) 573–85. On the place of Daniel in the Qumran library see P. W. Flint, "The Daniel Tradition at Qumran," in ibid., 329–67.

would regain their power and a new and better era would begin. The fact that there is no reference whatsoever to Antiochus' religious persecution, one of the most traumatic events in Jewish history, necessarily implies that the work was written before Antiochus issued his edicts. The composition of which this Qumran fragment is a remnant should therefore be dated to 168 B.C.E., just after Antiochus' second Egyptian campaign but before his anti-Jewish measures. The final redaction of the Book of Daniel is generally dated some time after 165 B.C.E., that is, after the edicts of 167 B.C.E. (Dan 7:25; 11:30–33; 12:1) and after Antiochus' defeat of the king of Armenia in the summer of 166 or 165 B.C.E. (7:24).[13] Based on this timeline, the work represented by this fragment was most likely written before the final redaction of Daniel, implying that the editor of the late stage of Daniel was not only influenced by this work found at Qumran, but in fact cited in 12:7.

I believe that the Book of Daniel's popularity at Qumran supports the contention that the Qumranites could have possessed one of its sources.[14] This small fragment from Cave 4 presents an interesting concentration of information about Antiochus Epiphanes and his activities. Moreover, the sale of land in Egypt is a new detail, which helps to understand an obscure verse in the Book of Daniel and indicates that Antiochus sold land in Judaea as well. Consequently, it is all the more likely that this fragment was composed shortly before the Book of Daniel was completed in its final form.

Broshi and Eshel have interpreted line 7 as proving the veracity of 1 Maccabees and confirming that the Temple was plundered after Antiochus' return from his first Egyptian campaign, before he set out on the second (as mentioned in line 8). According to Daniel Schwartz, however, the brevity of the account in the Qumran fragment and the simple statement that Antiochus came "to the Temple City and seized it with a[ll its treasures]," confirm the truth of Josephus' report in *Ant.* 12.246–52 that Antiochus came to Jerusalem twice, first upon his return from the first campaign, and second after the second campaign. Schwartz argues that Antiochus' first visit to Jerusalem passed relatively quietly, with no massacre having taken place, whereas the second was marked by considerable violence, involving a massacre and the looting of the Temple treasures.[15]

13 See Hartman and di Lella, *Daniel*, 253–54, 286–311, and bibliography; Goldstein, *II Maccabees*, 92–94. For the Book of Daniel as a collection of descriptive texts compiled by a late editor see E. Bickerman, *Four Strange Books of the Bible* (New York: Schocken, 1967) 53–126.

14 See E. Eshel, "Possible Sources of the Book of Daniel," in Collins and Flint, *Daniel*, 387–94.

15 See D. R. Schwartz, "Antiochus IV Epiphanes in Jerusalem," in *Historical Perspectives*

While the Qumran fragment yields nothing new about the anti-Jewish edicts and the course of the Hasmonean revolt, it does attest to the messianic expectations that were widespread in Judaea in 168 B.C.E., at the time of Antiochus' second Egyptian campaign, a few months before the outbreak of the Hasmonean Revolt in Modi'in. Perhaps this messianic anticipation accelerated the spread of rumors in Jerusalem that Antiochus had died during his second invasion of Egypt (2 Macc 5:1–5).[16] As will be shown in the next chapter, messianic sentiments in Jerusalem around 170 B.C.E. may well have inspired the formation of a new religious group in Judaea.

The text of Dan 11:25–31 describes Antiochus IV's incursions to Egypt and the desecration of the Temple in Jerusalem:

> He [= the king of the north] will muster his strength and courage against the king of the south with a great army. The king of the south will wage war with a very great and powerful army but will not stand fast... He [= the king of the north] will return to his land with great wealth... At the appointed time, he will again invade the south, but the second time will not be like the first. Ships from Kittim will come against him [= the king of the north]. He will be checked, and will turn back, raging against the holy covenant. Forces will be levied by him; they will desecrate the temple, the fortress; they will abolish the regular offering and set up the appalling abomination.[17]

---

from the Hasmoneans to Bar Kokhba in Light of the Dead Sea Scrolls (ed. D. Goodblatt, A. Pinnick, and D. R. Schwartz; STDJ 37; Leiden, Boston, and Köln: Brill, 2001) 45–56.

16 Various scholars have found possible references to Antiochus Epiphanes in four other Qumran scrolls. Maurya Horgan holds that the dirge over Jerusalem found in Cave 4 (4Q179) was written in the wake of Antiochus' campaigns and his visit to Jerusalem; see M. P. Horgan, "A Lament over Jerusalem (4Q179)," *JSS* 18 (1973) 222–34. Émile Puech suggested identifying the ominous protagonist of 4Q246 with Antiochus; see E. Puech, "4Q246. 4QApocryphe de Daniel ar," in *Qumran Cave 4.XVII: Parabiblical Texts, III* (DJD 22; Oxford: Clarendon, 1996) 165–84. Devorah Dimant suggested that the phrase "a king of the Gentiles, a blasphemer" in the Jeremiah Apocryphon 4Q388 and 4Q389 also alludes to Antiochus IV; see D. Dimant, in *Qumran Cave 4.XXI: Parabiblical Texts, IV* (DJD 30; Oxford: Clarendon, 2001) 112–16, 208–12, 228–32. However, even if these suggestions should be accepted, the texts provide no historical details. Dimant has identified an allusion to Antiochus' first invasion of Egypt in 4Q386; for a discussion of this suggestion and an alternative proposal see below, chapter eight.

17 For the historical background to these verses see J. J. Collins, *Daniel* (Hermeneia; Minneapolis: Fortress Press, 1993) 382–85.

As already mentioned, Flusser interpreted the first lines of the *War Scroll* as a Midrash on the unfulfilled prophecy in Daniel 11:41–45.[18] The opening section of the *War Scroll* should be read and reconstructed as follows:[19]

1. For the M[aster. The Rule] of War. The unleashing of the attack of the sons of light against the company of the sons of darkness, the army of Belial, against the band of Edom, Moab, and the sons of Amman,
2. and the ar[my of the people of] Philistia, and against the bands of the Kittim of Assyria and their allies the ungodly of the Covenant. The sons of Levi and the sons of Judah and the sons of Benjamin, the exiles of the wilderness, shall battle against them
3. in […] all their bands, when the exiled sons of light return from the Desert of the Peoples to camp in the Desert of Jerusalem; and after the battle they shall go up from there.
4. And [the king] of the Kittim [shall come] to Egypt, and in his time he shall set out in great wrath to wage war against the kings of the north, that his fury may destroy and cut the horn of
5. [Israel, and this shall] be a time of salvation for the people of God, an age of dominion for all the members of His company, and of everlasting destruction for all the company of Belial. And the confusion shall be
6. [great among] the sons of Japheth, and Assyria shall fall unassisted, and the dominion of the Kittim shall come to an end, and iniquity shall be vanquishe[d], leaving no remnant; and there shall be no escape
7. for [all the son]s of darkness.

Citing Flusser's study, Devorah Dimant suggested that this account, especially the words "And [the king] of the Kittim [shall come] to Egypt, and in his time he shall set out in great wrath to wage war against the kings of the north, that his fury may destroy and cut the horn of [Israel]," refers to "the two military campaigns of Antiochus IV Epiphanes to Egypt (170–168 B.C.E.), their failure owing to Roman pressure, Antiochus' return through Judaea and Jerusalem, the punitive

18 Flusser, "Apocalyptic Elements." This subject will be discussed in chapter nine.

19 Apart from Flusser's reconstruction of the Hebrew text, we read "For the M[aster. The Rule] of War" in line 1, based on the letters *lamed* and *mem* legible at the top of the scroll, read by neither Yadin nor Flusser. Thanks are due to Prof. Frank Cross for suggesting this reconstruction. The English translation is largely based on Geza Vermes, *The Complete Dead Sea Scrolls in English* (Harmondsworth: Penguin Books, 1998) 163, with minor emendations.

measures he imposed there, the looting of the temple and the persecution of the people of Jerusalem, and, finally, Epiphanes' death in Persia during a military campaign against the Parthians (164 B.C.E.)."[20] Dimant questioned Flusser's disregard of the similarity between the account at the beginning of the *War Scroll* and the historical events, that is, his failure to identify "the king of the Kittim" with Antiochus IV. I believe the reason was Flusser's conviction that a considerable length of time had to elapse between the composition of the Book of Daniel and that of the *War Scroll*, enough time for the author of the scroll to distinguish between the accounts of historical events in Daniel and the descriptions of events that had not yet occurred. Therefore, despite the *War Scroll*'s similarity to the events of 170–168 B.C.E. in Dan 11, the sectarian author seems not to have described Antiochus IV, but rather another evil king who would attack Israel in the future.[21] Nonetheless, Dimant was probably correct in her suggestion that the author of the *War Scroll* described the evil king in the image of Antiochus IV, who had invaded Egypt and desecrated the Temple.

None of the Qumran scrolls has produced a description of the Hasmonean Revolt, whether of Mattathias' exploits or of Judah Maccabee's battles.[22] As will be shown in the coming chapters, the Qumranites had no sympathy for the Hasmonean rulers, who had usurped the high priesthood as early as in the days of Mattathias' son Jonathan. Perhaps this was why they ignored Mattathias and Judah Maccabee.

20 D. Dimant, "Review of David Flusser, *Judaism in the Second Temple Period: Qumran and Apocalyptisim*," *Jewish Studies* 41 (2002) 192 (Hebrew).

21 Below, in chapter nine, we shall discuss the question of whether the "Kittim" of the *War Scroll* should be identified with the Seleucids or the Romans.

22 Most scholars have identified the large-horned ram of the *Animal Apocalypse* in *1 Enoch* 90:9–16 as Judah Maccabee; see for example J. J. Collins, "Pseudepigraphy and Group Formation in Second Temple Judaism," in *Pseudepigraphic Perspectives: The Apocrypha and Pseudepigrapha in Light of the Dead Sea Scrolls* (ed. E. G. Chazon and M. E. Stone; STDJ 31; Leiden, Boston, and Köln: Brill, 1999) 45–47. Menachem Kister, however, rejects the commonly held view, claiming that the ram should be identified with a leader of the Qumran community; see M. Kister, "Concerning the History of the Essenes," *Tarbiz* 56 (1987) 1–18 (Hebrew). For the moment, he is the only dissenter. While numerous fragments of *Enoch* were found at Qumran, no fragments of the *Animal Apocalypse* referring to the large-horned ram have been found. Since the *Animal Apocalypse* was known before the discovery of the scrolls, the identity of the ram will not be considered here. Some scholars have argued that the account of the wars of Jacob's sons in *Jubilees* alludes to Judah Maccabee's battles (34:1–10); see J. C. VanderKam, *Textual and Historical Studies in the Book of Jubilees* (Missoula, MT: Scholars Press, 1977) 218–29. However this seems to be a Samaritan tradition, which has nothing to do with Judah's battles; see E. Eshel and H. Eshel, "Toponymic Midrash in 1 Enoch and in Other Second Temple Jewish Literature," *Henoch* 24 (2002) 115–30.

Another scroll discovered at Qumran, 4Q390, reflects disapproval of the functioning of the priests throughout the Second Temple period. Among other things, the text states that the priests on the eve of the Hasmonean Revolt "forget law, festival, Sabbath, and covenant, and violate everything."[23]

4Q390 was apparently attributed to Jeremiah.[24] Having no sectarian features, it was probably not authored by a member of the sect.[25] The text levels grave accusations against the priests. Daniel 9:24–27 is an interpretation of Jeremiah's prophecy that the exile would last seventy years (Jer 25:8–14; 29:4–14). Jeremiah's prophecy is "updated" in Daniel 9, on the understanding that Jeremiah was not referring to seventy years but to seven seventy-year periods, that is, 490 years. Daniel divides this length of time into three periods: (a) seven seven-year periods, that is, forty-nine years of the Babylonian Exile;[26] (b) sixty-two seven-year periods, that is, 434 years from the reconstruction of Jerusalem to the time of Antiochus IV; and (c) one additional seven-year period, in the first half of which the sacrificial rites in the Temple would be discontinued because of the "appalling abomination" placed there, and in the second half of which redemption would take place.[27] The scroll 4Q390 from Qumran seems to

23 On this scroll see H. Eshel, "4Q390, the 490 Years Prophecy, and the Calendrical History of the Second Temple Period," in *Enoch and Qumran Origins* (ed. G. Boccaccini; Grand Rapids and Cambridge: Eerdmans, 2005) 102–10.

24 In John Strugnell's opinion, the fragment is part of a work that he called "Pseudo-Ezekiel." Dimant first believed it should be attributed to Moses; see D. Dimant, "New Light from Qumran on the Jewish Pseudepigrapha: 4Q390," in *The Madrid Qumran Congress* (2 vols; ed. J. Trebolle Barrera and L. Vegas Montaner; STDJ 11; Leiden, New York, Köln, and Madrid: Brill, 2002) 2.405–47. In the final publication, however (*Qumran Cave 4.XXI*), she identified it as part of a Pseudo-Jeremiah work.

25 Dimant holds that the non-sectarian writings are pre-sectarian. In keeping with her view that no further writings reached the sect after its establishment; she is therefore inclined to date all the works included in the non-sectarian scrolls to the second century B.C.E. However, it seems quite plausible that newcomers to the sect brought with them works that had been composed when the sect was already in existence. Paleographically speaking, Dimant dates the copying of 4Q390 to 30–20 B.C.E.; see Dimant, *Qumran Cave 4.XXI*, 236–37. There is no reason, therefore, not to assume that 4Q390 is a first century B.C.E. "update" of the late part of the Book of Daniel which was edited in 165 B.C.E.

26 Jerusalem was destroyed in 586 B.C.E.; Cyrus permitted the Jews to return to Judah in 538 B.C.E. Hence a time span of 49 years, as mentioned in Daniel 9, is very close to the historical fact.

27 See L. L. Grabbe, "The End of the Desolations of Jerusalem: From Jeremiah's 70 Years to Daniel's 70 Weeks of Years," in *Early Jewish and Christian Exegesis: Studies in Memory of W. H. Brownlee* (ed. C. A. Evans and W. F. Stinespring; Homage Series 10; Atlanta: Scholars Press, 1987) 67–72; D. Dimant, "The Seventy Weeks Chronology (Dan 9, 24–27) in the Light of New Qumranic

be a further "update" of 4Q390, pertaining to the 490-year prophecy of Daniel 9:24–27.[28] Fragment 1 of 4Q390 reads as follows:[29]

2. [... and a]gain I shall [deliver them] into the hand of the sons of Aar[on] seventy years [...]

3. the sons of Aaron shall rule over them, but they shall not walk [in] My [wa]ys which I am commanding you, so

4. you must warn them. And they also shall do evil before Me just as Israel did

5. in the days of the kingdom of their forefathers, except for those who are the first to go up from the land of captivity to rebuild

6. the Temple. I shall speak with them and send them a commandment and they shall comprehend completely: namely, what

7. they and their fathers had forsaken. But at the end of that generation, in the seventh jubilee

8. after the destruction of the land, they shall forget law, festival, Sabbath, and covenant, and shall violate everything and they shall do

9. evil before Me. So I shall hide my face from them, give them into the hand of their enemies and deliver [them] over

10. to the sword. But I shall cause a remnant of them to escape in order that they might not be completely [des]t[royed] in my wrath and when I turn [my face] away

11. from them. The angels of *Mastemot* will govern them and [. .. and they] shall again turn

12. and do ev[il] before [Me] and walk in the s[tubbornness of their heart...]

---

28 Dimant remarked that 4Q390 presents a historical account based on the Second Temple period calendar of "weeks," but overlooked the fact that the account amounts to a total of 490 years; see D. Dimant, "The Four Empires of Daniel, Chapter 2, in the Light of Texts from Qumran," in *Rivka Shatz-Uffenheimer Memorial Volume* (2 vols.; ed. R. Elior and Y. Dan; Jerusalem Studies in Jewish Thought 12; Jerusalem: Hebrew University, 1996) 1.40 (Hebrew).

Texts," in *The Book of Daniel in Light of New Findings* (ed. A. S. van der Woude; Leuven: Peeters, 1993) 57–76; G. Vermes, "Eschatological World View in the Dead Sea Scrolls and in the New Testament," in *Emanuel: Studies in Hebrew Bible, Septuagint and Dead Sea Scrolls in Honor of Emanuel Tov* (ed. S. M. Paul et al.; VTSup 94; Leiden and Boston: Brill, 2003) 481–84.

28 Dimant remarked that 4Q390 presents a historical account based on the Second Temple period calendar of "weeks," but overlooked the fact that the account amounts to a total of 490 years; see D. Dimant, "The Four Empires of Daniel, Chapter 2, in the Light of Texts from Qumran," in *Rivka Shatz-Uffenheimer Memorial Volume* (2 vols.; ed. R. Elior and Y. Dan; Jerusalem Studies in Jewish Thought 12; Jerusalem: Hebrew University, 1996) 1.40 (Hebrew).

29 The Hebrew text underlying this translation is that published by Dimant, *Qumran Cave 4.XXI*, 237–54; the translation is mine.

The historical survey is continued in the first column of Fragment 2:[30]

1.   [... They profaned]
2. [My] house [and My altar and th]e Holy of Ho[lies ...]
3. done and thus [.... all of] these things shall come upon them [...] and
4. the rule of Belial over them to hand them over to the sword for a week of (seven) years [... on] that Jubilee they shall be
5. violating all My laws and all My commandments which I shall command t[hem as sent by the han]d of my servants the prophets.
6. And they shall begin to contend with one another for seventy years from the day that they violate the covenant. Then I shall give them
7. [into the hand of the ang]els of *Mastemot* and they shall govern them and they shall not know or understand that I was angry with them for their unfaithfulness.
8. [...They shall fors]ake Me and do evil before Me. In that which I do not desire, they have chosen to enrich themselves by ill-gotten wealth and illegal profit
9. [...] they will rob, oppress one another, and they will defile My Temple
10. [they will profane My Sabbaths,] they will for[ge]t My [fes]tivals, and with fo[reign]ers [t]he[y] will profane their offspr[ing]. Their priests will commit violence

The beginning of Fragment 1 implies that the misbehavior of the priests during the Second Temple period is not surprising, since even during the "seventy years" mentioned in line 2, that is, the Babylonian Exile, the priests did not "walk in God's ways." The account reflects the idea that after the destruction of the First Temple the leadership of the people of Israel, previously entrusted to the House of David, fell into the hands of the priests who sinned by continuing to lead the exiles in Babylon in the same wrongful way as when they were in the land. God then sent His prophets to the returning exiles in Judah ("I shall speak with them and send them a commandment"), probably referring to Haggai and

30 In Dimant's view, all the fragments of the scroll attributed to Jeremiah are copies of a single work, which she calls the "Jeremiah Apocryphon." In the final publication she suggests that the two columns of 4Q390 were not contiguous, but separated by two other columns containing other parts of the Jeremiah Apocryphon, attested in other scrolls (Dimant, *Qumran Cave 4.XXI*, 236). Since the surviving parts of the other scrolls ascribed to Jeremiah do not overlap 4Q390, it would appear that 4Q390 is an independent work and that the second column is indeed the continuation of the first.

Zechariah. The attempt to reconstruct the Temple marked the beginning of a new era, during which the returnees understood "what they and their fathers had forsaken." This era ended "in the seventh jubilee after the destruction of the land,"[31] apparently referring to the 343rd year from the destruction of the First Temple ($343 = 7 \times 49$), when the priests forgot "law, festival, [and] Sabbath," that is to say, abandoned what the sectarians considered to be the correct calendar for the administration of the Temple service.[32] In addition to accusing the priests of desecrating the festivals, the author also protests that they had forgotten the covenant and "violated everything." Because of these sins, God delivered the Jews into the hands of their enemies (i.e., Antiochus IV), but nevertheless stopped short of destroying them completely.

The opening section of the first column in Fragment 2 refers to a "week of (seven) years" (line 4). Despite the fragmentary nature of lines 2–4, the "week of years" in which the people of Jerusalem were "handed over to the sword" and ruled by Belial is in all probability the same "week" as in Daniel 9:27: "For half a week he will put a stop to the sacrifice and the meal offering. At the corner [of the altar] will be an appalling abomination." Hence the "week" appearing both in Daniel and in 4Q390 is the three years of Antiochus' reign during which the Temple was desecrated and an idol placed in the Sanctuary.[33] I suggest that

31 Dates were commonly specified in the Second Temple period in terms of the number of jubilees and sabbaticals (= weeks of years). Such a division of time is documented in particular in the *Book of Jubilees* and in the *Vision of Weeks* (1 *Enoch* 93); see Dimant, *Seventy Weeks Chronology*, 61–72. As will be shown in the next chapter, the text in column I of the *Damascus Document* states that the origins of the sect lie in a group of Jews formed 390 years after the destruction of the First Temple. The chronological systems used by 4Q390 and the *Damascus Document* seem to be different, for, as we shall see, there is evidence that the group in question was established around 170 B.C.E. Hence the author of the *Damascus Document* believed that 390 years had elapsed from the destruction of the Temple to about 170 B.C.E., while the author of 4Q390 thought that the time that had elapsed from the destruction of the First Temple to the "week" of Antiochus' reign, which began in 167 B.C.E., was 343 years.

32 Daniel 7:25 states that Antiochus IV changed the calendar: "He will think of changing times and laws." The author of 4Q390 may have been referring to this event. For the change from the solar to the lunar calendar during Antiochus' reign see J. C. VanderKam, "2 Maccabees 6:7a and Calendrical Change in Jerusalem," *JSJ* 12 (1981) 52–74; G. Boccaccini, "The Solar Calendars of Daniel and Enoch," in Collins and Flint, *Daniel*, 311–28.

33 The half-week in which "the sacrifice and the meal offering" were discontinued and an "appalling abomination" placed at the corner of the altar surely refers to the time during which the idol was placed in the Temple, for we read in Dan 11:31: "They will desecrate the temple, the fortress; they will abolish the regular offering and set up the appalling abomination." See Collins, *Daniel*, 357–58.

the text at the end of line 1 in the second fragment should be reconstructed as "they profaned," reading "[they profaned My] house and My altar and the Holy of Holies." At this time the priests were "violating all My laws and all My commandments" (line 5), probably an allusion to the Hellenizing high priests Jason, Menelaus, and Alcimus, who officiated in the Temple during the seventies and sixties of the second century B.C.E. It cannot be ascertained whether the text in line 6, "they shall begin to contend with one another," alludes to the strife between the high priests Jason and Menelaus or to the Hasmonean Revolt.

The last historical stage described in 4Q390 is probably the reign of the Hasmoneans, which began after the "week" during which the Temple was desecrated. This period was to last for "seventy years" (line 6). During that time, Israel would be ruled by "angels of *Mastemot*" (line 7), for the Hasmoneans would not "know or understand." The accusation against the Hasmoneans for "unfaithfulness" at the end of line 7 may allude to the misuse of Temple funds.[34] Further on, as well, the author accuses them of choosing "to enrich themselves by ill-gotten wealth and illegal profit" (lines 8–9). In addition to accusing the Hasmoneans of avarice, the author notes that they oppressed one another, defiled the Temple, desecrated the Sabbath, and forgot the festivals (lines 9–10). In my view the last accusation is essentially an allegation that the Hasmoneans administered the Temple while using the wrong calendar. At the end of the fragment we read that "they," that is, the Hasmonean priests, defiled their offspring with foreigners and despoiled the priesthood.

It would appear that the author of 4Q390 favored a chronology of 490 years.[35] He divided the 490 years of Daniel 9:24 into four periods: (a) the seventy years of the Babylonian Exile;[36] (b) the 343 years during which the returnees followed the right path; (c) the seven years of Antiochus IV's reign; and (d) the seventy years of the Hasmonean rule.[37] Hence it seems probable that 4Q390 is an

---

34 The Hebrew root used here, *m'l*, as used in the Bible (see Lev 5:14–16), generally denotes illicit benefit derived from Temple property (this is indeed the topic dealt with in the mishnaic tractate *Me'ilah*). For the concept before and after the destruction of the Second Temple see B. M. Bokser, "*Ma'al* and Blessings over Food: Rabbinic Transformation of Cultic Terminology and Alternative Modes of Piety," *JBL* 100 (1981) 557–74. For the possibility that there are references to Jason, Menelaus, and Alcimus in another scroll (4Q387), see D. Dimant, *Qumran Cave* 4, 193; C. Werman, "Epochs and End-Time: The 490 Year Scheme in Second Temple Literature," *DSD* 13 (2006) 229–55.

35 See J. T. Milik, *The Books of Enoch* (Oxford: Clarendon, 1976) 254–55.

36 The author of 4Q390 seems to have believed that, in light of Jeremiah's prophecy, the Babylonian Exile had to last seventy years and not forty-nine.

37 This reconstruction involves a difficulty: The phrase "in the seventh jubilee after the

interpretation of Daniel 9, intended to "update" the prophecy of 490 years.[38] It is fiercely critical of the priests of the Second Temple period, perhaps confirming the thesis that Dan 7:25 documents the change of calendar used in the Temple during Antiochus' reign (Frg. 1, line 8). The end of Fragment 1 states that the Hellenizing priests "do ev[il] before [Me] and walk in the s[tubbornness of their heart...]," and the opening lines of Fragment 2 note that they defiled God's Temple. The author also accuses the Hellenizers of violating "all My laws and all My commandments" (Frg. 2, line 5). Perhaps the clause "they shall begin to contend with one another" in line 6 of the second fragment alludes to the internecine strife among the Hellenizing priests of Jerusalem on the eve of the Hasmonean Revolt, but the reference may even be to the revolt itself. Indeed, this author also disapproves of Hasmonean rule.[39]

To summarize: the two scrolls from Cave 4 provide significant supplementary information about events in Jerusalem prior to the outbreak of the Hasmonean Revolt in Modi'in. The first (4Q248) testifies to Antiochus' visit to Jerusalem between his two Egyptian campaigns, and to the Jews of Palestine's hopes that a new era would begin after the second campaign. The second document (4Q390) expresses harsh criticism of the high priests who led Judaea on the eve of the revolt. Neither contains allusions to Mattathias the Hasmonean or the battles of Judah Maccabee. The first historical figure of the Hasmonean dynasty alluded to in the Dead Sea scrolls is Mattathias' son Jonathan. Appointed high priest in 152 B.C.E., he was probably the figure designated by the Qumran authors as "the wicked priest." The next chapter will consider Jonathan the Hasmonean as reflected in the Dead Sea scrolls.

---

destruction of the land" in Fragment 1, lines 7–8, seems to indicate that the seventy years of the Babylonian Exile should be included in the 343 years. If that was indeed the author's intention, it is not inconceivable that, in order to reach the figure of 490 years, he described an additional seventy years after the Hasmonean period. Most of the second column of Fragment 2 has not survived. The few remaining traces may describe the seventy years of the era of redemption or an additional seventy-year period. Since 4Q390 was copied at some time in the last third of the first century B.C.E., the author may well have been alluding to events that occurred after Pompey's invasion. However, in light of my proposal at the end of chapter six, it is probably preferable to assume that the author of 4Q390 expected the redemption to come at the end of the seventy-year Hasmonean rule.

38 For such "updates," see L. L. Grabbe, "The Seventy-Weeks Prophecy (Daniel 9:24–27) in Early Jewish Interpretation," in *The Quest for Context and Meaning: Studies in Biblical Intertextuality in Honor of J. A. Sanders* (ed. C. A. Evans and S. Talmon; BIS 28; Leiden, New York, and Köln: Brill, 1997) 595–611.

39 For an attempt to determine the date of composition of the work copied in 4Q390 and its purpose, see below at the end of chapter six.

CHAPTER TWO

Questions of Identity:
The "Teacher of Righteousness," the "Man of Lies," and Jonathan the Hasmonean

The *Damascus Document* and some of the pesharim refer to a figure called the "Teacher of Righteousness" who played an important role in the formation of the Qumran sect. Any historian dealing with this sect must tackle two central questions: When was the sect established, and when was the Teacher of Righteousness active? The paucity of available information about this highly significant figure has inspired many conjectures.[1] The little that can be inferred from the pesharim and the *Damascus Document* may be summed up as follows: (a) there was a heated argument between the Teacher of Righteousness and a religious leader referred to as the "Man of Lies"; (b) a political leader, known as the "Wicked Priest," assaulted the Teacher of Righteousness; (c) the Teacher of Righteousness was forced into exile, probably after his confrontation with the Wicked Priest; (d) after the death of the Teacher of Righteousness, his disciples quarreled among themselves and some members of the sect seceded.

If we could identify the period in which the political leader referred to as the Wicked Priest was active, we would know when the Teacher of Righteousness

---

1   Most scholars identify the Teacher of Righteousness as the author of some of the hymns documented in the *Thanksgiving Scroll* (1QH), which are known in the scholarly literature as the "Teacher's Hymns." Joachim Jeremias was the first to propose that these hymns were composed by the Teacher of Righteousness, and it was he who coined the term "Teacher's Hymns"; see J. Jeremias, *Der Lehrer der Gerechtigkeit* (Göttingen: Vandenhoeck and Ruprecht, 1963) 168–239. For further discussion of this theory, see P. R. Callaway, *The History of the Qumran Community* (JSPSup; Sheffield, 1988) 185–97. Yadin identified the Teacher of Righteousness as the author of the *Temple Scroll*; see Y. Yadin, *The Temple Scroll* (3 vols.; Jerusalem: Israel Exploration Society, 1983) 1.393–97. Other conjectures concerning the Teacher of Righteousness, as well as his supposed authorship of *Miqṣat Maʿaśe ha-Torah*, will be considered below.

and the Man of Lies lived. In this chapter I shall argue that the Wicked Priest was none other than Jonathan the Hasmonean, son of Mattathias; hence all three figures—the Teacher of Righteousness, the Wicked Priest, and the Man of Lies—were active in the middle of the second century B.C.E.

Column 1 of the *Damascus Document* begins with a brief description of the destruction of the First Temple and then continues:[2]

5   ...And at the end of (His) wrath, three hundred

6   and ninety years after giving them into the hand of Nebuchadnezzar, king of Babylon,

7   He turned His attention to them and caused to grow out of Israel and Aaron a root of planting, to inherit

8   His land and grow fat in the goodness of His soil. And they discerned their iniquity and knew that

9   they were guilty people; yet they were as blind as those who grope for a way

10   for twenty years. But God discerned their works, (namely) that they sought Him wholeheartedly,

11   and He raised up for them (the) Teacher of Righteousness to guide them in the way of His heart...

The word פקדם, "turned His attention to them" (line 7), refers to the arrival of the group in Judaea, or, alternatively, to its formation. If the text is taken literally, this must have occurred around the beginning of the second century B.C.E., since the First Temple was destroyed in 586 B.C.E., so that 390 years after that event would bring us to 196 B.C.E.[3] It is not necessary, however, that the group actually became

---

2   Quotations from the *Damascus Document* generally follow the translation in J. H. Charlesworth et al., ed., *The Dead Sea Scrolls: Hebrew, Aramaic, and Greek Texts with English Translations*: Volume 2, *Damascus Document, War Scroll, and Related Documents* (Tübingen: Mohr Siebeck / Louisville: Westminster John Knox, 1995). For this particular passage see ibid., 13.

3   For the thesis that the group was formed in the Diaspora and came to Judaea as a group, see J. Murphy-O'Connor, "The Essenes and Their History," *RB* 81 (1974) 215–44. Murphy-O'Connor has suggested that "Damascus" was not the group's place of origin, but a designation for an unspecified location in the Diaspora, with reference to Amos 5:27: "I drove you into exile beyond Damascus." Since we know of no Jewish community in Damascus in the second century B.C.E., Murphy-O'Connor conjectures that the group had come from Babylonia. For a discussion of the subject, see C. Hempel, "Community Origins in the *Damascus Document* in the Light of Recent Scholarship," in *The Provo International Conference on the Dead Sea Scrolls: Technological Innovations, New Texts, and Reformulated Issues* (STDJ 30; ed. D. W. Parry and E. Ulrich; Leiden, Boston, and Köln: Brill, 1999) 316–29; idem, *The Damascus Texts* (London and

active precisely in 196 B.C.E., for the number 390 is clearly based on Ezekiel 4:5: "For I impose upon you three hundred and ninety days, corresponding to the number of the years of their punishment; and so you shall bear the punishment for the House of Israel." The number should not, therefore, be understood as an exact historical reckoning: the members of the group, believing that they bore "the punishment for the House of Israel," dated their origins to the 390th year after the destruction of the temple. However, since the Judaeans of the Second Temple period were not aware that the Persian period had lasted more than two hundred years (539–332 B.C.E.),[4] the Qumranites could not have accurately calculated the time that had elapsed from the destruction of the First Temple to their arrival in the country (or until the establishment of the group). Some scholars have associated the religious awakening that inspired the formation of the Qumran sect with the purification of the temple or other successful actions of Judah Maccabee. In any case, the group probably came into being before the Hasmonean revolt, most likely about the year 170 B.C.E.[5]

The passage quoted above from the *Damascus Document* describes the members of the group as "blind as those who grope for a way" for twenty years, after which God sent them the Teacher of Righteousness who guided them "in the way of His heart." This quite clearly implies that the Teacher of Righteousness

---

New York: T. & T. Clark, 2000) 56–60.

4 The evidence from Josephus' works and from *Seder Olam Rabbah* indicates that the Jews of the Land of Israel in the Second Temple period and the time of the Mishnah and the Talmud believed that the Persian period had been quite short. One reason for this was that by the end of the Second Temple period, it was no longer remembered that several similarly-named kings had reigned in succession during the Persian period: three were named Cyrus, three Darius, and three Artaxerxes; see J. Tabory, "The Persian Period according to Hazal," in *Milet: The Open University Studies in Jewish History and Culture* (ed. S. Ettinger et al.; Tel Aviv: The Open University, 1985) 2. 65–77 (Hebrew); D. Schwartz, "On Some Papyri and Josephus' Sources and Chronology for the Persian Period," *JSJ* 21 (1990) 175–99. On similar errors, indicating that this date should be viewed with some suspicion, see G. Vermes, "Eschatological World View in the Dead Sea Scrolls and in the New Testament," in *Emanuel: Studies in Hebrew Bible, Septuagint and Dead Sea Scrolls in Honor of Emanuel Tov* (ed. S. M. Paul et al.; VTSup 94; Leiden and Boston: Brill, 2003) 481–82, esp. n. 4.

5 Murphy-O'Connor ("The Essenes and their History," 224) suggested a connection between the arrival of the group in the Land of Israel and Judah Maccabee's successes. If, as Victor Tcherikover argued ("Antiochus' Persecution of Judaism," in idem, *Hellenistic Civilization and the Jews* [Philadelphia: Jewish Publication Society, 1959] 175–203), the religious persecution was sparked by a rebellion of conservative circles in Jerusalem in 168 B.C.E., it may be conjectured that the group first became active in the context of the religious awakening that inspired the revolt. The rebellion of conservative circles and the formation of the group may be associated with the religious awakening documented in 4Q248 (see the previous chapter).

did not head the group from its very beginning, but only some twenty years later.

One passage in the *Pesher on Habakkuk* (cols. 1–2) reports that the Teacher of Righteousness taught the members of the sect to "interpret" the words of the prophets:[6]

16   ["Look, O traitors and] s[ee;]

17   [and wonder (and) be amazed; for I am doing a deed in your days that you would not believe if]

1   it were told." [Interpreted, this concerns] the traitors together with the Man

2   of Lies, for (they did) not [listen to the words received by] the Teacher of Righteousness from the mouth

3   of God. And it concerns the tra[itors to] the New [Covenant], f[o]r they were not

4   faithful to the Covenant of God [and have profaned] His holy Name.

5   And thus, the interpretation of the passage [concerns the trai]tors at the End of

6   Days. They are the ruthless [ones of the Cove]nant who will not believe

7   when they hear all that is going to co[me up]on the last generation from the mouth of

8   the Priest, to whom God gave into [his heart discernme]nt to interpret all

9   the words of His servants the prophets [whom] by their hand God enumerated

10   all that is going to come upon His people and up[on His Community]...

This passage refers to three distinct groups of "traitors" (Heb. בוגדים): (a) traitors "together with the Man of Lies"; (b) traitors to the New Covenant; and (c) traitors "at the End of Days." The members of the third group are branded as traitors because they did not believe what the Priest had said about everything that was to happen to "the last generation" (that is, the period contemporary with

6   Quotations from the *Pesharim* generally follow translations in J. H. Charlesworth et al., ed., *The Dead Sea Scrolls: Hebrew, Aramaic, and Greek Texts with English Translations*: Volume 6B: *Pesharim, Other Commentaries, and Related Documents* (Tübingen: Mohr Siebeck / Louisville: Westminster John Knox, 2002). For this particular passage, see ibid., 162–63.

the pesharim since the Qumranites believed that they were living in the "last generation"). As the text continues, there are slight variations in the designation of the Teacher of Righteousness: מורה הצדקה instead of מורה הצדק; he is sometimes referred to as "the Priest, the Teacher of Righteousness," and sometimes as just the "Priest." This priest possessed divine knowledge that enabled him to interpret everything that the prophets had foretold. The designation מורה הצדק (*mwrh hzdk*), generally translated as "Teacher of Righteousness," probably means that the "Teacher" was a scion of the "House of Zadok," that is, of the priestly dynasty that claimed descent from Zadok the priest who served in the First Temple during the reign of King Solomon. This family held the High Priesthood until the crisis that led to the Hasmonean Revolt. In the course of that crisis, Menelaus, though not of the Zadokite dynasty, was appointed High Priest. It would seem that the first group, "the traitors together with the Man of Lies," rejected the Teacher of Righteousness' interpretation of God's words, that is, of the Torah.

Evidence that the sectarians learned from the Teacher of Righteousness not only how to explain the words of the prophets, but also how to interpret the laws of the Torah, is documented in the *Damascus Document* (col. 20):[7]

27 ...But all those who hold firmly to these precepts, to go out
28 and go in according to the Torah, and listen to the voice of the Teacher and confess before God, (saying,) "We have [sin]ned,
29 we have done wickedly, we and our fathers, by walking contrarily in the laws of the Covenant.
30 And Your judgments against us are true," and they are not to raise a hand against His holy laws and His righteous
31 precepts and His true testimonies; but rather, they are to be instructed in the first precepts in which
32 the men of the Community were judged, when they listened to the voice of (the) Teacher of Righteousness...

The new path preached by the Teacher of Righteousness must have aroused opposition, as indicated by the passage from the *Pesher on Habakkuk* quoted previously, which refers to a group of traitorous people, unwilling to obey the Teacher of Righteousness, who followed the "Man of Lies." The description in the *Damascus Document* implies that, in the view of the Qumran sectarians, the Teacher of Righteousness offered a new interpretation of the laws of the Torah.

7   Charlesworth, *Damascus Document*, 37.

In fact, before he became their leader, they believed, their observance of the Law had been inadequate and they had been sinning. In 4QpPs[a] (col. 3) we read that God had chosen the Teacher of Righteousness to lead those who had been designated as God's chosen community:[8]

> 14 "For from the Lor[d are the steps of a man. They] are established [and] He delights in his way, for [if] he should [char]ge, he would [not]
> 15 be hurled down, for the L[ord supports his hand]." Interpreted, this concerns the Priest, the [Righteous] Teacher, [whom]
> 16 God [ch]ose to stand (before Him). F[or] he established him to build for him the Congregation of [his true choice].

This passage implies that "the Priest, the Teacher of Righteousness" had so much influence on the group that their history before he joined their ranks could be ignored and he could be described as having founded the group.

A central event in the life of the Teacher of Righteousness was his confrontation with the religious leader referred to as "the Man of Lies," or sometimes as "the Preacher of Mockery" (מטיף הלצון). The conflict may be associated with the passage quoted above from the *Damascus Document*, according to which the Teacher of Righteousness departed from the "first precepts." Further evidence of this opposition to the Teacher of Righteousness comes from the following passage in the *Pesher on Habakkuk*, col. 5:[9]

> 8 "Why do you heed traitors, but are silent when a
> 9 wicked one swallows up one more righteous than he?" Its interpretation concerns the House of Absalom
> 10 and the men of their counsel, who were quiet at the rebuke of the Teacher of Righteousness
> 11 and did not support him against the Man of Lies who rejected
> 12 the Torah in the midst of all their counsel....

---

8 Charlesworth, *Pesharim*, 17. In light of this pesher, the suggestion of Mark Geller and Nikos Kokkinos that the Teacher of Righteousness did not head the Qumran sect, which was only influenced by his teachings, is untenable. Geller and Kokkinos identify the Teacher of Righteousness as Simeon the Just, see M. J. Geller, "Qumran's Teacher of Righteousness: Suggested Identification," *Scripta Judaica Cracoviensia* 1 (Krakow: Jagiellonian University, 2002) 9–19; N. Kokkinos, "Second Thoughts on the Date and Identity of the Teacher of Righteousness," *Scripta Judaica Cracoviensia* 2 (2003) 7–15.

9 Charlesworth, *Pesharim*, 169.

The Man of Lies headed a group that refused to obey the Teacher of Righteousness. Most scholars agree with Flusser's suggestion that the Man of Lies was the leader of the "Seekers of Smooth Things" (דורשי חלקות), namely, the Pharisees.[10] Judging from the above passage from the *Pesher on Habakkuk*, the party designated as the "House of Absalom" remained neutral when the followers of the Man of Lies rebuked the Teacher of Righteousness.[11] Another passage in the *Pesher on Habakkuk* (col. 10) relates that the Man (or Preacher) of Lies also gathered a group around himself:[12]

5   "Woe

6   to the one who builds a city with blood and founds a town on iniquity. Are not

7   these from the Lord of Hosts? Peoples toil for fire

8   and nations grow weary for nothing."

9   The interpretation of the passage concerns the Preacher of Lies, who caused many to err,

10   building a city of emptiness with bloodshed and establishing a congregation with falsehood,

11   for the sake of its glory making many toil in the service of emptiness and saturating them

12   with w[o]rks of falsehood, with the result that their labor is for nothing; so that they will come

---

10   D. Flusser, Review of J. T. Milik, "Dix ans de découvertes dans le Désert de Juda," *Kiryat Sefer* 33 (1958) 457–59 (Hebrew); J. J. Collins, "The Origin of the Qumran Community: A Review of the Evidence," in *To Touch the Text: Biblical and Related Studies in Honor of Joseph A. Fitzmyer* (ed. M. P. Horgan and P. J. Kobelski; New York: Crossroad, 1989) 172–77; B. Nitzan, *Pesher Habakkuk: A Scroll from the Wilderness of Judaea* (Jerusalem: Mossad Bialik, 1986) 136–38 (Hebrew).

11   The designation "House of Absalom" is an allusion to King David's son Absalom, who was unfaithful to his father. Alternatively, it may be that the group's leader was named Absalom (as in the "House of Shammai" and "House of Hillel" in the Rabbinic literature). In this connection, it is worth noting the reference to the so-called "Absalom's Tomb" in the *Copper Scroll*, that was written in the first century c.e.; see J. K. Lefkovits, *The Copper Scroll 3Q15: A Reevaluation* (STDJ 25; Leiden, Boston, and Köln: Brill, 2000) 348–51. The monument known as "Absalom's Tomb" in the Kidron Valley in Jerusalem, built in the Roman period, may have been erected by a rich priestly family, like the adjacent tomb of the "Sons of Hezir." However, since it dates to later than the second century b.c.e., an association with the "House of Absalom" mentioned in the *Pesher on Habakkuk* does not seem plausible. On the date of the monument, see N. Avigad, *Ancient Monuments in the Kidron Valley* (Jerusalem: Mossad Bialik, 1954) 91–130 (Hebrew); D. Barag, "2000–2001 Exploration of the Tombs of Benei Hezir and Zechariah," *IEJ* 53 (2003) 98.

12   Charlesworth, *Pesharim*, 179.

13 to the judgments of fire, because they reviled and reproached the elect of God.

Thus, besides the party of the Teacher of Righteousness, the Preacher of Lies formed his own group—albeit founded on falsehood.[13] It is also implied that the Man of Mockery—that is, the Preacher of Lies—was an influential figure in Judaea. This is clear from the beginning of the *Damascus Document* (col. 1):[14]

14 When the Man of Mockery arose, who sprinkled upon Israel
15 waters of falsehood and led them astray in a chaos without a way, bringing low the eternal heights and departing
16 from the paths of righteousness and moving the border marked out by the first ones in their inheritance...

Hence, the Man of Mockery was responsible for Israel's straying from the correct path, and it was he who altered the laws laid down by previous generations. In another passage of the *Damascus Document*, col. 8, we read:[15]

12 ....But none of this was understood by the "builders of the barrier" and the "whitewash-daubers," for
13 one who weighs the wind and the Preacher of Lies preached to them, against whose entire congregation God's anger was kindled.

Although the sect's scribes stress that the confrontation with the Man of Lies was the central, most crucial event in the life of the Teacher of Righteousness,[16] other

---

13 A similar interpretation may be found in 4QpPsᵃ (col. 1, 25 – col. 2, 1: " '[Moa]n before [the Lord and] writhe before Him. And do not be angry with the one who makes his way prosperous, with the man [who doe]s evil plans.' Its [interpretation] concerns the Man of the Lie, who led many astray with words of deceit, for they chose empty words and did not lis[ten] to the Interpreter of Knowledge, so that they will perish by the sword, by famine, and by plague." (Charlesworth, *Pesharim*, 9–11). The "Interpreter of Knowledge" mentioned here is probably the Teacher of Righteousness.

14 Charlesworth, *Damascus Document*, 13.

15 Ibid., 29.

16 For an attempt to identify the Man of Lies with Yose b. Yoezer, one of the leading Pharisees in the mid-second century B.C.E., see E. Regev, "Yose ben Yoezer and the Qumran Sectarians on Purity Laws: Agreement and Controversy," in *The Damascus Document: A Centennial of Discovery* (ed. J. M. Baumgarten et al., STDJ 34; Leiden, Boston, and Köln: Brill, 2000) 95–107, esp. n. 27.

accounts indicate that his life was not really endangered by the Man of Lies, who was a religious leader, but by the Wicked Priest, who was a political leader. This individual made an attempt to harm the Teacher of Righteousness, as recounted in 4QpPs[a] col. 4:[17]

> 7   "The wicked one lies in ambush for the righteous one and seeks [to murder him. The L]ord [will not abandon him into his hand,] n[or will he] let him be condemned as guilty when he comes to trial."
> 8   Its interpretation concerns [the] Wicked [Pri]est, who l[ay in ambush for the Teache]r of Righte[ousness and sought to] murder him [because of the words of the Law] and the Torah
> 9   that he sent to him...

In other words, the Wicked Priest tried to kill the Teacher of Righteousness because of "the Law and the Torah" that the latter had sent him. The identity of the work that the Teacher of Righteousness sent the Wicked Priest will be discussed below. In the meantime, a more detailed description of one of the Wicked Priest's assaults on the Teacher of Righteousness, possibly the same incident as alluded to 4QpPs[a], may be found in the *Pesher on Habakkuk* (col. 11):[18]

> 2   "...Woe to him who gives his neighbors to drink, mixing in
> 3   his poison, indeed, making (them) drunk in order that he might look upon their feasts."
> 4   Its interpretation concerns the Wicked Priest, who
> 5   pursued the Teacher of Righteousness—to swallow him up with his poisonous
> 6   vexation—to his house of exile. And at the end of the feast, (during) the repose of
> 7   the Day of Atonement, he appeared to them to swallow them up
> 8   and to make them stumble on the fast day, their restful Sabbath.

The text is clearly concerned with an attempt by the Wicked Priest on the lives of the Teacher of Righteousness and his followers.

17 Charlesworth, *Pesharim*, 19. This reading is based on the convincing reconstructions of E. Qimron and J. Strugnell, *Qumran Cave 4, V: Miqṣat Maʿaśe ha-Torah* (DJD 10; Oxford: Clarendon, 1994) 120.

18 Charlesworth, *Pesharim*, 181.

The clash was probably due to differences over calendrical matters, in particular, the date of the Day of Atonement.[19] Since it is generally agreed that the Wicked Priest was a High Priest, he would have been occupied in the temple on the Day of Atonement, and surely would not have been able to leave Jerusalem on that day to pursue the Teacher of Righteousness in his place of exile. Clearly then, the Wicked Priest and the Teacher of Righteousness disagreed as to the date of the Day of Atonement. The incident described in the *Pesher on Habakkuk* must have taken place on the Teacher of Righteousness' Day of Atonement, which did not fall on the same day as determined by the Wicked Priest.[20] As a result of this attempt, the Teacher of Righteousness was obliged to go into exile.

Another source, 4QpPs[a] (col. 2), states that the Teacher of Righteousness was persecuted not only by the Wicked Priest but by two groups referred to as "Ephraim and Manasseh":[21]

16 "The wicked drew the sword and bent their bow to fell the afflicted and the poor,

19 S. Talmon, "Yom Hakippurim in the Habakkuk Scrolls," *Biblica* 32 (1951) 549–63; S. Talmon and J. Ben-Dov, *Qumran Cave 4, XVI: Calendrical Texts* (DJD 21; Oxford: Clarendon, 2001) 1–36.

20 It is clear from the Dead Sea scrolls that the Qumranites followed a 364-day solar year; see J. C. VanderKam, *Calendars in the Dead Sea Scrolls: Measuring Time* (London and New York: Routledge, 1998). In the biblical period, however, a lunar calendar was undoubtedly in use. The advantage of the lunar cycle was that any person, even if illiterate, could go out at nightfall, observe the moon, and determine the day of the month. The use of this calendar in early Israelite history is attested by the use of the Hebrew words "moon" (ירח) and "new" (חדש) for "month," both of which are associated with the moon's monthly cycle. The great disadvantage of the lunar calendar, however, is the need to correct it every three years by adding a month. In the Second Temple period, when many Judaeans were literate, it was possible to institute a solar year of 365 or 364 days. The astronomical section of the *Book of Enoch* (chaps. 72–82) and the *Aramaic Levi Document* indicate that, probably as early as the third century B.C.E., the priests in the Jerusalem Temple began to use a solar calendar. This change was apparently unopposed until 167 B.C.E. As a consequence of the shock caused by the erection of an idol in the temple during the religious persecution of 167–164 B.C.E., and the fact that some priests (mainly from the house of Bilgah) continued on unabated with the temple ritual despite the presence of the idol in the Holy of Holies, faith in the priestly circles was undermined. The dispute over the adoption of the solar over the lunar calendar was revived. In my opinion, some circles demanded restoration of the lunar calendar in the Temple, as in the First Temple period after the stormy events of the second quarter of the second century B.C.E.; see H. Eshel, "4Q390, the 490 Years Prophecy and the Calendrical History of the Second Temple Period," in *Enoch and Qumran Origins* (ed. G. Boccaccini; Grand Rapids and Cambridge: Eerdmans, 2005) 102–10.

21 Charlesworth, *Pesharim*, 13.

17 and to slaughter those who are upright of way. Their sword will enter their (own) heart, and their bows will be broken."

18 Its interpretation concerns the wicked ones of Ephraim and Manasseh, who will seek to lay (their) hand(s)

19 on the priest and on the men of his counsel in the time of refining that is coming upon them. But God will ransom them

20 from their hand, and afterwards they will be given into the hand of the ruthless ones of the Gentiles for judgment.

In other words, the "wicked ones of Ephraim and Manasseh" tried to assault the Teacher of Righteousness. In the *Pesher on Nahum*, "Ephraim" denotes "the Seekers of Smooth Things," meaning the Pharisees, while "Manasseh" refers to the Sadducees.[22] The author of 4QpPs^a also used these terms, noting that the Teacher of Righteousness was persecuted by the members of both groups.[23] As we have seen, the Man of Lies (or the Preacher of Lies or Mockery) established a community, whose members are referred to in the *Pesher on Nahum* as "Seekers of Smooth Things" or "Ephraim."

From 4QpPs^a we learn that "Manasseh," that is the Sadducees, were also active at the same time as the Teacher of Righteousness. According to the *Damascus Document*, the clash in Judaea between the Pharisees (Ephraim), the Sadducees (Manasseh), and the sectarians (probably members of the Essene movement, referred to in the pesharim as "Judah"), erupted all at once. This is the implication of an interpretation of Isaiah 7:17 that appears in the *Damascus Document*, col. 7:[24]

22 The use of these terms was noted by the following scholars: J. D. Amoussine, "Ephraim et Manassé dans le Péshèr de Nahum (4Q p Nahum)," *RQ* 4 (1963) 389–96; A. Dupont-Sommer, "Le Commentaire de Nahum découvert près de la Mer Morte (4Q p Nah): Traduction et notes," *Semitica* 13 (1963) 55–58; D. Flusser, "Pharisäer, Sadduzäer un Essener im Pescher Nahum," in *Qumran: Wege der Forschung* (ed. K. E. Grözinger; Darmstadt: Wissenschaftliche Buchgesellschaft, 1981) 121–66; Y. Yadin, "Pesher Nahum (4QpNahum) Reconsidered," *IEJ* 21 (1971) 1–12. The same terms are used in other sectarian writings; see D. R. Schwartz, "To Join Oneself to the House of Judah (*Damascus Document* IV, 11)," *RQ* 10 (1981) 440 n. 15.

23 There is no reason to assume that the phrase "wicked ones of Ephraim and Manasseh" refers to members of a single group. Ephraim and Manasseh are not mentioned in Psalm 37, so that the author of the pesher did not have to refer to them in his interpretation. In col. I, line 24, of the same pesher (4QpPs^a), only Ephraim is mentioned. It would seem, therefore, that the author of this pesher, like the author of the *Pesher on Nahum*, was referring to two distinct groups.

24 Charlesworth, *Damascus Document*, 25–27.

39

10 …when that happens of which is written in the words of Isaiah, son of Amoz, the prophet,

11 who said: "There shall come days upon you and upon your people and upon your fathers' house, such as did <not>

12 come since the day Ephraim departed over Judah." (This refers to) when the two houses of Israel split,

13 Ephraim lorded over Judah…

The phrase "the two houses of Israel" at the end of line 12 is quoted from Isaiah 8:14, which states that whoever disobeys God, whether from Judah or from the Northern Kingdom, will become "a trap and a snare for those who dwell in Jerusalem." The author of the *Damascus Document* was describing events that took place when "Ephraim departed over Judah, when the two houses of Israel split." Clearly, he did not count Judah—his own community—as one of the two "houses of Israel," for it is surely inconceivable that he believed the members of his own group to be disobeying God and becoming a stumbling-block to the people of Jerusalem. "The two houses of Israel" are then Ephraim (the Pharisees) and Manasseh (the Sadducees), both of which became religious communities when the Pharisees seceded from "Judah" (the Essenes).[25] The implication is that the dispute between all the sects in Judaea broke out during the time of the Teacher of Righteousness and the Wicked Priest.[26]

What can be learned of the Wicked Priest who persecuted the Teacher of Righteousness? The *Pesher on Habakkuk*, col. 8, supplies some details of his beginnings:[27]

25 M. Kister, "Concerning the History of the Essenes," *Tarbiz* 56 (1987) 16–17 (Hebrew).

26 Since Josephus' description of the three sects is part of his account of the reign of Jonathan the Hasmonean, the generally held view of the scholarly world is that the sectarian schism took place at that time, when the Hasmonean state was established; see for example, L. I. Levine, "The Political Struggle between Pharisees and Sadducees in the Hasmonean Period," in *Jerusalem in the Second Temple Period* (Abraham Schalit Memorial Volume; ed. A. Oppenheimer, U. Rappaport, and M. Stern; Jerusalem: Ben-Zvi, 1981) 61–83 (Hebrew); S. Mason, *Flavius Josephus on the Pharisees* (Leiden: Brill, 1991) 129–30, 196–202. Joseph Sievers, in a brilliant paper ("Josephus, First Maccabees, Sparta, the Three *Haireseis* and Cicero," *JSJ* 32 [2001] 241–51), has shown that no chronological conclusions may be drawn from the fact that Josephus first mentions the sects under Jonathan, which he believes is due to differences between the various editions of *Antiquities*. If I have correctly analyzed the above passages from the *Damascus Document*, it would appear that despite Sievers' study, the original thesis that the sectarian split took place at the time of Jonathan the Hasmonean is still valid.

27 Charlesworth, *Pesharim*, 175.

3   … "And moreover, wealth betrays a haughty man, and

4   he is unseemly, who opens his soul wide like Sheol; and like death he cannot be sated.

5   And all the nations are gathered about him, and all the peoples are assembled to him.

6   Do not all of them raise a taunt against him and interpreters of riddles about him,

7   who say: Woe to the one who multiplies what is not his own! How long will he weigh himself down with

8   debt?" Its interpretation concerns the Wicked Priest, who

9   was called by the true name at the beginning of his standing, but when he ruled

10   in Israel, his heart became large, and he abandoned God, and betrayed the laws for the sake of

11   wealth. And he stole and amassed the wealth of the men of violence who had rebelled against God,

12   and he took the wealth of peoples to add to himself guilty iniquity. And the abominable

13   ways he pursued with every sort of unclean impurity…

The Wicked Priest was "called by the true name at the beginning of his standing," most probably meaning at the outset of his public activities. However, when he became Israel's ruler, he abandoned God and began to betray the laws in his quest for riches. It is striking that the verse from Habakkuk does not describe an originally good person who then sinned; it would seem, therefore, that the author of the *Pesher on Habakkuk* had his own reason for stressing that the Wicked Priest was not originally wicked.[28]

Another passage in the same work (cols. 11–12), accuses the Wicked Priest of persecuting the members of the sect and illegally amassing riches:[29]

17   [.… "For the violence to Lebanon will cover you and the assault of beasts]

---

28   The author seems to have understood the word יבגוד, here translated as "betrays," as referring to an originally good person who has fallen into evil ways. Nevertheless, the interpretation of these verses is rather surprising; a simpler interpretation would be that since the rulers of Judaea had amassed wealth, the nations gathered against them and burdened them with "debt." This reading would be quite consistent with the general approach of the pesharim.

29   Charlesworth, *Pesharim*, 181–82.

1   will destroy. On account of human bloodshed and violence (done to) the land, the town and all who inhabit it."

2   The interpretation of the passage concerns the Wicked Priest—to pay him

3   his due inasmuch as he dealt wickedly with the Poor Ones; for "Lebanon" is

4   the Council of the Community, and the "beasts" are the simple ones of Judah, those who observe

5   the Torah—(he it is) whom God will condemn to complete destruction

6   because he plotted to destroy completely the Poor Ones. And when it says, "On account of the bloodshed of

7   the town and violence (done to) the land," its interpretation: the "town" is Jerusalem,

8   where the Wicked Priest committed abominable deeds and defiled

9   God's sanctuary. And "violence (done to) the land" (refers to) the cities of Judah, where

10   he stole the wealth of the Poor Ones...

In other words, God will punish the Wicked Priest for what he did to "the Council of the Community" (עצת היחד, that is, the sectarians) and the "simple ones" (פתאים), namely people associated with the sect. The Wicked Priest is accused not only of persecuting the sectarians (the Council of the Community, or "Judah"—hence the expression "simple ones of Judah") and robbing the "Poor Ones" of their wealth, but also of defiling the temple. God punished the Wicked Priest for plotting to destroy the Poor Ones.

Qumran scholars have disputed the identity of the Wicked Priest. Most of them agree with the proposal of Geza Vermes and Józef Milik identifying him as Jonathan the Hasmonean, who officiated as High Priest in the years 152–143 B.C.E.[30] Frank Cross identifies him with Simeon, Jonathan's brother, High Priest and *nasi* of Judaea in 143–134 B.C.E.[31] Others, mainly Israeli scholars, have suggested the identification with Alexander Jannaeus, who reigned as king in

---

30 G. Vermes, *Discovery in the Judean Desert* (New York: Desclee, 1956) 88–97; J. T. Milik, *Ten Years of Discovery in the Wilderness of Judaea* (Studies in Biblical Theology 26; London: SCM Press, 1959) 74–78.

31 F. M. Cross, *The Ancient Library of Qumran and Modern Biblical Studies* (Garden City, NY: Anchor Books, 1961) 141–56.

103–76 B.C.E.[32] It has even been suggested that there was more than one "wicked priest."[33] The identification with Simeon may be rejected, as it is based on the pesher to Joshua 6:26, which is concerned not with the Wicked Priest but with the "man of Belial."[34] The debate is therefore between scholars who identify the Wicked Priest with Jonathan the Hasmonean and those who prefer the figure of Alexander Jannaeus.[35]

We have an account of the Wicked Priest's violent death in the *Pesher on Habakkuk*, col. 9:[36]

32 J. van der Ploeg, *The Excavations at Qumran* (London, New York, and Toronto: Longmans and Green, 1958) 59–62; Yadin, "Pesher Nahum," 12; D. Flusser, "Pharisäer, Sadduzäer und Essener," 131–35; Nitzan, *Pesher Habakkuk*, 132–36.

33 A. S. van der Woude, "Wicked Priest or Wicked Priests? Reflections on the Identification of the Wicked Priest in the Habakkuk Commentary," *JJS* 33 (1982) 349–59; idem, "Once Again: The Wicked Priests in the Habakkuk Pesher from Cave 1 of Qumran," *RQ* 17 (1996) 375–84; I. R. Tantlevskij, *The Two Wicked Priests in the Qumran Commentary on Habakkuk* (Krakow and St. Petersburg: Enigma Press, 1995). This view is contested by T. H. Lim, "The Wicked Priests of the Groningen Hypothesis," *JBL* 112 (1993) 415–25. See also J. H. Charlesworth, *The Pesharim and Qumran History* (Grand Rapids and Cambridge: Eerdmans, 2002) 36–37.

34 The "man of Belial" mentioned in the pesher to Joshua 6:26 is most likely John Hyrcanus; see the next chapter.

35 Besides those mentioned, there are also a few far-fetched hypotheses. Thus, Barbara Thiering contends that the Wicked Priest was Jesus, and the Teacher of Righteousness John the Baptist; see B. E. Thiering, *Redating the Teacher of Righteousness* (Sydney: Theological Explorations, 1979). Robert Eisenman has suggested the identification of Paul as the Wicked Priest and Jesus' brother James as the Teacher of Righteousness; see R. H. Eisenman, *James the Just in the Habakkuk Pesher* (Leiden: Brill, 1986). Michael Wise argues that the Teacher of Righteousness should be some figure active in the first century B.C.E.; see M. O. Wise, *The First Messiah: Investigating the Savior before Jesus* (San Francisco: HarperSanFrancisco, 2000); idem, "Dating the Teacher of Righteousness and the *Floruit* of His Movement," *JBL* 122 (2003) 53–87; J. J. Collins, "The Time of Teacher: An Old Debate Renewed," in *Studies in the Hebrew Bible, Qumran, and the Septuagint Presented to Eugene Ulrich* (ed. P. W. Flint, E. Tov, and J. C. VanderKam; VTSup 101; Leiden and Boston: Brill, 2006) 212–29. In those studies, Wise and Collins do not discuss one of the three major arguments for the identification of the Wicked Priest with Jonathan the Hasmonean, namely, the 390 years of col. 1 of the *Damascus Document* (together with his death at the hands of his enemies, who abused his body; and the fact that he was first associated with the true faith and betrayed the laws only after becoming ruler of Israel). Another recent proposal (G. L. Doudna, *4QpNah: A Critical Edition* [JSPSup, 35; Sheffield: Sheffield Academic Press, 2001] 683–754) identifies the Wicked Priest and the Teacher of Righteousness as Aristobulus and Hyrcanus, Alexander Jannaeus' two sons, respectively. Most of these hypotheses may be refuted by paleographic considerations and the results of Carbon 14 tests; see M. A. Knibb, "Teacher of Righteousness," in *Encyclopedia of the Dead Sea Scrolls* (2 vols.; ed. L. H. Schiffman and J. C. VanderKam; Oxford: Oxford University Press, 2000) 2.918–21.

36 Charlesworth, *Pesharim*, 177.

8   "On account of human bloodshed and violence (done to) the land, the town, and its inhabitants."

9   Its interpretation concerns the [Wi]cked Priest, whom—because of wrong done to the Teacher of

10   Righteousness and the men of his counsel—God gave into the hand of his enemies to humble him

11   with disease for annihilation in bitterness of soul, beca[u]se he had acted wickedly

12   against His chosen one…

In other words, God delivered the Wicked Priest into his enemies' hands as punishment for having wronged the Teacher of Righteousness, who is referred to in this passage as God's "chosen one" (בחירו). The Wicked Priest's fate is also mentioned in three additional passages of the same work. In one of these descriptions we read (cols. 8–9):[37]

13   …"Will it not be sudden, that your cre[di]tors

14   will arise? And will those who make you tremble awake, and will you become their booty?

15   For you have plundered many nations, but all the rest of the peoples will plunder you."

16   [The interpretation of the passage] concerns the priest, who rebelled

17   [and transgre]ssed the laws of [God. And all his enemies will rise and pl]under him to [make]

1   his injury on account of wicked judgments. And horrors of evil

2   diseases were at work in him, and acts of vengeance on his carcass of flesh…

The Wicked Priest rebelled and violated God's laws. Because of his sins, he did not die a natural death, but was executed by his enemies, but only after these had tortured "his carcass of flesh."

In another passage in the *Pesher on Habakkuk*, cols. 11–12, we find a description of the suffering of the Wicked Priest:[38]

---

37 Ibid., 175–77.
38 Ibid., 180–83.

8   …"You will be sated

9   with shame rather than glory. Drink then, you yourself, and totter.

10   The cup in the right hand of the Lord will come around to you, and disgrace (will come)

11   upon your glory" *vacat*

12   Its interpretation concerns the priest whose shame prevailed over his glory,

13   for he did not circumcise the foreskin of his heart, but he walked in the ways of

14   inebriety in order that the thirst might be consumed, but the cup of the wrath of

15   [G]od will swallow him up, ad[d]ing [t]o [all] [s]ha[me] and a wound

16   […]

17   [… "For the violence to Lebanon will cover you and the assault of beasts]

1   will destroy. On account of human bloodshed and violence (done to) the land, the town and all who inhabit it."

2   The interpretation of the passage concerns the Wicked Priest – to pay him

3   his due inasmuch as he dealt wickedly with the Poor Ones…

4QpPs^a (col. 4) also describes the Wicked Priest as being captured and slaughtered by ruthless Gentiles:[39]

7   "The wicked one lies in ambush for the righteous one and seeks [to murder him. The L]ord [will not abandon him into his hand,] n[or will he] let him be condemned as guilty when he comes to trial."

8   Its interpretation concerns [the] Wicked [Pri]est, who l[ay in ambush for the Teache]r of Righte[ousness and sought to] murder him [because of the words of the Law] and the Torah

9   that he sent to him; but God will not ab[andon him into his hand,] nor [will he let him be condemned as guilty when] he comes to trial. But as for [him, God will] pay [him] his due, giving him

10   into the hand of the ruthless ones of the Gentiles to do [vengeance] against him…

39   Charlesworth, *Pesharim*, 19. See also Qimron and Strugnell, *Miqṣat Maʿasé ha-Torah*, 120.

From these five pesharim we learn that the Wicked Priest did not die a natural death, but was handed over to his enemies, who tortured him and put him to death. These descriptions are consistent with the execution of Jonathan by Tryphon in 143 B.C.E. (1 Macc 12:39–13:25), but not with the death of Alexander Jannaeus, who died a natural death during his campaign against the city of Ragaba in Transjordan (*J.W.* 1.106; *Ant.* 13.398–404). Hence the identification of the Wicked Priest as Jonathan.

The publication of the scroll known as *Miqṣat Maʿaśe ha-Torah* (MMT; "Some Observances of the Law") provides another confirmation of the identification of the Wicked Priest with Jonathan the Hasmonean.[40] Here and there in the Qumran scrolls, some otherwise unknown compositions are mentioned by name, such as *Sefer he-Hago*, *The Sealed Book of the Torah*, and *The Book of the Second Torah*.[41] Since the works discovered at Qumran are mostly untitled, it seems plausible that fragments of some of the compositions referred to in the scrolls have actually been discovered at Qumran. Elisha Qimron and John Strugnell, editors of the *editio princeps* of MMT, suggested that this text might in fact be "the Law and the Torah" mentioned in 4QpPsᵃ quoted above as having been sent by the Teacher of Righteousness to the Wicked Priest.[42] Since the publication of 4QpPsᵃ, scholars have debated the identity of "the Law and the Torah." Yigael Yadin believed that it might have been the *Temple Scroll*;[43] at that time, however, the scholarly world was unaware of the existence of MMT. Now that the latter has been published, it seems to be the most likely candidate for the role of "the Law and the Torah" mentioned in 4QpPsᵃ.[44] At the end of MMT, we read:[45]

40 The following discussion of MMT is based on H. Eshel, "4QMMT and the History of the Hasmonean Period," in *Reading 4QMMT: New Perspectives on Qumran Law and History* (ed. J. Kampen and M. S. Bernstein; Atlanta: Scholars Press, 1996) 53–65.

41 *Sefer he-Hago* is mentioned in the *Damascus Document* (10:4–6; 13:2–3; 14:6–8) and in the *Rule of the Congregation* (1:6–8); *The Sealed Book of the Torah* is mentioned in the *Damascus Document* (5:1–5); and *The Book of the Second Torah* in 4QCatena A (4Q177 fr. 2: 1, 14). For a discussion of the first work, see D. Steinmetz, "Sefer HeHago: The Community and the Book," *JJS* 52 (2001) 50–58.

42 Qimron and Strugnell, *Miqṣat Maʿaśe ha-Torah*, 120; see also J. Strugnell, "MMT: Second Thoughts on a Forthcoming Edition," in *The Community of the Renewed Covenant* (ed. E. Ulrich and J. C. VanderKam; Notre Dame: University of Notre Dame Press, 1994) 70–73.

43 Yadin, *Temple Scroll*, 396; but Qimron and Strugnell, *Miqṣat Maʿaśe ha-Torah*, 120 n. 24.

44 Both terms חוק ("law, statute") and תורה ("Torah") occur in *Miqṣat Maʿaśe ha-Torah*. The first is mentioned in part B, line 52 (Qimron and Strugnell, ibid., 52) in the context of the laws of purity and impurity, which take up much of the work's attention. The term Torah, in the passage quoted below, is used to define the work: "We have sent you *some of the precepts of the Torah*…"

45 Qimron and Strugnell, *Miqṣat Maʿaśe ha-Torah*, 62–63.

26   ...We have (indeed) sent you

27   some of the precepts of the Torah according to our decision, for the
     welfare of you and of your people. For we have seen (that)

28   you have wisdom and knowledge of the Torah. Consider all these
     things and ask Him that He strengthen

29   your will and remove from you the plans of evil and the device of
     Belial

30   so that you may rejoice at the end of time, finding that some of our
     practices are correct.

31   And this will be counted as a virtuous deed of yours, since you will be
     doing what is righteous and good in His eyes, for your own welfare
     and

32   for the welfare of Israel.

MMT is written in the first person plural and addressed to a single person,
always in the second person. Qimron and Strugnell therefore describe the work
as a legal letter. Even if one challenges the conjecture that it was a real letter, sent
to a specific addressee, and assumes instead that it is a pseudepigraphic work,[46]
one may still suppose that it was the "Law and the Torah" mentioned in 4QpPs[a].
The question of the author's identity as perceived by the readers of MMT is no
less important than the question of the author's actual identity. Given the fact
that six copies of MMT were found in Qumran Cave 4, the sectarians clearly
held it in great regard and devoted time to its study. Notably, one copy of MMT
(4Q394) begins with a list of calendrical items and festivals. Clearly then, one
of the controversies between the author of MMT and his correspondent was
the question of the calendar.[47] The passage quoted above from the *Pesher on*

---

46   Strugnell, "Second Thoughts," 67, expresses his doubts as to the definition of the work
as an "epistle." He notes that since the author was careful to use only first person plural to avoid
giving the impression of a work written by a single author, it cannot be so defined.

47   Qimron and Strugnell, *Miqṣat Maʿaśé ha-Torah*, 7–9 and Strugnell, "Second Thoughts,"
61–62, address the question whether or not the calendar is indeed part of *Miqṣat Maʿaśé ha-Torah*,
because of the two manuscripts preserving the opening sections of the work, only one contains
traces of the calendrical passages. Since 4Q394 contains an account of the calendar on the same
parchment as *Miqṣat Maʿaśé ha-Torah*, it may be assumed that at least one scribe believed there
was a connection between the calendar and the Halakhic work. If some copies of the work were
made for study by the sectarians, perhaps the calendar was not included in 4Q395 (see Qimron and
Strugnell, *Miqṣat Maʿaśé ha-Torah*, 203), possibly because the Halakhic sections were significant for
the legal differences between the sectarians and their opponents whereas the laconic calendrical
section and the beginning of the work are technical and not easily studied. It may therefore have

Habakkuk, col. 11, indicates that the reason for the Wicked Priest's persecution of the Teacher of Righteousness was specifically about the date of the Day of Atonement. At the same time, 4QpPsᵃ states that the Wicked Priest tried to kill the Teacher of Righteousness because of the "Law and the Torah" that the latter had sent him.

Since the temple service was necessarily based on an established calendar, the High Priest could hardly have agreed with a group of priests who were rejecting it and celebrating the festivals on different dates. Neither is it conceivable that the priests, following a calendar which they believed to be the true one, would consent to offer sacrifices according to an alternate calendar. Consequently, with the very validity of the temple calendar being put into question, it would have been extremely difficult for both sides to agree upon a solution. Disagreement over calendrical matters were potentials for vehement disputes, ones that could easily turn violent (a danger referred to in the Mishnah, *Rosh ha-Shanah* 2:8–9).[48]

According to the passage quoted above from the *Pesher on Habakkuk* (col. 8), the Wicked Priest "was called by the true name at the beginning of his standing." Since the verse being interpreted gives no grounds for describing the Wicked Priest in this way, the author clearly had good reason for stressing the change in the Wicked Priest's behavior.[49] Furthermore, since the author of the *Pesher on Habakkuk* states that the Wicked Priest harassed the Teacher of Righteousness and tried to harm him, he surely would not have described any part of the Wicked Priest's life in a positive light unless he wished to convey to his readers that the latter, at the beginning of his career, had not been an evil person. Presumably, the author of the *Pesher on Habakkuk* and his readers had studied MMT, or were at least familiar with it. Since the closing sections of MMT are favorably disposed toward the addressee, the author of the *Pesher on Habakkuk* had to point out that the Wicked Priest had originally been "called by the true name," and that only when he "ruled in Israel" did he abandon God and betray the Law. If this is indeed the reason for the positive reference to the Wicked Priest, it would follow that the author and his readers believed that MMT was written by the Teacher of Righteousness, who indeed addressed the Wicked Priest "at the beginning of his standing," before he began to sin and amass wealth.

---

been omitted from some copies. On the distinction between the two first fragments of 4Q394 (the calendrical fragments) and the rest of the work, see Talmon and Ben-Dov, *Calendrical Texts*, 157–66.

48 See Talmon, "Yom Hakippurim."

49 But see above, n. 28.

Another famous passage from MMT (part C) reads as follows:[50]

7   ... [And you know that] we have separated ourselves from the multitude of the people [and from all their impurity]

8   and from being involved with these matters and from participating with [them] in these things. And you [know that no]

9   *ma'al*[51] or deceit or evil can be found in our hand (i.e., in us), since for [these things] we give [... And]

10   we have [written] to you so that you may study (carefully) the book of Moses and the books of the Prophets and (the writings of) David...

Three different groups are alluded to here: "We," (אנחנו) namely, the author's own group; "you," that is, the addressee's group (אתם); and the "multitude of the people" (רוב העם).[52] In this passage, the author is trying to persuade the addressee of his own group's credentials; accordingly, he would hardly have written to him that they had "separated" from the addressee's group—a statement that might have alienated the latter. The implication is that the writer's group was not "the multitude of the people." Presumably, "the multitude of the people" had the support of most of the inhabitants of Judaea, contrary to the writer's own group and that of the addressee, both of which were comprised of fewer members.[53]

50 Qimron and Strugnell, *Miqṣat Ma'aśé ha-Torah*, 58–59.

51 Qimron and Strugnell seem to have misunderstood the precise meaning of the term מעל, which they translated as "treachery," on the basis of Lev. 5:15–16: "When a person commits a trespass (נפש כי תמעל מעל), being unwittingly remiss about any of the Lord's sacred things, he shall bring as his penalty to the Lord.... He shall make restitution... and he shall add a fifth part to it and give it to the priest." The original context of the root מע"ל is thus the misappropriation or derivation of benefit from consecrated property, as is indeed the subject-matter of Tractate Me'ilah in the Mishnah. Such an accusation was undoubtedly leveled against the priests who were in charge of the temple. For the concept of *me'ilah* before and after the destruction of the Second Temple, see B. M. Bokser, "*Ma'al* and Blessings over Food: Rabbinic Transformation of Cultic Terminology and Alternative Modes of Piety," *JBL* 100 (1981) 557–74. I am indebted to Professor Daniel Schwartz for bringing Bokser's article to my attention.

52 Qimron and Strugnell, *Miqṣat Ma'aśé ha-Torah*, 114–15. Qimron and Strugnell saw a connection between the expressions "the multitude of the people" (רוב העם) and "of you and of your people" (לך ולעמך; MMT, line 27) and therefore concluded that "the multitude of the people" was the addressee's group. However, I believe a distinction should be made between the "you" group and the "multitude," who are apparently another, third, group. See below and D. R. Schwartz, "MMT, Josephus and the Pharisees," in *Reading 4QMMT: New Perspectives on Qumran Law and History* (ed. J. Kampen and M. S. Bernstein; Atlanta: Scholars Press, 1996) 67–80.

53 Flusser suggested that the phrase "the multitude of the people" in this passage of MMT

Hence MMT reflects a situation in which the addressee was not the leader of a majority of the people, but nevertheless headed a sizable community as a recognized leader.[54] It is clear from this passage that the division of the people of Judaea into three main groups or parties already existed at the time MMT was written. Most probably, the members of the addressee's group were those later referred to as Pharisees, whereas the "multitude" mentioned in MMT eventually became known as Sadducees. The situation arising from MMT is thus consistent with the indications in 4QpPs[a] and the *Damascus Document*, as quoted above, that the other two groups were already active in Judaea during the lifetime of the Teacher of Righteousness.

The text of MMT lists more than twenty laws about which the author adhered to a more rigorous interpretation than the addressee. The dispute over these matters was most probably the core of the Halakhic controversy between the groups in the Second Temple period, but presumably it was not over these laws only that the author and his group seceded from the majority of the community. One additional reason is alluded to in lines 8–9 of the above passage: "And you know that no *ma'al* or deceit or evil can be found in our hand." This implies that there had been some who had misappropriated consecrated property, not to mention doing deceitful and evil things.[55] It was because of such misdeeds by the priests in Jerusalem, as well as Halakhic and calendrical differences, that the author of MMT and his associates broke away from the multitude of the people.[56]

---

is similar to the term "the many" (הרבים) in the sectarian scrolls; see D. Flusser, "Some of the Precepts of the Torah from Qumran (4QMMT) and the Benediction against the Heretics," *Tarbiz* 61 (1992) 366 (Hebrew). For the meaning of the term "the many" in the sectarian scrolls, see L. H. Schiffman, *The Eschatological Community of the Dead Sea Scrolls* (Atlanta: Scholars Press, 1989) 94. Given the context of MMT, the suggestion that the terms "the multitude of the people" and "the many" have the same meaning does not seem plausible.

54 Qimron and Strugnell (*Miqṣat Ma'asé ha-Torah*, 115, 117) believed that MMT was written at a time when the addressee was the leader of the "multitude of the people." Relying on the passage from the *Pesher on Habakkuk* discussed above, they suggested (ibid., 118) that MMT had been sent to the Wicked Priest "at the beginning of his standing," before "his heart became large" and he betrayed the Law. Presumably, they concluded from the words "when he ruled" in the pesher that the Wicked Priest had strayed from the straight path during his term of office, not immediately upon assuming power. Since it may well have been the appointment of the Wicked Priest as High Priest that inspired the sectarians' assault upon him, we may perhaps suggest that, if the favorable passage at the end of MMT was indeed addressed to the Wicked Priest, it reflects the sectarians' attitude before he was appointed.

55 See above, n. 51.

56 Qumran scholars have concluded that the sectarians left Jerusalem for three reasons:

All writers about the Halakhah reflected in MMT agree that the addressee's Halakhah was close to Pharisaic law.[57] This conclusion rests mainly on two well-known controversies featured both in MMT and in the Mishnah, concerning the pouring of liquid from a pure vessel into an impure one,[58] and the level of purity required of the priest charged with burning the red heifer.[59] In light of these two examples, we may conclude that the addressee of MMT favored the Pharisaic version of the Halakhah. In that case, if MMT was indeed the "Law and the Torah" that the Teacher of Righteousness sent the Wicked Priest as mentioned in 4QpPs[a], the Wicked Priest cannot possibly be identified as Alexander Jannaeus, who was a Sadducee his entire life. Jonathan the Hasmonean, however, subscribed to a Pharisaic outlook. Presumably, then, the object of MMT was to persuade him to observe the stricter halakhic norms of the Qumran community.

Yet another implication of Qimron and Strugnell's identification of

---

(a) The calendrical dispute; (b) the laws listed in MMT; (c) ideological criticism of the Jerusalem priests. One of the passages quoted above from MMT reads: "[And you know that] we have separated ourselves from the multitude of the people... And you [know that no] *ma'al* or deceit or evil can be found in our hand..." There may be a correlation between the three reasons given above—calendar, laws, and criticism of the priests—and the reference to "*ma'al*... deceit... evil" in MMT. For a dissenting view, see A. Baumgarten, "But Touch the Law and the Sect Will Split: Legal Dispute as the Cause of Sectarian Schism," *Review of Rabbinic Judaism* 5 (2002) 301–15.

57 See Y. Sussmann, "The History of the Halakha and the Dead Sea Scrolls," in Qimron and Strugnell, *Miqṣat Ma'ase ha-Torah*, 185–91; Qimron and Strugnell, *Miqṣat Ma'asé ha-Torah*, 110–11; L. Schiffman, "The New Halakhic Letter (4QMMT) and the Origins of the Dead Sea Sect," *BA* 33 (1990) 69; J. M. Baumgarten, "Sadducean Elements in Qumran Law," in *The Community of the Renewed Covenant* (ed. R. Ulrich and J. VanderKam; Notre Dame: University of Notre Dame Press, 1994) 29–30.

58 According to the Rabbinical laws of ritual purity and impurity, a food can contract impurity by contact with an impure object or substance. One question disputed in the sources is whether a (ritually pure) liquid being poured into a vessel containing impure liquid is rendered impure, being considered as "in contact" with the lower vessel through the stream of liquid being poured. The author of MMT argued that the poured liquid and that in the lower vessel are "alike, (being) a single liquid," so that the upper vessel indeed becomes impure. The Pharisees, however, ruled that the upper vessel remains pure. The same controversy is mentioned in *m. Yadayim* 4:7, as being between Pharisees and Sadducees.

59 See Num 19. The author of MMT held that the priest who burns the heifer and the priest who collects the heifer's ashes should be in a state of complete ritual purity, whereas the Pharisees held that even an impure person who had already undergone ritual immersion, but still needing to wait until sunset to be declared pure (see Lev 22:6–7), was qualified for those tasks. This particular disagreement is also documented in *m. Parah* 3:7. Yaakov Sussmann, "The History of the Halakha," 187–89, has traced other controversies mentioned in MMT to Rabbinic literature; in those cases, too, the addressee's Halakhah is that of the Pharisees.

MMT with the "Law and the Torah" sent to the Wicked Priest is that the scroll describes a situation in which most of the people followed neither the Teacher of Righteousness nor the Wicked Priest—most probably, they looked to the Hellenizers for leadership. Nevertheless, judging from MMT, the addressee did have considerable influence on the people of Judaea, as the work closes with the statement that if the addressee accepts the writer's halakhic positions, he will be doing what is right and good for himself as for all of Israel.[60]

On the basis of the pesharim and the passages quoted from the *Damascus Document*, the Vermes–Milik identification of the Wicked Priest with Jonathan the Hasmonean is highly plausible. In light of the passages quoted from the *Pesher on Habakkuk*, the reality described in MMT reflects the situation in Judaea around the year 152 B.C.E. After Judah Maccabee's death in 160 B.C.E., Jonathan became the leader of the group of people who fought the Seleucids—people who refused to give up and continued the struggle even after Judah had fallen in battle. After the death of the Hellenizing High Priest Alcimus in 159 B.C.E., Jonathan consolidated his power, until he was appointed High Priest in 152 B.C.E., replacing the unnamed High Priest who officiated from 159 to 152 B.C.E.[61] The period described in the *Pesher on Habakkuk*—the beginning of the Wicked Priest's "standing," before he became ruler of Israel—is the time of Jonathan's sojourn in Michmash, where he "began to judge the people" (1 Macc 9:70–73). During these years, Jonathan apparently had a considerable following among the people of Judaea, particularly those living outside Jerusalem. The majority, however, still considered the Hellenizers as the religious and political leadership of Judaea.[62] Presumably, even after Jonathan had become High Priest in Jerusalem, the

---

60 See the first passage quoted above from MMT (part C, lines 26–27). The phrase "for the welfare of you and of Israel" does not necessarily imply that the addressee was a leader, but that for the good of Israel, the addressee was advised to accept the writer's views. According to Qimron and Strugnell (*Miqṣat Maʿaśé ha-Torah*, 117) and Schiffman, ("New Halakhic Letter," 18–20), the comparison with Solomon and other kings of Israel indicates that the addressee was an important leader at the time MMT was written.

61 The identity of this High Priest will be discussed below.

62 Roland Deines has challenged this assumption. There is no hint in the sources, he argues, that the Hellenizers still wielded influence in Judaea after Judah Maccabee purged the temple in 164 B.C.E.; see R. Deines, "The Pharisees between 'Judaisms' and 'Common Judaism,'" in *Justification and Variegated Nomism* (ed. D. A. Carson, P. T. O'Brien, and M. A. Seifried; Tübingen and Grand Rapids: Mohr Siebeck and Baker Academic, 2001), 465–74. However, it should be remembered that history is written by the victorious party, so that even if the Hellenizers still enjoyed support in Judaea after the purification of the temple, that would hardly have been mentioned by supporters of the Hasmoneans.

priestly families of Jerusalem had not lost their influence in Judaea. The reality described in MMT, therefore, may reflect the situation when Jonathan was still at Michmash, or immediately after his appointment as High Priest in Jerusalem. Even if one assumes that MMT reflects conditions prior to his appointment, the circles opposed to the Hellenizing priests of Jerusalem must have understood by now that the hegemony of those priests was drawing to a close, and that Jonathan would soon become the ruler of Judaea. This would explain why the author of MMT included laws relating to the temple service in his work.

The separation from the "multitude of the people," as mentioned in MMT, did not necessarily involve a retreat to the desert; rather what is implied there is an ideological schism, motivated by misuse of temple funds and by the laws of ritual purity. It cannot be determined whether the followers of the Teacher of Righteousness retired to the desert in the wake of the dispute with the "Man of Lies" or the Wicked Priest. Neither can it be determined whether the Teacher of Righteousness' place of exile— where, according to the *Pesher on Habakkuk*, he was assaulted by the Wicked Priest on the Day of Atonement—was indeed Qumran. There is no way to determine whether the Teacher of Righteousness first went into exile at Qumran or whether he lived somewhere else before settling there. The earliest published pottery finds from Qumran most likely date to the beginning of the first century B.C.E.[63] Hence the Teacher of Righteousness and his disciples could have resided somewhere else before moving to Qumran. The Teacher of Righteousness is not mentioned in the *Rule of the Community* found in Cave 1, but there are two indications in that scroll that the members of the community had left their original homes and retreated to the desert. In col. 8 we read:[64]

12 ...When these become the Community in Israel
13 they shall separate themselves by these laws from the session of the men of deceit in order to depart into the wilderness to prepare there the Way of the Lord(?);
14 as it is written: "In the wilderness prepare the way of the Lord, make level in the desert a highway for our God."

63 J. Magness, "A Reassessment of the Excavations of Qumran," in *The Dead Sea Scrolls: Fifty Years after Their Discovery* (ed. L. H. Schiffman, E. Tov, and J. C. VanderKam; Jerusalem: Israel Exploration Society, 2000) 713–14.

64 J. H. Charlesworth et al., ed., *The Dead Sea Scrolls: Hebrew, Aramaic, and Greek Texts with English Translations:* Volume 1, *Rule of the Community and Related Documents* (Tübingen: Mohr Siebeck; Louisville / Westminster John Knox, 1994) 34–37.

Hence the members of the group sought—and found—ideological justification for their abandonment of Jerusalem and withdrawal to the desert. Their exile was motivated, they claimed, not only by persecution but mainly by Isaiah's prophecy in chapter 40. The next column of the scroll (col. 9) offers a similar reference:[65]

18 He shall guide them with knowledge, and instruct them in the mysteries of wonder and truth in the midst of

19 the men of the Community, so that they may walk perfectly each one with his fellow in everything which has been revealed to them. That is the time to prepare the way

20 to the wilderness...

In the middle of the second century B.C.E., three High Priests from Hellenizing circles officiated. The first was Jason, whose term lasted from 175 to 172 B.C.E. He was followed by Menelaus (172–163 B.C.E.), and then Alcimus, who served in the temple from 163 to 159 B.C.E.[66] Josephus, in *Jewish Antiquities* 20.237, relates that after the death of Alcimus, there was no High Priest for seven years.[67] However, since the Day of Atonement could not be celebrated in the temple without a High Priest, someone must have officiated during the years 159–152 B.C.E. This is confirmed by 1 Macc 10:25–45, a letter which is directed to "the nation of the Jews," such an address being different from that of all of the other letters quoted in 1 Maccabees which are addressed to the High Priest.[68] In this letter, Demetrius I promises to give the citadel in Jerusalem (the Accra) to the High Priest (v. 32). The accepted date of this letter is 152 B.C.E., before Jonathan

---

65 Ibid., 40–41; but see D. Dimant, "Not Exile in the Desert but Exile in Spirit: The Pesher of Isa. 40:3 in the *Rule of the Community*," *Meghillot* 2 (2004) 21–36 (Hebrew).

66 J. C. VanderKam, *From Joshua to Caiaphas: High Priests after the Exile* (Minneapolis: Fortress Press, 2004) 197–239. The Midrash, *Genesis Rabbah* 65:27 (ed. Theodor–Albeck, 472–73), presents a legendary account of the death of "Yakum of Zerorot" [= Alcimus], a nephew of R. Yose ben Yoezer. It has been suggested that this legend has some historical basis; see M. Hengel, *Judaism and Hellenism* (2 vols.; Philadelphia: Fortress Press, 1974) 1.80; J. A. Goldstein, *I Maccabees* (AB; Garden City, NY: Doubleday, 1976) 334–36.

67 In *Ant.* 13.46, Josephus writes that there was no High Priest for four years, from the death of Judah Maccabee until the appointment of Jonathan the Hasmonean. The number "four" is probably a mistake, relying on the erroneous tradition of *Ant.* 12.434 that Judah Maccabee served as High Priest for three years.

68 On this letter, see M. Stern, *The Documents on the History of the Hasmonaean Revolt, with a Commentary and Introductions* (Tel Aviv: Hakibbutz Hameuchad, 1973) 95–106 (Hebrew).

the Hasmonean was appointed High Priest, that is, at the end of the time during which, according to Josephus, there was no High Priest in Jerusalem.[69] It would seem, therefore, that someone took the trouble to delete the name of the High Priest from the beginning of the letter, but the text itself attests to the fact that there was a High Priest at the time.

After the discovery of the Qumran scrolls, it was suggested that the anonymous High Priest who officiated from 159 to 152 B.C.E. was the Teacher of Righteousness.[70] This hypothesis is based on the fact that the pesharim sometimes refer to the Teacher of Righteousness as "the priest," and some scholars have suggested that this designation, with the definite article (הכהן), always refers to the High Priest rather than to a common priest. The author of 1 Maccabees and the person who compiled the list of High Priests reflected in Josephus' *Jewish Antiquities* presumably tried to suppress memory of the priest who had officiated in the years 159–152 B.C.E.; for had there been no High Priest at that time, Jonathan would not have had to dispossess anyone in order to secure his own appointment as High Priest. Furthermore, had the temple indeed functioned for seven years without a High Priest, it would have been easier to agree to the appointment of a Hasmonean High Priest, who belonged to the "course" (*mishmar*) of Jehoiarib and not to the Zadok family.[71]

Another question, related to that of the identification of the Teacher of Righteousness with the anonymous High Priest, concerns the date of the secession from the "multitude of the people," mentioned in MMT. On the assumption that the author of MMT was referring to an event in the late seventies or early sixties of the second century B.C.E.—that is, that the secession took place at the time the priests in Jerusalem were the Hellenizers guilty of *ma'al*, such as Menelaus who delivered the treasures of the temple to Antiochus IV—it might be suggested that

---

69 J. G. Bunge, "Zur Geschichte und Chrolonogie des Untergangs der Oniaden und des Aufstiegs der Hasmonäer," *JSJ* 6 (1975) 27–43; J. Murphy-O'Connor, "Demetrius I and the Teacher of Righteousness," *RB* 83 (1976) 400–20.

70 On the possibility that the Teacher of Righteousness served as High Priest while Jonathan was living in Michmash, see J. Jeremias, *Der Lehrer der Gerechtigkeit*, 79–125, and also H. Stegemann, *Die Entstehung der Qumrangemeinde* (Bonn: Rheinischen Friedrich-Wilhelms-Universität, 1971).

71 As opposed to Alison Schofield and James VanderKam, it seems that since we do not find explicit statement saying that the Hasmoneans were Zadokites, we should assume that they were not from this family. Schofield and VanderKam believe that since we do not find an explicit accusation saying that the Hasmoneans were not from the House of Zadok, we must assume that they were; see A. Schofield and J. C. VanderKam, "Were the Hasmoneans Zadokites?" *JBL* 124 (2005) 73–87.

after Alcimus' death in 159 B.C.E., the Teacher of Righteousness was appointed High Priest, although probably not in an official capacity. The Teacher of Righteousness was a conservative opponent of the Hellenizing circles. On the other hand, if the description in MMT reflects the reality of the 150's B.C.E., around the time of Jonathan the Hasmonean's appointment as High Priest in 152 B.C.E., the above passage from MMT, from which we infer that most of the people did not consider the writer and the addressee as their leaders, indicates that the Teacher of Righteousness could not have been the High Priest in 159–152 B.C.E..

If the term *ma'al* indeed refers to the Hellenizers, we may suppose that the author of MMT reminded the addressee that his own group, like the Hasmoneans, had seceded from the majority, refusing to accept the leadership of the Hellenizing High Priests.[72] On the assumption that the "separation" referred to in MMT took place in the period of religious persecution, the conjecture that the Teacher of Righteousness was the High Priest in the 150's B.C.E. seems plausible. However, one must then assume that his term of office was not accompanied by any real change in the status of the group of the author of MMT, which continued to exist as a small group exercising no leadership over the majority of the people. Hence, even if the Teacher of Righteousness was indeed the High Priest in the 150's, he surely did not enjoy the support of the majority of the people of Judaea.[73]

Despite the fact that the term "*the* priest" frequently does denote the High Priest, it is not inconceivable that an important priest like the Teacher of Righteousness would be referred to by his followers as "the priest," though he may never have served as High Priest.[74] Whatever the case may be, the data

---

72 Flight to the wilderness during religious persecution is mentioned in 1 Macc 2:29–38. All that is known of the fugitives is that they were called *hasidim* and meticulously observed the Sabbath laws. One possible explanation is that they may have originated in the same conservative circles as the Teacher of Righteousness; see Hengel, *Judaism and Hellenism*, 1.175–81; see also J. Schwartz and J. Spanier, "On Mattathias and the Desert of Samaria," *RB* 98 (1991) 252–71.

73 If indeed the Teacher of Righteousness served as the High Priest in the period when the sectarians were likened to "blind men groping for the way" (CD 1:7–11), it must be assumed that his influence was so limited that not only did the majority of the people not follow him, but he could not even enlighten the sectarians and teach them the true path. More plausibly, therefore, the Teacher of Righteousness never served as High Priest.

74 See M. O. Wise, "The Teacher of Righteousness and the High Priest of the Intersacerdotium: Two Approaches," *RQ* 14 (1990) 589–602. Wise does not discuss the Yoḥanan ha-Kohen coin—the strongest evidence that any priest referred to as "*the* priest" in the Second Temple period was a High Priest; see D. Barag, "A Silver Coin of Yohanan the High Priest and the Coinage of

reviewed thus far is that, given our present state of knowledge on the matter, the identity of the anonymous priest who officiated as High Priest in the 150's B.C.E. cannot be determined. It cannot be definitively stated whether he was the Teacher of Righteousness, another conservative priest, or a fourth High Priest from the Hellenizing circles.[75]

While we have no proof that MMT is identical with the "Law and the Torah" that the Teacher of Righteousness sent to the Wicked Priest (as mentioned in 4QpPsᵃ), the content of MMT supports such a conjecture. The evidence of the pesharim favors the identification of the Wicked Priest with Jonathan the Hasmonean. The political situation reflected in MMT is consistent with that of Judaea around the year 152 B.C.E.. Tension later arose between the Teacher of Righteousness and the Wicked Priest around the question of the calendar. Thus MMT reflects the sectarians' hopes that Jonathan and his followers would adopt their strict Halakhic point of view—hopes that were dashed when Jonathan preferred the more lenient approach of the Pharisees.

It is difficult to determine the date of the Teacher of Righteousness' death.[76] As long as he was alive, his followers' messianic hopes focused on him.[77] Two

Judaea in the Fourth Century B.C.," *INJ* (1986–87) 4–21. Nevertheless, I am inclined to agree with Wise's first conclusion that the designation *"the* priest" did not necessarily refer to the High Priest. However, there are no grounds for his second conclusion, that the Teacher of Righteousness wrote the *Temple Scroll*, and that, based on the similarity between 1 Macc 10:34 and the *Temple Scroll*, it follows that the Teacher of Righteousness was the High Priest in the years 159–152 B.C.E.

75 See E. Schürer, *The History of the Jewish People in the Age of Jesus Christ* (3 vols.; rev. and ed. G. Vermes, F. Millar, and M. Black; Edinburgh:T. & T. Clark, 1973–87) 2.587.

76 Hartmut Stegemann was of the opinion, that the Teacher of Righteousness died around 110 B.C.E., see H. Stegemann, *The Library of Qumran* (Leiden: Brill, 1998) 123. His conclusion is based on the assumption that the author of the *Damascus Document* believed, based on Dan 9:24–26, that the End of Days will come 490 years after the destruction of the First Temple. Thus, the author of the *Damascus Document* divided these years into four sub-periods: 390 until the sect was established (CD 1:5–8); twenty years during which the sect members were "blind" until the Teacher of Righteousness started leading the group (CD 1: 9–11); the period in which the Teacher of Righteousness was actually leading the sect; and 40 years which will then pass between the death of the Teacher of Righteousness and the time when the messiahs from Aaron and Israel will start leading the people of Israel (CD 19:33–20:1; 20:13–15). The length of the third period was not specified in the *Damascus Document*. If we accept the assumption, that the author of the *Damascus Document* believed that the End of Days will start 490 years after the destruction of the First Temple, in order to reach the 490 years, it would appear that the Teacher of Righteousness led the sect for 40 years. Since there is evidence that the Teacher of Righteousness joined the sect around 150 B.C.E., it seems that the Teacher of Righteousness died around 110 B.C.E.; see H. Eshel, "The Two Historical Layers of *Pesher Habakkuk*," *Zion* 71 (2006) 143–52, esp. n. 3 (Hebrew).

77 For the crisis that emerged among the followers of the Teacher of Righteousness after

passages in the *Damascus Document* (cols. 19–20) indicate that the sectarians experienced a major crisis after his death:[78]

33   ...Thus all the men who entered the new Covenant
34   in the land of Damascus and returned and betrayed and departed from the well of living water
35   will not be accounted among the council of the people; and when (the latter) are written, they will not be written from the day
1   the unique Teacher was gathered in until there arises the Messiah from Aaron and from Israel...

There is little doubt that some disciples of the Teacher of Righteousness left the sect after his death. The author of the *Damascus Document* labeled them "betrayers" or traitors who had abandoned the Teacher's teachings. The gist of this passage is that people who had subscribed to the Covenant and then violated it were no longer considered "among the council of the people" and that they would not be counted among the Sons of Light when the hour of redemption would arrive. Since the revolution awaited by the sectarians failed to materialize and they did not gain control of the leadership or the temple, some members must have begun to question whether the path mapped out by the Teacher was indeed the correct one. These doubts are alluded to in the *Damascus Document* (col. 20):[79]

13   ...And from the day
14   the unique Teacher was gathered in until the end of all the men of war who turned away
15   with the Man of Lies there will be about forty years...

---

his death see H. Eshel, "The Meaning and Significance of CD 20:13–15," in *The Provo International Conference on the Dead Sea Scrolls* (ed. D. W. Parry and E. Ulrich; STDJ 30; Leiden, Boston, and Köln: Brill, 1999) 330–36.

78 Charlesworth, *Damascus Document*, 33–35. Ben Zion Wacholder has argued that these passages do not attest to the death of the Teacher of Righteousness, who he believes was not a historical but an eschatological figure; see B. Z. Wacholder, "Does Qumran Record the Death of the *Moreh*? The Meaning of *he'aseph* in *Damascus Covenant* XIX,35–XX,14," *RQ* 13 (1988) 323–30. After the publication of Wacholder's article, Joseph Fitzmyer devoted an important article to these passages, in which he proved that the Teacher had indeed died; see J. A. Fitzmyer, "The Gathering In of the Community's Teacher," *Maarav* 8 (1992) 223–28. Wacholder, however, has not changed his mind; see B. Z. Wacholder, "The Teacher of Righteousness is Alive, Awaiting the Messiah," *HUCA* 70–71 (1999–2000) 75–92.

79 Charlesworth, *Damascus Document*, 35.

The faithful were hereby informed that they needed not question the delay in the advent of redemption, for they were to wait until all the "men of war" who had strayed from the path of the Teacher of Righteousness and followed the Man of Lies had died. Only then would the messiahs "from Aaron and from Israel" arrive. This was the author's answer to those who questioned the delay in redemption's promised arrival. In effect, he compared the Teacher of Righteousness to Moses and the Teacher's generation to the generation of Israelites in the wilderness. Because of the sin of the spies and Moses' betrayal, the Israelites had to wait forty years in the wilderness until all the sinners had perished.[80] This passage in the *Damascus Document* seems to be a Midrash on the verse: "The time that we spent in travel from Kadesh-Barnea until we crossed the wadi Zered was thirty-eight years, until that whole generation of warriors had perished from the camp, as the Lord had sworn concerning them" (Deut 2:14), and the verses: "But your carcasses shall drop in this wilderness, while your children roam the wilderness for forty years, suffering for your faithlessness, until the last of your carcasses is down in the wilderness. You shall bear your punishment for forty years, corresponding to the number of days—forty days—that you scouted the land: a year for each day. Thus you shall know what it means to thwart Me" (Num 14:32–34). This Midrash-like exposition in the *Damascus Document* was intended to explain to the disciples of the Teacher of Righteousness why the expected revolution was late in coming: they would have to wait until the death of all those who had betrayed their Teacher. The comparison with Moses is based on Moses' leadership of the Israelites in the Sinai Desert and the Teacher's leadership of his followers in the Judaean Desert. Both leaders passed away before their faithful followers were admitted to the Promised Land.

To summarize: In this chapter I have tried to demonstrate a certain historical reconstruction, involving a group of Jews who first gathered together as a religious sect in Judaea around the year 170 B.C.E. (possibly in the wake of messianic expectations in Jerusalem under Antiochus IV). Some of those Jews joined forces with conservative circles in Jerusalem who were opposed to the Hellenizing priests and accused the Hellenizers of *ma'al*, that is, the

---

80 The forty years to elapse after the death of the Teacher of Righteousness are also alluded to in 4QpPs[a] (col. 2, lines 5–9): "And again a little while, and the wicked one will be no more. When I look carefully at his territory, he will not be there. Its interpretation concerns all the wicked at the end of forty years: they will be consumed, and there will not be found on earth any [wi]cked man." (Charlesworth, *Pesharim*, 11). The meaning seems to be that forty years after the death of the Teacher of Righteousness the wicked will have perished, at which point redemption will then take place.

misappropriation of temple funds for improper use. These circles probably suffered severe losses when Antiochus IV massacred large numbers of people in Jerusalem upon returning from his second campaign to Egypt in 168 B.C.E. Some of them fled to caves in the desert and were slaughtered there, having refused to fight on the Sabbath (1 Macc 2:29–38). As a result, the members of the sect could not have taken part in the Hasmonean revolt that broke out in 167 B.C.E. and which continued until Judah Maccabee's death in battle in 160 B.C.E. It is conceivable that after the Hellenizing High Priest Alcimus died in 159 B.C.E., one of the priests of those conservative circles served unofficially as High Priest on the Day of Atonement, though he probably considered himself a legitimate High Priest, as did his associates. In 152 B.C.E., Jonathan, son of Mattathias, was appointed High Priest by the Seleucid king Alexander Balas, thereby wresting the High Priesthood from the Zadokite dynasty and giving it to the Hasmoneans. The deposed priest and his followers surely could not accept such a development. After Jonathan's appointment, probably around 150 B.C.E., the Teacher of Righteousness threw his lot in with the people described in the opening lines of the *Damascus Document* and became their leader. During Jonathan's priesthood, three religious factions were solidified in Judaea—Pharisees, Sadducees, and Essenes. The Teacher of Righteousness was involved in a fundamental argument with the religious leader of the Pharisees, who is referred to in the scrolls as the "Man of Lies." The Teacher tried to persuade Jonathan the Hasmonean to adopt the solar calendar and his sect's rigorous system of Halakhah. The attempt failed and Jonathan tried to assault the Teacher of Righteousness in his place of exile, on the date of the Day of Atonement according to the Teacher's reckoning. Because of such attempts on the Teacher's life, Jonathan is referred to in the scrolls as the "Wicked Priest," and when Jonathan was put to death by Tryphon in 143 B.C.E., the sectarians saw this event as God's revenge on the Wicked Priest.[81] The death of the Teacher of Righteousness toward the end of the second century B.C.E. created a crisis

---

81 A para-Danielic scroll fragment (4Q245) contains a list of High Priests, beginning with [Lev]i and Qahat, and going on to mention Bukki, Uzzi, [Zado]k, Ebiathar, and Hi[l]kiah. Line 9 contains the name Onias, and another name, in line 10, may be restored as [Jona]than Simeon. If this reconstruction is accepted, it seems reasonable to identify Onias in line 9 with the High Priest Onias III or IV, and Jonathan and Simeon with Mattathias' sons. However, the scroll is extremely fragmentary and provides little if any historical information; see J. J. Collins and P. W. Flint, "245. 4Qpseudo–Daniel ar," in *Qumran Cave 4. XVII: Parabiblical Texts, III* (DJD 22; Oxford: Clarendon, 1996) 159–61; M. O. Wise, 4Q245 (psDan^c ar) and the High Priesthood of Judas Maccabaeus," *DSD* 12 (2005) 313–62.

among his followers and diminished its numbers. The author of the *Damascus Document* compares the Teacher of Righteousness to Moses, predicting that the time of redemption would begin only forty years later, after the death of all the traitors who has transferred their loyalties to the Man of Lies.

CHAPTER THREE

The Succession of High Priests:
John Hyrcanus and his Sons
in the Pesher to Joshua 6:26

When John Hyracus was appointed High Priest in 134 B.C.E. after his father
Simeon, the last of Mattathias' sons, was assassinated, he inherited a rather small
kingdom. In the west, Judaea had access to the Mediterranean Sea only at Jaffa;
in the east the kingdom reached as far as Jericho; its northern districts were
Ophrah, Gophnah, and Timnah; and the border between Judaea and Idumea
passed through Bet Zur, north of Hebron. John Hyrcanus ruled Judaea for
thirty-one years, and by the time he died in 104 B.C.E. he had gained control of
the Hebron Hills, Samaria, Galilee, and some areas in Transjordan. As well, most
of the coastal plane, with the exception of Ptolemais (Acre), Dor, and Gaza, were
under Judaean rule. As the first Hasmonean High Priest to rule in Judaea for an
extended period, he successfully consolidated the Hasmonean state. An allusion
to John Hyrcanus can be found in the Dead Sea scrolls, in a passage interpreting
Joshua's curse on whoever rebuilds the city of Jericho (Josh 6:26).

In 1956, John Allegro published a text found in Qumran Cave 4, known
as 4QTestimonia (4QTest) or 4Q175.[1] The text, written on a single sheet by the
same scribe who copied the *Rule of the Community* from Cave 1,[2] quotes three
passages from the Torah and ends with an interpretation of Josh 6:26. Allegro

---

1   J.M. Allegro, "Further Messianic References in Qumran," *JBL* 75 (1956) 182–87.
2   The same scribe also copied 4QSam^c, corrected the great Isaiah scroll (1QIsa^a) and perhaps other scrolls as well. See E. C. Ulrich, "4QSam^c: A Fragmentary Manuscript of 2 Samuel 14
– 15 from the Scribe of the *Serek Ha-yahad* (1QS)," *BASOR* 235 (1979) 3; E. J. C. Tigchelaar, "In
Search of the Scribe of 1QS," in *Emanuel: Studies in Hebrew Bible, Septuagint and Dead Sea Scrolls
in Honor of Emanuel Tov* (ed. S. M. Paul, R. A. Kraft, L. H. Schiffman, and W. W. Fields; VTSup 94;
Leiden and Boston: Brill, 2003) 439–52.

called the text *Testimonia*, a title given by the Church Fathers to collections of proof texts for a specific religious idea, particularly when relating to messianism.[3] The scroll has survived almost in its entirety, except for a missing fragment in the lower right-hand corner, which contained the beginnings of the lines in the passage dealing with Josh 6:26. Whenever the scribe began a passage dealing with a new subject, he made a hook-shaped mark between the lines; this mark is visible at the beginnings of the last three sections. The text reads as follows:[4]

1 And **** spoke to Moses, saying: "You have heard the words that this people
2 have spoken to you; all they have said is right.
3 that their heart were always like this, to fear me and to keep all
4 My commandments always, that it might be well with them and their children forever!
5 I will raise up for them a Prophet like you from among their brethren. I will put My words
6 into his mouth and he shall tell them all that I command him. And it shall come to pass, that man
7 who will not listen to My words that the Prophet shall speak in My name, I
8 shall require [a reckoning] from him.

9 And he took up his parable, and said: Oracle of Balaam son of Beor, and oracle of the man
10 whose eye is penetrating. Oracle of Him who has heard the words of God, who knows the wisdom of the Most High, who
11 sees the vision of the Almighty, who falls and his eyes are opened. I see him but not now.
12 I behold him but not near. A star shall come out of Jacob and a scepter shall rise out of Israel; and he shall crush

---

3   J.A. Fitzmyer, "4QTestimonia and the New Testament," *Theological Studies* 18 (1975) 513–37.

4   The version of the scroll is based on Allegro's addition and Strugnell's emendations. See J. M. Allegro, *Qumran Cave 4, I (4Q158-4Q186)*, (DJD 5; Oxford: Clarendon, 1968) 57–60; J. Strugnell, "Notes en marge du volume V des *Discoveries in the Judaean Desert of Jordan*," *RQ* 7 (1970) 225–29. The reconstruction of line 25 "made rulers of his sons" (והמשיל את בניו) is based on Milik's suggestion. See J. T. Milik, *Ten Years of Discovery in the Wilderness of Judaea* (Studies in Biblical Theology 26; London: SCM Press, 1959) 61–62, n. 1.

13 the temples of Moab and destroy all the children of Sheth.

14 And of Levi he said: Give Your Tummim to Levi, and your Urim to Your pious one, whom

15 You tested at Massah, and with whom You quarreled at the waters of Meribah; who said to his father, <"I do not>

16 <see you,"> and to his mother, "I do not know you," and who did not acknowledge his brother and did not know

17 his sons. For he observed Your word and kept Your covenant. And they shall cause Your precepts to shine for Jacob

18 and Your law for Israel. They shall place incense before Your nostrils and a burnt-offering upon Your altar.

19 Bless, O ****, his power and delight in the work of his hands. Smite the loins of his adversaries and let his enemies

20 rise no more.

21 <And it came to pass,> at the time when Joshua finished praising and giving thanks with his praises,

22 he said, "Cursed be the man who builds this city; with his firstborn

23 shall he lay its foundations, and with his youngest shall he set up its gates." And behold, ᵃ man accursed, a man of Belial,

24 shall arise to be a fowl[er's sn]are to his people, and destruction to all his neighbors. And he shall arise

25 [and appoint his sons to rule,] so that the two of them will be instruments of violence. And they will again build

26 [this city. And they will es]tablish for it a wall and towers, to make a refuge of wickedness

27 [and a great evil] in Israel and a horrible thing in Ephraim and in Judah

28 [... and they] shall cause pollution in the land, and great contempt among the sons of

29 [Jacob, and they shall pour out bl]ood like water upon the ramparts of the Daughter of Zion, and within the precincts of

30 <the daughter of> Jerusalem.

The scribe who wrote 4QTest and the *Rule of the Community* (1QS) never wrote the Tetragrammaton, writing instead four dots. When he wrote 4QTest he occasionally erased incorrectly written words and added words between the lines.[5] Paleographic studies indicate that this scribe worked in the first quarter of the first century B.C.E.[6] In his 1956 article Allegro noted that the first three passages deal with "good" leaders: the true prophet, the ruler chosen by God to rule Israel, and the priest described by Moses in his blessing of the tribe of Levi. The last passage, however, refers to a negative personality. In describing 4QTest as a series of quotations, Allegro believed that the last passage in the scroll was taken from a work that was customarily referred to as 4Q*Psalms of Joshua,* noting that Strugnell had recognized that this identical passage appeared in a scroll describing Joshua. However, in his first publication, Allegro did not notice that the first passage in 4QTest was taken from a harmonistic version of the Book of Exodus, similar to the Samaritan version of Exodus.[7] Instead, he wrote that the text consisted of quotations from Deut 5:28–29, 18:18–19, Num 24:16–17, Deut 33:8–11, followed by the passage from the *Psalms of Joshua.* Immediately after the publication, Patrick Skehan pointed out Allegro's oversight.[8] The harmonistic editors of the Masoretic Text of the Pentateuch were trying to establish a text free of inner contradictions. They were aware of two passages in Deuteronomy, both relating to the true prophet and Mount Sinai, that are not in the Book of Exodus. In Deut 5:24 we read that God heard the people's appeal to Moses at Sinai to be their intermediary as the one to relay God's words to them, and that God responded to their request by commenting "all they have said is right." In Deut 18:16 we read that God would raise up a prophet for the Israelites, and that this request was in line with "what [they] asked of the Lord [their] God at

5   When the scribe wished to erase letters or words written on the scroll, he rubbed the scroll with a knife. With the aid of infrared photographs we are now able to read the erased words. These letters appear here in < >.

6   Nahman Avigad dated the script of the *Rule of the Community* from cave 1 (1QS) to the period of the great Isaiah scroll, that is to the second half of the second century B.C.E., or slightly later. See N. Avigad, "The Paleography of the Dead Sea Scrolls and Related Documents," in *Aspects of the Dead Sea Scrolls* (eds. C. Rabin and Y. Yadin; Scripta Hierosolymitana 4; Jerusalem: Magnes, 1958) 71. Cross dated the scroll to the first quarter of the first century B.C.E. See F. M. Cross, "The Development of the Jewish Scripts," in *The Bible and the Ancient Near East: Essays in Honor of William Foxwell Albright* (ed. G. E. Wright; Garden City, New York: Doubleday, 1965) 198, n. 116. Birnbaum dated this scroll to the last quarter of the second century B.C.E. See S. A. Birnbaum, *The Hebrew Scripts, I: The Text* (Leiden: Brill, 1971) 134. There is no doubt that the scribe of 1QS is the same scribe of 4QTest.

7   On the character of the harmonistic editing see E. Tov, "The Nature and Background of Harmonizations in Biblical Manuscripts," *JSOT* 31 (1985) 3–29; E. Eshel, "4QDeut^n: A Text that has Undergone Harmonistic Editing," *HUCA* 62 (1991) 117–54.

8   P. W. Skehan, "The Period of the Biblical Texts from Khirbet Qumran," *CBQ* 19 (1957) 435.

Horeb, on the day of the Assembly..." Since these details are not mentioned in the description of the theophany at Sinai in Exodus, the harmonistic redactor added these verses to Exodus 20 after v. 17. Since these passages appear one after the other in the Samaritan Pentateuch, as in the first passage of the 4QTest, the scribe who wrote the scroll probably quoted the first passage from a harmonistic version of the Book of Exodus. This would suggest that 4QTest is comprised of quotations from Exodus, as well as from Numbers and Deuteronomy, followed by the passage interpreting Josh 6:26.

The last passage in 4QTest is also documented in a different fragmentary scroll from Qumran Cave 4, 4Q379. The scroll, an account of Joshua's deeds, was first called *Psalms of Joshua* (because of the first sentence in our passage), but since the work contains no psalms, it would perhaps be better to refer to it as the *Deeds of Joshua*. It is also documented in another scroll, 4Q378, but the passage interpreting Josh 6:26 has survived only in 4Q379.[9] Some scholars believe that the *Psalms of Joshua* enjoyed canonical status in the Qumran sect and that this would explain why it was quoted together with pentateuchal passages in 4QTest.[10] The text interpreting Josh 6:26 in 4Q379 reads as follows:[11]

7 At the time when Josh[u]a fin[ish]ed pr[aising and giving] than[ks] with [his] praises, [he said:]

8 C[ursed be the m]an who bu[il]ds this [ci]ty. With [his] firstborn [shall he lay its foundations]

9 and with [his yo]ung[est] shall he set up its gates. *vacat* And behold, [a man ac]cursed, a m[an of Belial,]

10 [shall arise] to b[e] a fowler's snare to his people, and destruction to all hi[s] neighbors. And he shall ari[se]

11 [and appoint his sons to rule,] so that the two of them will be vessels of violence, and they will again build

9 For the preliminary publication of the fragment, see C. Newsom, "The 'Psalms of Joshua' from Qumran Cave 4," *JJS* 39 (1988) 56–73. It was later discussed by Lim, who offered some emendations to Newsom's reconstructions. Among these reconstructions some seem correct, while others seem less plausible. See T. H. Lim, "The *Psalms of Joshua* (4Q37 fr. 22 col. 2): A Reconsideration of Its Text," *JJS* 44 (1993) 309–12. For the *editio princeps* see C. Newsom, "379. 4QApocryphon of Joshua[b]," in *Qumran Cave 4, XVIII: Parabiblical Texts, III* (DJD 22; Oxford: Clarendon, 1996) 263–88.

10 See Milik, *Ten Years*, 61; Newsom, "Psalms of Joshua," 59.

11 Newsom, "Apocryphon of Joshua," 278–81. Newsom did not reconstruct the beginning of line 11, but it seems that Milik's reading here is correct (Milik, *Ten Years*, 61–62, n. 1) and should be accepted.

12 [t]his [city]. And they will establish for it a wall and towers in order to make [a refuge of wickedness] {in Israel and a horrible thing in Ephraim [and in Judah]}

13 [in the land,] a great [w]ickedness among the sons of Jacob. And [they] will po[ur out blood.]

14 [And they will cause pollution] in the land and great contempt like wa[ter upon the ramparts of the Daughter of Zion]

15 [and within the precincts of Jerusalem]...

On the basis of paleographic considerations, 4Q379 should be dated to the middle of the first century B.C.E.[12] The scribe who copied the text omitted nine words due to a *homoioteleuton*, meaning that he skipped the text because of the two occurrences of the word גדלה ("great"). After line 13 and the words "and they will pour out blood", he realized the omission and added four words between lines 12 and 13, inserting the remaining five words at the beginning of line 14. However, he did not rewrite the words "and they will pour out blood", continuing instead from the middle of the sentence, "like water upon the ramparts of the Daughter of Zion."[13]

When 4QTest was published, considerable scholarly attention was directed to the historical background of the passage which mirrored Josh 6:26. The passage is strongly reminiscent of a pesher, since it interprets a biblical verse in light of contemporary events.[14] Accordingly, it is assumed that the author of the passage believed that Joshua's curse was still in effect in his time as well.[15] Consequently,

12 Newsom, "Apocryphon of Joshua," 263. 4Q378 is written in a script dated to the beginning of the first century C.E. (ibid. 241).

13 Ibid. 279.

14 Yadin was the first to define this paragraph as a pesher. See Y. Yadin, "Recent Developments in the Dead Sea Scrolls Research," in *Studies in the Dead Sea Scrolls* (ed. J. Liver; Jerusalem: Kiryat Sepher, 1957) 53–54 [Hebrew]. On the definition of the literary genre of the pesharim found at Qumran see G. J. Brooke, "Qumran Pesher: Towards the Redefinition of a Genre," *RQ* 10 (1981) 483–503. Even though the word "pesher" is not mentioned in the last paragraph of 4QTest, the fact that it includes contemporizing exegesis of biblical verses justifies its classification as a pesher. See H. Eshel, "The Historical Background of the Pesher – Interpreting Joshua's Curse on the Rebuilder of Jericho," *RQ* 15 (1991) 409–20.

15 Though the people of Qumran knew the prophecies had a meaning relevant to the time they were uttered, they believed the prophecies include an additional meaning relating to the end of time, thought by them to be their own time. Accordingly, they considered Joshua's curse to apply both to Hiel of Bethel who built Jericho in the days of Ahab (1 Kgs 16:34) as well as to John Hyrcanus who built Jericho in the Second Temple period, since two of his sons died in a short period of time under what could appear to be unnatural circumstances.

he expanded and elaborated upon the evil deeds of the man of Belial and his sons, associating them with the bloodshed in Jerusalem. While many scholars believe that they have successfully deciphered the historical allusions in the last passage, there is little consensus as almost all the Hasmonean rulers have in turn been identified as being the "man of Belial" in question.

The proposed interpretations of the historical background of the last passage of 4QTest may be classified according to whether they identify the "city" in question as Jerusalem or as Jericho. Those who believe that the passage refers to Jerusalem point to the fact that Jericho is not mentioned at all in the passage, whereas Jerusalem receives explicit mention. Moreover, the phrase העיר הזאת ("this city") occurs fifty-six times in the Bible, fifty-three of them in reference to Jerusalem. Scholars of this school therefore believed that the author of the pesher interpreted Joshua's curse as aimed at the ruler who had built Jerusalem. It should be noted that the version of Josh 6:26 in the Septuagint is shorter than in the Masoretic version, and moreover does not mention Jericho. In the Masoretic Text, the verse reads as follows: "At that time Joshua pronounced this oath: 'Cursed of the Lord shall be the man who shall undertake to build this city of Jericho; with his firstborn shall he lay its foundations, and with his youngest shall he set up its gates.'" In the Septuagint version, however, it reads: "On that day Joshua pronounced this oath before the Lord: 'Cursed shall be the man who shall build *that city*. With his firstborn…'" Presumably, therefore, the author of our passage quoted the verse from a text similar to that of the Septuagint.[16]

Several different explanations proposed for the historical background of the last passage of 4QTest will be reviewed in chronological order, beginning with the suggestion that the events occurred in the fourth century B.C.E. and ending with to the proposal that the events date to the first century B.C.E. Carol Newsom contends that by the time the scroll was copied, the passage interpreting Joshua's curse possessed canonical status at Qumran, and that the pesher was probably written before the second century B.C.E. As a result, she suggests that the historical events that led to the fortification of Jericho took place in the fourth century B.C.E. when the people of that city rebelled against Artaxerxes III (ca. 343 B.C.E.). Even so, it may be appropriate to distinguish between the historical background that inspired the *composition* of the pesher in the fourth or third century B.C.E., and the background of its *quotation* in 4QTest. As Newsom

16 On this matter see F. M. Cross, *The Ancient Library of Qumran and Modern Biblical Studies* (Garden City, NY: Anchor Books, 1961) 151, n. 84; Strugnell, "Notes," 228; L. Mazor, "The Origin and Evolution of the Curse upon the Rebuilder of Jericho: A Contribution of Textual Criticism to Biblical Historiography," *Textus* 14 (1988) 4–7.

herself notes, one needs to reserve judgment and allow for the possibility that the quotation could have been referring to later events.[17]

In Milik's view, the passage alludes to Mattathias the Hasmonean and his two sons, Simeon and Jonathan.[18] The pesher would then be referring to the rebuilding of a city by the two sons, namely, the fortification of Jerusalem under the two Hasmonean brothers before Tryphon's 146 B.C.E. campaign.[19]

Cross understands the passage as describing the rebuilding of Jericho under Simeon and the murder of his two sons, Mattathias and Judah, in the fortress of Doq, above Jericho, in 134 B.C.E.[20] The bloodshed in Jerusalem alluded to in the passage is Antiochus Sidetes' attempt to conquer Judaea and Jerusalem in 134–132 B.C.E.[21]

Skehan suggests that the passage refers to the fortification of Jerusalem with the accursed man being Jonathan, the son of Mattathias. He proposes that the use of the plural in the phrase "they will again rebuild" indicates that it was Simeon who completed the work of fortification. He regards the phrase "so that the two of them will be vessels of violence [כלי חמס]" as a reference to Gen 49:5: "Simeon and Levi are brothers; their weapons are tools of lawlessness [כלי חמס]," and therefore as proof that Simeon and his brother Jonathan were indeed the persons who shed blood in Jerusalem. The pesher was written, he believes, after the assassination of Simeon and his two sons near Jericho, justified, as it were, by Joshua's curse on whoever rebuilt that city.[22]

Otto Betz and William Brownlee identify the accursed man as John Hyrcanus I and the two sons who ruled Judaea as Aristobulus I and Alexander Jannaeus.[23] Jean Starcky similarly suggested that the "man of Belial" was John Hyrcanus I, but identified the sons as Aristobulus and Antigonus.[24]

17 Newsom, "Psalms of Joshua," 69–73.

18 Milik, *Ten Years*, 61–64. Knibb also adopted this view. See M. A. Knibb, *The Qumran Community* (Cambridge: Cambridge University Press, 1987) 266.

19 1 Macc 10:45, 12:36–37; *Ant.* 13.57, 181, 202.

20 Cross, *Ancient Library*, 147–52; idem, "The Early History of the Apocalyptic Community at Qumran," in *Canaanite Myth and Hebrew Epic: Essays in History of the Religion of Israel* (Cambridge, MA: Harvard U. P., 1973) 326–42. See also H. Burgmann, "Gerichtsherr und Generalankläger: Jonathan und Simon," *RQ* 9 (1977) 12. Possibly Simeon's eldest son was John Hyrcanus, not Judah; see W. H. Brownlee, *The Meaning of the Qumran Scrolls for the Bible* (New York: Oxford U. P., 1964) 102.

21 *J.W.* 1.61; *Ant.* 13.236–47.

22 W. Skehan, "Two Books on Qumran Studies," *CBQ* 21 (1959) 74–75.

23 O. Betz, "Donnersöhne, Menschenfischer und der davidische Messias," *RQ* 3 (1961) 42, n. 4; Brownlee, *Meaning* 101-4.

24 J. Starcky, "Les Maîtres de Justice et la chronologie de Qumrân," in *Qumrân: Sa Piété, sa*

Allegro, Dupont-Sommer, and Yadin believe that the reference is to Alexander Jannaeus and his sons Hyrcanus and Aristobulus, since according to Josephus it was their struggle for dominion that brought Pompey to Judaea in 63 B.C.E.[25] In Yadin's view, the passage alludes to the fortresses built by the Hasmoneans at Jericho, while Allegro and Dupont-Sommer believed that the allusion is to Jerusalem.[26]

In summary, Newsom, Cross, and Yadin associate the pesher to Josh 6:26 to the city of Jericho.[27] Newsom reached this conclusion on the basis of the surviving fragments of the *Deeds of Joshua*, in which the pesher recounts Joshua's activities and does not contain any additions not found in the biblical account.[28] Since she believes the pesher to be part of the *Deeds of Joshua*, it is not plausible that the writer should redirect Joshua's curse from Jericho to Jerusalem.[29] To quote Yadin, "it is not plausible that the author of the pesher rejected the plain sense of the explicit prohibition on rebuilding Jericho, especially as the rebuilding of Jerusalem surely would not have been considered a sinful act, the city having been rebuilt after its destruction in periods preceding the composition of the

---

théologie et son milieu (ed. M. Delcor; BETL 46; Paris: Duculot, 1978) 253.

25 J. M. Allegro, "Further Messianic References in Qumran Literature," *JBL* 75 (1956) 187, n. 109; A. Dupont-Sommer, *The Essene Writings from Qumran* (Cleveland and New York: World Publishing Company, 1962) 355–56; Yadin, "Recent Developments," 53–54.

26 Driver and Vermes also argued that the city was Jerusalem. See G. R. Driver, *The Judaean Scrolls* (Oxford: Blackwell, 1965) 138–40; G. Vermes, *The Dead Sea Scrolls: Qumran in Perspective* (London: Collins, 1977) 80–81.

27 Doudna argued that the composition should not be associated with Jericho, following his argument that the pesharim refer only to Jerusalem, and not to other towns in Judaea. See G. L. Doudna, *4Q Pesher Nahum: A Critical Edition* (JSPSup 35; Sheffield: Sheffield Academic Press, 2001) 467–68, n. 526.

28 But see E. Qimron, "Concerning 'Joshua Cycles' from Qumran (4Q522)," *Tarbiz* 63 (1994) 503–8 (Hebrew). Still, it is not certain that 4Q522 is indeed related to 4Q378 and 4Q379, in contrast to Emanuel Tov and Devorah Dimant who considered these three scrolls to be part of a single composition which they entitled "The Apocryphon of Joshua." See E. Tov, "The Rewritten Book of Joshua as found at Qumran and Masada," in *Biblical Perspectives: Early Use and Interpretation of the Bible in Light of the Dead Sea Scrolls* (ed. M. E. Stone and G. E. Chazon; STDJ 28; Leiden, Boston, and Köln: Brill, 1998) 233–56; D. Dimant, "*The Apocryphon of Joshua: 4Q522 9 ii:* A Reappraisal," in *Emanuel: Studies in Hebrew Bible, Septuagint and Dead Sea Scrolls in Honor of Emanuel Tov* (ed. S. M. Paul, R. A. Kraft, L. H. Schiffman, and W. W. Fields; VTSup 94; Leiden and Boston: Brill, 2003), 179–204; D. Dimant, "Between Sectarian and Non-Sectarian: The Case of the *Apocryphon of Joshua*," in *Reworking the Bible: Apocryphal and Related Texts from Qumran* (ed. E.G. Chazon, D. Dimant, and R. A. Clements; STDJ 58; Leiden and Boston: Brill, 2005) 105–34.

29 Newsom, "Psalms of Joshua," 69–70.

pesher."[30] We possess insufficient information about the history of Jericho in particular, and of Judaea in general, during the fourth and third centuries B.C.E.,[31] but given the nature of the historical allusions documented in the scrolls, the idea that the pesher would be alluding to such an early period does not seem well founded. Furthermore, Yadin's suggestion should be rejected for paleographic reasons, since it indicates that 4QTest was copied before the time of Jannaus' sons, Hyrcanus and Aristobulus.[32]

In order to evaluate Cross' interpretation, I quote here below the available information about the events in Jericho in 134 B.C.E. The final chapter in 1 Maccabees is devoted to the assassination of Simeon at Jericho:[33]

> Ptolemy the son of Abubos received the post of commander over the plain of Jericho, and he had much gold and silver, for he was the son-in-law of the high priest. Intoxicated with his success, he formed the desire to seize control over the country and treacherously plotted to do away with Simeon and his sons. Simeon was conducting a tour of inspection of the towns of his country and looking to their needs when he came down to Jericho with his sons Mattathias and Judas, in the year 177 in the eleventh month, which is the month of Shebat. The son of Abubos treacherously received them in the castle called Doq, which he had built; there he concealed men while he set a sumptuous banquet before his guests. When Simeon and his sons became drunk, Ptolemy and his men emerged from hiding, seized their arms, and rushed into the banquet hall upon Simeon and killed him and his two sons and some of their servants. Thus Ptolemy committed high treason and returned evil for good.
>
> He then wrote an account of what he had done and sent a messenger with it to the king, asking the king to send him troops to assist him, offering to deliver to the king the cities and the taxes. He sent other men to Gazara to do away with John, and to the regimental commanders he sent letters to come to him, intending to bribe them with silver and gold and with gifts.

30 Yadin, "Recent Developments," 54.

31 On the revolt of Jericho in the days of Artaxerxes Ochus, see E. Schürer, *The History of the Jewish People in the Age of Jesus Christ* (3 vols.; rev. and ed. G. Vermes, F. Millar, and M. Goodman; Edinburgh: T. & T. Clark, 1973–87) 1.6; H. Eshel and H. Misgav, "A Fourth Century B.C.E. Document from Ketef Yeriho," *IEJ* 38 (1988) 175–76.

32 See the paleographic studies mentioned above, n. 6.

33 The translation is based on J. A. Goldstein, *I Maccabees* (AB; Garden City, NY: Doubleday, 1976) 523.

Others he sent to seize Jerusalem and the temple mount. However, a man ran up to John at Gazara and informed him that his father and brothers had perished and told him, "He has also sent men to kill you." On hearing the news, John was stunned, but he seized the men who had come to kill him and slew them, for he knew that they sought to do away with him.

Josephus describes the same events but, contrary to the account in 1 Maccabees,[34] in which Simon and his two sons, Judah and Mattathias, were killed in Jericho in the fortress of Doq, no mention is made of Simon's wife (the mother of John Hyrcanus). Josephus' description in *Jewish War* I and in *Jewish Antiquities* XIII is much more dramatic:[35]

> Now he ruled over the Jews for eight years in all, and died while at a banquet, as a result of the plot formed against him by his son-in-law Ptolemy, who then seized and imprisoned his wife and two sons, and also sent men to put to death his third son John, also called Hyrcanus. But the youth, being aware of their coming, escaped danger at their hands and hastened to the city, trusting in the people to help him because of his father's good deeds and the masses' hatred of Ptolemy. When, therefore, Ptolemy also made an effort to enter through another gate, the populace drove him away, for they had already admitted Hyrcanus.
>
> And so Ptolemy withdrew to one of the fortresses above Jericho, which was called Dagon. But Hyrcanus, having assumed the high-priestly office of his father, first propitiated God with sacrifices, and then marched out against Ptolemy and attacked his stronghold; and though in all other respects he was superior to him, in one thing he was at a disadvantage, that is, in feeling pity for his mother and brothers. For Ptolemy had brought them up on to the wall and maltreated them in the sight of all, threatening to hurl them down headlong if Hyrcanus did not give up the siege. And so, reflecting that the more he slackened his efforts to capture the place, the

---

34 On the use of Josephus of the first chapters of 1 Maccabees see I. M. Gafni, "Josephus and I Maccabees," in *Josephus, the Bible and History* (ed. L. H. Feldman and G. Hata; Detroit: Wayne State University Press, 1989) 116–31; L. H. Feldman, "Josephus' Portrayal of the Hasmoneans Compared with 1 Maccabees," in *Josephus and the History of the Greco-Roman Period* (ed. F. Parente and J. Sievers; Leiden, New York, and Köln: Brill, 1994) 41–68; still, it seems that Josephus did not have the last three chapters of the book in front of him, where most of Simon's acts are described.

35 The translation is based on R. Marcus, *Josephus, Jewish Antiquities Books XII–XIV* (Loeb Classical Library; Cambridge, MA: Harvard University Press, 1933) 343–47.

greater was the kindness he would show those dearest to him by sparing them suffering, Hyrcanus relaxed his eagerness. His mother, however, stretched out her hands, beseeching him not to weaken on her account, but to give way to his anger all the more, and make every effort to take the place and get his foe into his power and avenge those dearest to him. For, she said, it would be pleasant for her to die in torment if the enemy, who was doing these things to them, paid the penalty for his crimes against them. Now when his mother said these things, Hyrcanus was seized with a powerful desire to capture the fortress, but when he saw her being beaten and torn apart, he became unnerved and was overcome with compassion at the way in which his mother was being treated. But while the siege was being protracted in this manner, there came round the year in which the Jews are wont to remain inactive, for they observe this custom every seventh year, just as on the seventh day. And Ptolemy, being relieved from the war for this reason, killed the brothers and mother of Hyrcanus, and after doing so, fled to Zenon, surnamed Cotylas, who was ruler of the city of Philadelphia (*Ant.* 13.228–35; *J.W.* 1.54–60 with slight changes).

Josephus presumably described these incidents on the basis of a Hellenistic work, written in a vivid style. The source was probably the world history of Nicholas of Damascus, who generally described the history of the Hasmoneans with much drama, emphasizing their internecine strife and belittling their military victories.[36] Since the historical accuracy of Josephus' report is suspect, the archaeological remains around the fortress of Doq are of particular importance. The ruins of siege works attest to an attempt to besiege the fortress and capture it—possibly John Hyrcanus' attempt to punish Ptolemy as described above.[37] Another plausible point in Josephus' account is the *halakhah* prohibiting all warfare during the sabbatical year, as indeed documented in the *War Scroll*.[38]

36 M. Stern, *Greek and Latin Authors on Jews and Judaism*, (3 vols.; Jerusalem: Israel Academy of Sciences, 1976–84) 1.229–31.

37 On the remains of the siege system around the fortress of Doq, see Z. Meshel, "The Siege Systems during the Hasmonean Period," in *Zev Vilnay's Jubilee Volume* (2 vols.; ed. E. Schiller; Jerusalem: Ariel, 1984–87) 1.256–58 (Hebrew).

38 Y. Yadin, *The Scroll of the War of the Sons of Light against the Sons of Darkness* (Oxford: Oxford University Press, 1962) 20, n.1; further evidence that John Hyrcanus followed the halakhic system documented in the Qumran scrolls in his early years may also be found in the writings of Josephus. Josephus quotes Nicholas as saying that when John Hyrcanus joined Antiochus VII's campaign to conquer Babylon, the entire army was forced to wait two days because of Pentecost, see *Ant.* 13.250–53. Such an incident, in which Pentecost falls on a Sunday is possible in the Phari-

Then it is quite plausible that John Hyrcanus would have had to interrupt the siege because of the sabbatical year. Nevertheless, these particulars by no means confirm all the details of Josephus' dramatic account.

Returning to Cross' contention that the last passage in 4QTest, interpreting Josh 6:26, alludes to the murder of Simeon and his sons at Jericho,[39] I reject it for several reasons: (a) there is no evidence that Simeon built Jericho and the information in 1 Maccabees cites Ptolemy as the builder of the Doq fortress; (b) Simeon's two sons Judah and Mattathias built neither Jericho nor Jerusalem; (c) as to the bloodshed, while we are indeed told that Simeon's son Judah fought Candebius in the region of Kedron near Jamnia and was wounded in this battle (1Macc 16:1–10), we know nothing of his brother Mattathias, who was probably too young when he was killed to have had any opportunity to personally shed blood. There is no reason, therefore, to assume that the two sons had shed blood in Jerusalem; (d) if one accepts Milik's reconstruction of line 25, "[and appoint his sons to rule]," Cross' interpretation is no longer possible, since Judah and Mattathias never ruled Judaea. As a result, the pesher cannot refer to the events of 134 B.C.E.

I am inclined to agree with Yadin and Cross that the pesher is alluding to events that took place in Jericho. The events, however, were not the assassination of Simeon in 134 B.C.E. but the construction of the Hasmonean estate and winter palace at Jericho during the reign of John Hyrcanus, Simeon's son. In the years 1973–87, archeological excavations directed by Ehud Netzer near Jericho uncovered this estate with several Hasmonean and Herodian palaces.[40] The finds at the site of the early Hasmonean palace indicate that it was built by John Hyrcanus I and his successors further fortified it, adding a defensive moat. Netzer conjectured that the palace was fortified during the civil war in the days of Alexander Jannaeus (94–88 B.C.E.).[41] The finds at Jericho and Josephus' account support Starcky's view that the author of the last passage in 4QTest was applying Joshua's curse to John Hyrcanus I and his sons, Aristobulus and Antigonus after

---

saic lunar calendar. According to the 364-day calendar used in Qumran, Pentecost always occurred on a Sunday.

39 Cross, *Ancient Library*, 147–52.

40 See E. Netzer, "The Hasmonean and Herodian Winter Palaces at Jericho," *IEJ* 25 (1975) 89–100; idem, *Hasmonean and Herodian Palaces at Jericho, 1: Stratigraphy and Architecture* (Jerusalem: Israel Exploration Society, 2001) 1–49; idem, *Hasmonean and Herodian Palaces at Jericho: Stratigraphy and Architecture, 2* (Jerusalem: Israel Exploration Society, 2004) 3–38; R. Bar-Nathan, *Hasmonean and Herodian Palaces at Jericho: The Pottery* (Jerusalem: Israel Exploration Society, 2002) 14.

41 Netzer, *Hasmonean and Herodian Palaces*, vols. 1–2.

their deaths in 104/3 B.C.E. Josephus describes John Hyrcanus I's activities in both *The Jewish War* and *Jewish Antiquities*. Here is his account in the former work:[42]

> The prosperous fortunes of John and his sons, however, provoked a sedition among his envious countrymen, large numbers of whom held meetings to oppose them and continued to agitate, until the smoldering flames burst out in open war and the rebels were defeated. For the rest of his days John lived in prosperity, and, after excellently directing the government for thirty-one whole years, died leaving five sons; truly a blessed individual and one who left no ground for complaint against fortune as regards himself. He was the only man to unite in his person three of the highest privileges: the supreme command of the nation, the high priesthood, and the gift of prophecy. For so closely was he in touch with the Deity, that he was never ignorant of the future; thus he foresaw and predicted that his two elder sons would not remain at the head of affairs. The story of their downfall is worth relating, and will show how great was the decline from their father's good fortune (*J.W.* 1.67–69).

Jewish Antiquities renders a somewhat different report:[43]

> And so Hyrcanus quieted the outbreak, and lived happily thereafter; and when he died after administering the government excellently for thirty-one years, he left five sons. Now he was accounted by God worthy of three of the greatest privileges, the rule of the nation, the office of high-priest, and the gift of prophecy; for the Deity was with him and enabled him to foresee and foretell the future; so, for example, he foretold of his two elder sons that they would not remain masters of the state. And the story of their downfall is worth relating, to show how far they were from having their father's good fortune (*Ant.* 13.299–300).

Comparison of the two accounts shows that in the latter Josephus did not mention the civil war that broke out during John Hyrcanus' reign, which is mentioned in

42 The translation is based on M. St. J. Thackeray, *Josephus: The Jewish War, Books I–III* (Loeb Classical Library; Cambridge, MA: Harvard University Press, 1927) 33–35.
43 Marcus, *Jewish Antiquities*, 377–79; On the reliability of this tradition see C. Thoma, "John Hyrcanus I as Seen by Josephus and Other Early Jewish Sources," in *Josephus and the History of the Greco-Roman Period* (ed. F. Parente and J. Sievers; Leiden, New York and Köln: Brill, 1994) 138–40.

76

The Jewish War.[44] Some of the details in both reports seem to derive from Jewish legends.[45] The motif of "three gifts" (which later became "three crowns") surely comes from a Jewish tradition.[46] Immediately following the summary of John Hyrcanus' reign, Josephus describes Aristobulus' single year as king:[47]

> After their father's death the eldest son Aristobulus saw fit to transform the government into a kingdom, which he judged the best form, and he was the first to put a diadem on his head, four hundred and eighty-one years and three months after the time when the people were released from the Babylonian captivity and returned to their own country. Now of his brothers he loved only Antigonus, who was next in age, and considered him worthy of a position like his own, while he kept his other brothers in chains. He also imprisoned his mother, who had disputed the royal power with him—for Hyrcanus had left her mistress of the realm—, and carried his cruelty so far that he caused her to die of starvation in prison. And to the death of his mother he added that of his brother Antigonus, whom he seemed especially to love and had made his associate in the kingdom, for he was alienated from him by calumnies which at first he did not believe, disregarding the things that were said, partly because he loved Antigonus and partly because he believed that he was being calumniated out of envy. But on one occasion when Antigonus had returned from a campaign with glory, as the season of the festival during which tabernacles are erected to God was at hand, it chanced that Aristobulus fell ill, and Antigonus, arrayed in great splendour and with his heavy-armed soldiers about him,

44 The opponents of John Hyrcanus seem to be the Pharisees. It is plausible that Nicholas specified this, while Josephus decided to obscure this fact in *The Jewish War* and chose not to identify them by name. In *Jewish Antiquities* XIII, Josephus decided not to mention any conflict at all between John Hyrcanus and the Jews in order not to portray the Pharisees as an inciting factor responsible for causing revolts; see D. R. Schwartz, "Josephus and Nicolaus on the Pharisees," *JSJ* 14 (1983) 158–59; idem, *Studies in the Jewish Background of Christianity* (Tübingen: Mohr, 1992) 44–56.

45 This tradition appears in the *t. Sotah* 13.5. On motifs which Josephus imported from Jewish legends see the studies by Schwartz mentioned in the previous note.

46 The tradition of the three gifts was probably developed later than the tradition of the three crowns. At first, these three included prophecy, leadership, and priesthood, and later the prophecy was replaced by the Torah. See M. Beer, "The Term 'Crown of Torah' in Rabbinic Literature and its Social Significance," *Zion* 56 (1990) 397–417 (Hebrew); S. A. Cohen, *The Three Crowns: Structures of Communal Politics in Early Rabbinic Jewry* (Cambridge: Cambridge University Press, 1990) 7–28.

47 Marcus, *Jewish Antiquities*, 379–83.

went up to the temple to celebrate the festival and to pray earnestly for his brother's recovery; thereupon the unscrupulous men who were bent on disrupting the harmonious relation between them, found in Antigonus' ambitious display and in the successes he had achieved, a pretext to go to the king and maliciously exaggerate the pomp of his appearance at the festival, saying that everything that had been done was out of keeping with the behaviour of a private person and that his actions rather had the indications of one who imagined himself a king, and that he had come with a strong body of troops with the intention of killing Aristobulus, reasoning that it would be absurd for him to believe that he had won any great distinction in having a share in high office when he might just as well be king himself.

Aristobulus reluctantly began to believe these charges, and taking care not to be suspected by his brother and at the same time thinking of his own safety, stationed his bodyguards at intervals in a dark underground passage—for he was lying ill in the castle afterwards called Antonia—and gave orders that none of them should touch Antigonus if he were unarmed, but should kill him if he came to the king with his armour on. Moreover he himself sent to Antigonus, asking him to come unarmed. But the queen and the men who were plotting with her against Antigonus persuaded the messenger to say the opposite, namely that his brother had heard that he had equipped himself with arms and military gear, and invited him to come to him armed, in order that he might see his equipment. Accordingly, Antigonus, who had no suspicion of foul play and was confident of his brother's friendly feeling towards him, came to Aristobulus just as he was, in full armour, to show him his arms. But when he reached Straton's Tower, as it is called, just where the very dark passage was, the bodyguards killed him (*Ant.* 13.301–9, *J.W.* 1.70–77 with slight changes).

After the dramatic story of the murder of Antigonus, and before reporting Aristobulus' punishment, Josephus adds a tradition concerning a certain "Judas the Essene" (*J.W.* 1.78–80; *Ant.* 13.310–13), possibly borrowed from a Jewish source.[48] He then goes on with a description taken from Nicholas:[49]

But Aristobulus was soon seized by remorse for the murder of his brother,

48 M. Stern, "Nicholaus of Damascus as a Source of Jewish History in the Herodian and Hasmonean Age," in *Bible and Jewish History* (ed. B. Uffenheimer; Tel Aviv: Peli, 1972) 393 (Hebrew).

49 Marcus, *Jewish Antiquities*, 385–87.

and this was followed by illness, his mind being so troubled by his guilty deed that his inward parts were corrupted by intense pain, and he vomited blood. And once one of the servants who waited on him was carrying this blood away and slipped and spilled it—by divine providence, I believe— on the very spot where the stains made by the blood of the murdered Antigonus were still to be seen. Thereupon a cry went up from those who saw this that the servant had spilled the blood there deliberately, and when Aristobulus heard it, he asked what the reason for it was, and as they did not tell him, he became still more determined to find out, for in such cases men naturally suspect the worst in what is covered by silence. But when, under his threats and the constraint of fear, they told him the truth, he was stricken in mind by his consciousness of guilt, and weeping freely, with deep groans exclaimed, "I was not destined, I see, to escape the notice of God in committing such impious and unholy crimes, but swift punishment has overtaken me for the murder of my kin. How long, then, O most shameless body, will you keep within you the life that is forfeit to the spirits of my brother and mother? Why, instead of giving this up to them at one stroke, do I merely offer my blood drop by drop as a libation to those who have been so foully murdered?" And scarcely had he spoken these words when he died (*Ant.* 13.314–18, see also *J.W.* 1.81–84).

This account is followed in *Jewish Antiquities* XIII by details of Aristobulus not mentioned in *The Jewish War*, which Josephus learned from Strabo:[50]

...In his reign of one year, with the title of Philhellene, he conferred many benefits on his country, for he made war on the Ituraeans and acquired a good part of their territory for Judaea and compelled the inhabitants, if they wished to remain in their country, to be circumcised and to live in accordance with the laws of the Jews. He had a kindly nature, and was wholly given to modesty, as Strabo also testifies on the authority of Timagenes, writing as follows. "This man was a kindly person and very serviceable to the Jews, for he acquired additional territory for them, and brought over to them a portion of the Ituraean nation, whom he joined to them by the bond of circumcision" (*Ant.* 13.318–19).

This passage was written in a spirit very different from those cited previously,

---

50 Ibid., 387.

portraying Aristobulus in a much more positive light than Nicholas' description of the man who died shortly after assassinating his brother.[51]

Returning to the last passage in 4QTest, I will now explain it in light of Nicholas' account and the archeological data that point to John Hyrcanus as the builder of the Jericho estate and palaces. The passage interpreting Josh 6:26 may be divided into two parts, the first referring to John Hyrcanus, the "man accursed," and the second to his two dead sons, Aristobulus and Antigonus, the "instruments of violence."

The passage seems to incorporate various phrases taken from the Bible designed to demonstrate that the figures in question are not the positive ones described in the three first sections of the document. For example, "instruments of violence" (כלי חמס) is taken from Gen 49:5, where Simeon and Levi are called such in connection with their attack on the city of Shechem after the rape of Dinah. The author of the pesher may have associated the capture of Shechem by Simeon and Levi with the capture of the city of Samaria by Aristobulus and Antigonus in 108 B.C.E.,[52] because in both cases two brothers captured a city without the participation of their father and brothers. Perhaps the geographical proximity of Shechem and Samaria inspired the comparison.

Phrases occurring in the pesher of Joshua's curse are associated with passages quoted previously in 4QTest. In line 24, the man of Belial is called a "fowler's snare" (פח יקוש), a phrase occurring in Hosea 9:7–8: "The days of punishment have come for your heavy guilt; the days of requital have come—Let Israel know it! The prophet was distraught, the inspired man driven mad by constant harassment. Ephraim watches for my God. As for the prophet, *fowlers' snares* [my emphasis—H. E.] are on all his paths, harassment in the House of his God." The use of the phrase seems to imply that the man of Belial is nothing but a false prophet, hence not to be mistaken for a true prophet such as what is described in the first passage of the scroll.[53]

---

51 Stern, *Greek and Latin Authors*, 1.222–26; M. Stern, "Timagenes of Alexandria as a Source for the History of the Hasmonean Monarchy," in *Jews and Judaism in the Second Temple, and Mishnah and Talmud Period: Studies in Honor of Shmuel Safrai* (ed. I. M. Gafni, A. Oppenheimer, and M. Stern; Jerusalem: Ben-Zvi, 1993) 8–11 (Hebrew).

52 *J.W.* 1.64–66; *Ant.* 13.275–83. A Greek inscription found in the town of Samaria may verify Josephus' description. See A. D. Tushingham, "A Hellenistic Inscription from Samaria-Sebaste," *PEQ* 104 (1972) 59–63. For the different aspects of Josephus' description, see B. Bar-Kochva, "The Conquest of Samaria by John Hyrcanus," *Cathedra* 106 (2003) 7–34 (Hebrew).

53 The description of "a great evil in Israel and a horrible thing in Ephraim and in Judah" which the pesher associates with the two sons of the man of Belial, alludes to Hos 6:10-11: "In the house of Israel I have seen a horrible thing; there harlotry is found in Ephraim, Israel is defiled.

Another phrase in the same line, "destruction to all his neighbors," also refers to the man of Belial. Josephus reports that John Hyrcanus conquered cities in Transjordan, Samaria, Idumea, and the coastal plane.[54] Archeological finds in several cities mentioned in the list of John Hyrcanus' conquests indicate that they were indeed conquered during his reign.[55] For our purposes, it is important to note that according to Josephus, John Hyrcanus conquered Moab.[56] His success in Moab may have prompted his followers to interpret the verses in Balaam's prophecy, concerning a ruler who would crush Moab, as referring to John Hyrcanus. The phrase "destruction to all his neighbors" (ומחתה לכל שכניו) may allude to Jeremiah 48:39: "How he is dismayed (חתה)! Wail! How Moab has turned his back in shame! Moab shall be a laughingstock and a shock to all those near him (ולמחתה לכל סביביו)." The similarity between "destruction to all his neighbors" and "destruction to all those near him" is meant to convey that, contrary to Balaam's prophecy as quoted in the second part of 4QTest, which alludes to an Israelite ruler who would come and crush the temples of Moab,

---

Also, O Judah, there is a harvest appointed for thee! When I would turn the captivity of My people." This has been pointed out by Newsom, "Apocryphon of Joshua," 281. The authors of Qumran referred to this verse since they called themselves "Judah," the Pharisees "Ephraim" and the Sadducees "Manasseh" (see the discussion in the previous chapter). This midrash may indicate that the Pharisees and the Qumran sect were weakened in the days of Aristobulus. See the following discussion of the word "horrible thing" (שערוריה) which alludes mainly to Jer 5:30–31, and 23:14–15.

54   *J.W.* 1.62–63; *Ant.* 13.254–58. This list is based on a Hellenistic source that states that these towns were Syrian. The *Prayer of Joseph*, found in three scrolls from Qumran (4Q371, 4Q372, and 4Q373a), seems to relate to the conquest of Mount Gerizim by John Hyrcanus. See E. Schuller, "4Q372 1: A Text about Joseph," *RQ* 14 (1990) 349–76; H. Eshel, "The Prayer of Joseph, a Papyrus from Masada and the Samaritan Temple on ΑΡΓΑΡΙΖΙΝ," *Zion* 56 (1991) 125–36 (Hebrew); E. M. Schuller and M. J. Bernstein, "371–373. 4QNarrative and Poetic Composition^{a-c}," in *Wadi Daliyeh II: The Samaria Papyri from Wadi Daliyeh and Qumran Cave 4. XXVIII: Miscellanea, II* (DJD 28; Oxford: Clarendon, 2001) 167–78; E. Tigchelaar, "On the Unidentified Fragments of DJD 33 and PAM 43.680: A New Manuscript of 4QNarrative and Poetic Composition, and Fragments of 4Q13, 4Q269, 4Q525 and 4QSb," *RQ* 21 (2004) 477–83.

55   On the conquest of Mount Gerizim see Y. Magen, "Mount Gerizim and the Samaritans," in *Early Christianity in Context* (ed. F. Manns and E. Alliata; Jerusalem: Franciscan Printing Press, 1993) 91–148; Y. Magen, H. Misgav, and L. Tsfania, *Mount Gerizim Excavations* (Jerusalem: Israel Antiquities Authority, 2004) 1.1–13; D. Barag, "New Evidence on the Foreign Policy of John Hyrcanus I," *INJ* 12 (1992–93) 1–12; G. Finkielsztejn, "More Evidence on John Hyrcanus I's Conquests: Lead Weights and Rhodian Amphora Stamps," *BAIAS* 16 (1998) 33–63. See also the following note.

56   On the attempt to identify one of the towns conquered by John Hyrcanus with Mount Nebo, see G. Foerster, "The Conquests of John Hyrcanus I in Moab and the Identification of Samaga-Samoge," *Eretz-Israel* 15 (1981) 353–55 (Hebrew).

the writer wished to stress that although the man of Belial had indeed defeated Moab, Moab's neighbors would be intimidated not by the latter's power, but by his fate when he would be defeated by his enemies.[57] The writer was thus arguing with John Hyrcanus' followers, that Balaam's prophecy could not possibly refer to John Hyrcanus, since while he had indeed conquered several Moabite cities, his kingdom was doomed, as in Jeremiah's description of the future fall of Moab. The Qumran authors interpreted Balaam's prophecy as referring to the "interpreter of the Law" who would come from Damascus: "And the 'star' is the Interpreter of the Torah who came to Damascus; as it is written: 'A star stepped forth out of Jacob, and a staff arose out of Israel.' The staff is the Prince of the whole congregation, and when he will arise he will 'destroy all the sons of Seth'" (Damascus Document VII, 18–21).[58] These authors surely could not accept the interpretation of the verses as referring to the Hasmonean rulers.[59]

I believe that the author of the pesher also intended to refer to the third passage, describing the ideal priest, and therefore used the word שערוריה, here translated as "horrible thing" (line 27), probably alluding to Jer 5:30–31: "An appalling, horrible thing (שערוריה) has happened in the land: The prophets prophesy falsely, and the priests rule accordingly; and My people like it so." These verses are aimed at the false prophets and the priests. [60] The words "horrible thing" (line 27) and "pollution" (חנופה, line 28) can be linked to Jeremiah 23. In this chapter Jeremiah attacks the false prophets, but it seems that the author of

57   A similar use of the word מחתה can be found in Ps 89:41–42: "Thou hast broken down all his fences; Thou hast brought his strongholds to ruin (מחתה). All that pass by the way spoil him; he is become a taunt to his neighbors." Besides these two occurrences (Jer 48:39 and Ps 89:41), the other occurrences of מחתה in the Hebrew Bible indicate something frightening. It seems the phrase in the pesher was mainly influenced by Jer 48:39 due to its connection to Moab.

58   See M. Broshi, *The Damascus Document Reconsidered* (Jerusalem: Israel Exploration Society, 1992) 22–23.

59   An interpretation of Balaam's oracle on the star as relating to the priest who will make true judgment at the End of Days is found in the *T. Levi* 18:1–5. This interpretation may originate from the *Aramaic Levi Document* which was known to the Qumran sectarians. In any case, this interpretation testifies, as does the passage in the Damascus Document, that the opponents of the Hasmoneans did not believe that Balaam's oracle can be associated with John Hyrcanus, even though he did conquer Moab.

60   I wish to thank Moshe Ben-Baruch for drawing my attention to this verse. It seems that the word "horrible thing" (שערוריה) in the pesher relates not only to Jer 5:30–31 and 23:14, but also to Hos 6:10–11: "In the house of Israel I have seen a horrible thing; there harlotry is found in Ephraim, Israel is defiled. Also, O Judah, there is a harvest appointed for thee! When I would turn the captivity of My people," since the "horrible thing" in Ephraim could also be associated with the Pharisees, whereas Judah was associated with the return of Israel.

the pesher deliberately chose words that speak about the priests as well. Jer 23:11 reads: "For both prophet and priest are godless (חנפו). Even in my house I find wickedness." In Jer 23:14-15 we read: "But what I see in the prophets of Jerusalem is something horrifying (שערורה): adultery and false dealing. They encourage evildoers, so that no one turns back from his wickedness. To me they are all like Sodom and [all] its inhabitants like Gomorrah. Assuredly, thus said the Lord of Hosts concerning the prophets: I am going to make them eat wormwood and drink a bitter draft; for from the prophets of Jerusalem godlessness has gone forth (חנפה) to the whole land."[61]

I suggest that the phrases in this passage were carefully chosen and arranged in a particular order to demonstrate that John Hyrcanus should not be identified as the ideal prophet, the ruler who would crush Moab, nor as the perfect priest who is described in Moses' blessing of Levi.

Since 4QTest contains three quotations from the Torah, some scholars have suggested that the pesher to Josh 6:26 is also a quotation, from the work entitled the *Deeds of Joshua*.[62] This argument needs to be reevaluated for five reasons, all of which indicate that the pesher was written specifically to be incorporated as the last passage in 4QTest, and that only later was it added to the apocryphal work on Joshua:

1. Of the surviving fragments of the *Deeds of Joshua*, only this one would include allusions to contemporary affairs. Furthermore, it is the only fragment resembling a pesher, so that at the very least it should be suspected as being an addition to the original work. All other surviving fragments describing Joshua's activities are free of any eschatological motives.[63]

---

61 This was pointed out by Katell Berthelot in her lecture: "4QTestimonia as a Polemic against the Prophetic Claims of John Hyrcanus," delivered at the Society of Biblical Literature International Meeting in Edinburgh on July 4, 2006.

62 Milik, *Ten Years*, 61; Newsom, "Psalms of Joshua," 59. My proposal that this passage was composed for 4QTest and later added to the *Deeds of Joshua* was rejected by Lim, Tov, and Dimant, since they consider 4QTest to be a sequence of quotations, and that therefore this passage should be considered as yet another quote in 4QTest, imported from the *Deeds of Joshua*. See Lim, "Psalms of Joshua," 309, n. 8; Tov, "The Rewritten Book of Joshua," 255–56; Dimant, "Apocryphon of Joshua," 182, n. 13; Dimant, "Between Sectarian," 130–33.

63 A similar process is apparently documented in 4Q252, "Commentary on Genesis," where an eschatological interpretation of Jacob's blessing of Judah was incorporated. See D. R. Schwartz, "The Messianic Departure from Judah (4QPatriarchal Blessings)," *Theologische Zeitschrift* 37 (1981) 257–66. Other fragments of 4Q252 do not include sectarian indications. See C. Niccum,

2. The scribe who copied 4QTest was careful not to spell out the Tetragrammaton. Instead, when he had to quote a verse containing the Tetragrammaton, he used four dots. The sectarian scribes never used the Tetragrammaton in their works, and in the pesharim the Tetragrammaton occurs only in quoted passages.[64] Even so, the author of the passage dealing with Joshua's curse quoted only the last part of the verse, probably to avoid writing the Tetragrammaton.[65] This is in contrast to the other parts of the *Deeds of Joshua* which do use the Tetragrammaton.[66] Hence, it seems probable that the pesher was written by a sectarian author and added at a later date to the *Deeds of Joshua*.

3. The opening sentence of the passage, "At the time when Joshua finished praising and giving thanks with his praises," which appears in both 4QTest and 4Q379 further suggests that the passage was written specifically for 4QTest. In it, all four passages feature a proper name in the opening line, as if to inform the reader of the source of the quotation.[67] Because the author of the pesher on Josh 6:26 decided to omit the beginning of the verse (in order to avoid writing the Tetragrammaton), Joshua's name, which occurs at the beginning of the verse is no longer mentioned. This explains why the writer of 4QTest had to add a connecting phrase, "At the time when Joshua finished..." On the other hand, this sentence and the ensuing passage taken together do not seem to be an organic part of the *Deeds of Joshua*.

"The Blessing of Judah in 4Q252," in *Studies in the Hebrew Bible, Qumran, and the Septuagint Presented to Eugene Ulrich* (ed. P. W. Flint, E. Tov, and J. C. VanderKam; VTSup 101; Leiden and Boston: Brill, 2006) 250–60.

64 H. Stegemann, "Religionsgeschichtliche Erwägungen zu den Gottesbezeichnungen in den Qumrantexten," in *Qumrân: Sa piété, sa théologie et son milieu* (ed. M. Delcor; BETL 46; Paris: Duculot, 1978) 195–217.

65 As mentioned above, the verse was quoted according to the version preserved in the Septuagint. This version is also reflected in the ending clause of the verse. According to the Masoretic text, "before the Lord" is placed between "cursed be the man" and "who rises up and rebuilds the city." If indeed the scribe were quoting from the Masoretic text, he would have omitted these words from his quote. Furthermore, he wrote "who will build" (אשר יבנה) and not "who rises up and rebuild" (אשר יקום ובנה). The only detail in which the version of the pesher is close to the Masoretic text is in its reading "this city" (העיר הזאת), instead of "that city" as it appears in the Septuagint.

66 See Newsom, "Psalms of Joshua," 59.

67 In 4QTest, line 1 mentions Moses; line 9, Balaam; line 14, Levi; and line 21, Joshua.

4. Various features of 4QTest categorize it as an autograph, that is, a first copy made by the author himself and not by a copyist.[68] Such features include deletions and additions as well as indications that the writer did not consult his sources while writing 4QTest, but quoting the verses needed in the first three passages from memory.[69] Even when writing the portion interpreting Josh 6:26, his memory seems to have been wavering, as he ended up deleting the word ויהי ("and it came to pass") in line 21 and the word בת ("daughter") in line 30, and adding the word איש ("a man") above line 23. These are all indications that the pesher to Josh 6:26 is an autograph, written specially for 4QTest.[70]

5. As already noted, there are links between the passage interpreting Josh 6:26 and the passages quoted previously in 4QTest, yet another indication that the pesher was written with those passages particularly in mind, and was not a quotation from the *Deeds of Joshua*.

For all these reasons, it would appear that the pesher interpreting Josh 6:26 was composed by a scribe of the Qumran sect while writing 4QTest. Later, another

---

68 See A. Steudel, "Testimonia," in *Encyclopedia of the Dead Sea Scrolls* (2 vols.; ed. L. H. Schiffman and J. C. VanderKam; Oxford: Oxford University Press, 2000) 2.936.

69 An example for this can be found in lines 15–17 of 4QTest, where the scribe originally wrote: "who said to his father, 'I do not see you', and to his mother, '<I> do not know you', and who did not acknowledge his brother and did not know his sons." The scribe later returned to this verse and erased two words, one at the beginning of line 15 and the other at the beginning of line 16, and changed the last letter of the third word of line 16 from *yod* to *waw*, thus changing the verse from stating "I did not know you" to "I did not know him." The Masoretic text of Deuteronomy 33:9 reads: "Who said of his father and of his mother: 'I have not seen him'; neither did he acknowledge his brothers, nor knew he his own sons." On this matter, see Skehan, "Biblical Texts," 436. These details show that 4QTest is an autograph and that its scribe probably quoted the verses from memory rather than from other scrolls. Edward Greenstein argued that many of the textual variants between the Qumran scrolls and the ancient manuscripts of the Hebrew Bible are due to scribes who wrote the scrolls and quoted biblical verses based on their memory. Greenstein held this view also in regarding to 4QTest and provided several examples, such as the version in line 20: "let his enemies rise no more" (בל יקומו) which stands in contradiction to the Masoretic text and to all the other major versions "that they rise not again" (מן יקומון). The same is true for line 17: "And they shall cause Your precepts to shine for Jacob" (יאירו משפטיך ליעקב) instead of "they shall teach Jacob Thine ordinances" (יורו משפטיך ליעקב) (Deut. 33:10). See E. L. Greenstein, "Misquotation of Scripture in the Dead Sea Scrolls," in *The Frank Talmage Memorial Volume* (2 vols.; ed. B. Walfish; Haifa: Haifa University Press, 1993) 1.71–83.

70 The word "and was" (ויהי) which was erased in 4QTest, apparently did not exist in 4Q379, providing further evidence that the passage in discussion was incorporated from 4QTest into 4Q379.

scribe, copying the work recounting Joshua's actions, added the sectarian passage to the non-sectarian work he was copying, so that the same pesher found its way to 4Q379.[71] There are indications that the pesher to Josh 6:26 was familiar to the scribes of Qumran, and they in fact alluded to it in another sectarian work, 4Q460, discovered in the same cave.[72]

4QTest consists of one page containing different biblical passages relating to prophecy, leadership, and priesthood. It ends with the passage recounting Joshua's curse on the builder of Jericho. Various scholars have tried to explain the purpose of the work,[73] but a plausible explanation of the relationship between the various parts of the scroll is forthcoming only if one associates this last passage with John Hyrcanus.[74] The selection of the passages that comprise

71 The orthography of 4QTest is different from the one found in 4Q379. 4QTest is written in an orthographic system characteristic of some of the scrolls found at Qumran, while 4Q379 is written in the Masoretic orthography. On the orthography of 4QTest, see E. Tov, "The Orthography and Language of the Hebrew Scrolls found at Qumran and the Origin of These Scrolls," *Textus* 13 (1986) 31–57. It should be noted that this orthography was not particular to the scribes at Qumran; see S. Talmon and Y. Yadin, *Masada VI: Yigael Yadin Excavations 1963-1965, Final Report* (Jerusalem: Israel Exploration Society, 1999) 22–24. It is hard to accept Tov's suggestion that the scrolls found at Masada originated in Qumran. See E. Tov, "A Qumran Origin for the Masada Non-Biblical Texts?" *DSD* 7 (2000) 57–73. Furthermore, not all the sectarian scrolls were written in this orthography. See E. Qimron and J. H. Charlesworth, "4QS MS D," in *The Dead Sea Scrolls: Hebrew, Aramaic, and Greek Texts with English Translations: Volume 1, Rule of the Community and Related Documents* (ed. J. H. Charlesworth, et al.; Tübingen: Mohr Siebeck / Louisville: Westminster John Knox, 1994) 72–83. It is therefore possible that a sectarian scribe from Qumran could convert a text he was copying from the Qumran orthography to the Masoretic orthography when he was copying a composition that was written in the Masoretic orthography.

72 See E. Larson, "460. 4QNarrative Work and Prayer," in *Qumran Cave 4, XXVI* (DJD 36; Oxford: Clarendon, 2000) 369–86. This is a sectarian polemic composition addressing the sect's adversaries who are designated here as "Ephraim and Israel," such as "When you abandoned your God, O Israel" or "for by no one in Ephraim will the statute be understood." This composition also includes the phrase "for confusion in Israel and for something horrible in Jerusalem." There is no doubt that this sentence, like the sentence "a great evil in Israel and a horrible thing in Ephraim and in Judah" in the pesher on Josh 6:26, is based on Hos 6:10–11: "In the house of Israel I have seen a horrible thing; there harlotry is found in Ephraim, Israel is defiled. Also, O Judah…." But it seems that the phrase "something horrible in Ephraim," which appears both in the pesher and in 4Q460 but does not appear in Hosea, points to a relationship between the pesher on Joshua 6 and 4Q460. Though other possibilities cannot be overruled it seems that the author of 4Q460 was familiar with the pesher to Josh 6:26, and alluded to it when attacking the Pharisees.

73 For a bibliography on 4QTest, see J. Carmignac, E. Cothenet, and H. Lignée, *Les textes de Qumran* (Paris: Letouzey et Ané, 1963) 273–78; and also J. A. Fitzmyer, "A Bibliographical Aid to the Study of the Qumran Cave IV Texts 158–186," *CBQ* 31 (1969) 68–70.

74 See Knibb, *Qumran Community*, 264–66; G. J. Brooke, *Exegesis at Qumran* (JSOTSup

4QTest may be explained if we regard this critical passage as John Hyrcanus' construction of the Hasmonean palace and manor at Jericho. As we have seen, Josephus describes him explicitly as a ruler, High Priest, and prophet. Dupont-Sommer and Flusser have pointed out the connection between this description and the biblical passages of 4QTest,[75] and accordingly, Treves has suggested that the work be dated to John Hyrcanus' rule.[76]

Given this date, the archeological findings at Jericho also point to the identification of the "man of Belial" in the pesher to Josh 6:26 with John Hyrcanus, who ruled Judaea from 134 to 104 B.C.E. John Hyrcanus appointed his two sons to succeed him. After their deaths a few months after his own death, in circumstances that seem far from natural, one of the Qumran authors claimed that Joshua's curse of the person who would build Jericho applied to John Hyrcanus. It may be assumed that the people of Qumran, living about three hours walk from the Hasmonean palace at Jericho, were aware of the construction there and considered the deaths of Antigonus and Aristobulus as proof that the Hasmoneans were not worthy of ruling the nation. The writer of 4QTest held that, although John Hyrcanus' followers believed that God had bestowed upon him the gifts of prophecy, the rule of the nation, and priesthood, he could not be considered a prophet of the kind promised to the Jewish people at Sinai, neither was he the ruler described in Balaam's prophecy, nor the perfect priest described in Moses' blessing of Levi. The proof that he was not a positive figure was the fulfillment of Joshua's curse, for he had built the palace and the estate at Jericho, and within a year both his sons died in mysterious circumstances.[77]

29; Sheffield: JSOT Press, 1985) 309–19; J. Lübbe, "A Reinterpretation of 4QTestimonia," *RQ* 12 (1986) 187–97. See also the complex explanation provided by Vermes on this issue: G. Vermes, "Bible Interpretation at Qumran," *Eretz Israel* 20 (1989) *190.

75 Dupont-Sommer, *Essene Writings,* 318; D. Flusser, *The Spiritual History of the Dead Sea Sect* (Tel Aviv: MOD Books, 1989) 87–88, n. 46.

76 M. Treves, "On the Meaning of the Qumran Testimonia," *RQ* 2 (1960) 569–71. According to Treves, the author of 4QTest was pro-Hasmonean who believed that John Hyrcanus fulfilled the biblical verses collated in the scroll. On the last passage he comments: "What about the curses against the city? I do not find that Jericho played any important role in Jewish history in the days of Hyrcanus." However, it seems that the author of 4QTest, like the authors of the other pesharim, was anti-Hasmonean. The curse is not on the city, but on its builder. During the days of John Hyrcanus, Jericho became the second major city of Judah, due to the agricultural estate and palaces built there.

77 The man of Belial is used in the pesher to designate John Hyrcanus and is not derived from Joshua 6. If that were the case, he would surely be designated as "cursed" (ארור) rather than "Belial." I did not find that this term is used as a designation for John Hyrcanus in any other of the Qumran scrolls. Though Callaway did try to associate the Belial described in 4QTest with other

Appendix: The List of False Prophets (4Q339) and John Hyrcanus

A small fragment, consisting of only nine lines, found in Cave 4, lists various false prophets of Jewish history. Two scholars have suggested that the list polemicizes against John Hyrcanus and his adherents, who considered him a true prophet. The fragment may be read as follows:[78]

1   The false prophets who arose in [Israel]
2   Balaam [son of] Beor
3   [the] Old Man from Bethel
4   [Zede]kiah son of Cha[na]anah
5   [Aha]b son of K]ol]iah
6   [Zede]kiah son of Ma[a]seiah
7   [Shemaiah the Ne]lemite
8   [Hananiah son of Azz]ur
9   [   ]eon

After this list was published, Elisha Qimron and Alexander Rofé, independently, proposed the reconstruction of line 9 as "[Yoḥanan (John) son of Sim]eon," and the identification of the prophet in that line with John Hyrcanus, whose followers, as noted previously, considered him a prophet.[79] They therefore suggested that the purpose of the list was to oppose John Hyrcanus' followers and compare him to the false prophets who had harmed the Jewish people in the past.

Somewhat later, Qimron proposed a different reconstruction for lines 8 and 9: "[Hananiah son of Azz]ur, [prophet that is from Gib]eon" (ונביאה די] [מגב]עון), referring to the false prophet mentioned in Jer 28:1. Qimron wrote that the new reconstruction was preferable to the old, and virtually disowned his previous version of line 9 as well as his former view on the purpose of the list.[80]

"Belial" phrases found in Qumran, his arguments are not convincing. See P. R. Callaway, *The History of the Qumran Community* (JSPSup 3; Sheffield: Sheffield Academic Press, 1988) 181–82.

78 M. Broshi and A. Yardeni, "On Netinim and False Prophets," in *Solving Riddles and Untying Knots: Biblical, Epigraphic and Semitic Studies in Honor of Jonas C. Greenfield* (ed. Z. Zevit, S. Gitin, and M. Sokoloff; Winona Lake, IN: Eisenbrauns, 1995) 33–37; idem., "339. 4QList of False Prophets ar," in *Qumran Cave 4. XIV: Parabiblical Texts, II* (DJD 19; Oxford: Clarendon, 1995) 77–79.

79 E. Qimron, "On the List of False Prophets from Qumran," *Tarbiz* 63 (1994) 273–75 (Hebrew); A. Rofé, "A List of False Prophets from Qumran: Two Riddles and Their Solution," *Haaretz* April 13, 1994 (Hebrew).

80 E. Qimron, "An Additional Note on the List of False Prophets," *Tarbiz* 63 (1994) 508 (Hebrew).

The editors of *DJD* agreed with the new reconstruction, in keeping with the "minimalist" approach, preferring a more modest conclusion that relies less on conjecture.[81] Despite the fact that the hypothesis of the link between the list of false prophets and John Hyrcanus is dubious, since it is based on a questionable reconstruction for which there is a plausible alternative, some scholars still believe such a link with John Hyrcanus exists. Assuming that to be the case, the list could then be associated with the pesher to Josh 6:26 documented in two Qumran fragments (4QTest and 4Q379) as yet another composition criticizing the perception that John Hyrcanus was a true prophet.[82]

---

81 J. Naveh, *On Sherd and Papyrus. Aramaic and Hebrew Inscriptions from the Second Temple, Mishnaic and Talmudic Periods* (Jerusalem: Magnes, 1992) 209 (Hebrew).

82 For further discussions of the *List of False Prophets*, see S. J. D. Cohen, "Hellenism in Unexpected Places," in *Hellenism in the Land of Israel* (ed. J. J. Collins and G. E. Sterling; Notre Dame: University of Notre Dame Press, 2001) 216–23; A. Shemesh, "A Note on 4Q339 'List of False Prophets'," *RQ* 20 (2001) 319–20.

CHAPTER FOUR

Alexander Jannaeus and His War against Ptolemy Lathyrus

After the death of Aristobulus in 103 B.C.E., a third son of John Hyrcanus was appointed as king. His Greek name was Alexander, his Hebrew name Jonathan, and his Aramaic name Jannaeus. From the writings of Josephus it is clear that immediately after his ascent to power, Alexander Jannaeus became entangled in a war against Ptolemy Lathyrus. There are substantial differences between the short account of this event in *The Jewish War* I and the long account given in *Jewish Antiquities* XIII. The account in *The Jewish War* is as follows:[1]

> He also had an encounter with Ptolemy, surnamed Lathyrus, who had taken the town of Asochis; although he killed many, victory inclined to his opponent. But when Ptolemy, pursued by his mother Cleopatra, retired to Egypt, Alexander besieged and took Gadra and Amathus (*J. W.* 1. 86).

This account does not provide an explanation as to the reasons that led Ptolemy to fight Jannaeus. In contrast, *Jewish Antiquities* XIII provides a much longer account of the same events:[2]

> Then, leaving his realm in a condition which he thought advantageous to himself, Alexander marched against Ptolemais, and after defeating

1   The translation is based on M. St. J. Thackery, *Josephus: The Jewish War, Books I–III* (Loeb Classical Library; Cambridge, MA: Harvard University Press, 1927) 43.
2   The translation is based on R. Marcus, *Josephus: Jewish Antiquities, Books XII–XIV* (Loeb Classical Library; Cambridge, MA: Harvard University Press, 1933) 391–405.

its inhabitants in battle, he shut them up in the city and surrounding it, besieged them. For of the cities on the coast there remained only Ptolemais and Gaza to be surrounded by him, and also Straton's Tower and Dora, which the local ruler Zoilus held. Now as Antiochus Philometor and his brother Antiochus, surnamed Cyzicenus, were fighting each other and destroyed their own forces, no help could be given by them to the people of Ptolemais; but while they were being hard pressed in the siege, Zoilus, who held Straton's Tower, appeared with a company of soldiers that he maintained, and as he had ambitions to make himself absolute ruler because of the struggle between the two kings, he gave some slight help to the people of Ptolemais. Nor were the kings so friendly to them that they could hope for any assistance from them, for both of them were in the position of athletes whose strength is exhausted but who are ashamed to yield, and so continue to prolong the contest by periods of inactivity and rest. The only hope that was left them was in sovereigns of Egypt and in Ptolemy Lathyrus, the ruler of Cyprus, who had been driven from his realm by his mother Cleopatra, and had come to Cyprus. And so the people of Ptolemais sent to him and begged him to come to their aid and save them from the hand of Alexander, by whom they were endangered. The envoys led him to hope that when he crossed to Syria, he would have the people of Gaza on the side of those of Ptolemais, as well as Zoilus, and they told him further that the Sidonians and many others would join him; being, therefore, full of high hope, he made haste to sail.

Meanwhile, however, the people of Ptolmais had been persuaded to change their plans by Demaenetus, who had their confidence at that time and influenced the people; he said that it would be better for them to risk a contest with the Jews, although the outcome was uncertain, than to accept open servitude by delivering themselves up to an absolute ruler, and in addition not only have the present war on their hands, but also a much more serious one arising from Egypt. For Cleopatra would not permit Ptolemy to provide himself with an army from the neighboring cities but would come against them with great force, since she was eager to drive her son out of Cyprus too. Moreover, if Ptolemy was disappointed in his expectations, he could again find a refuge in Cyprus, whereas they themselves would be in the greatest danger. Now though Ptolemy on the way over learned of the change of mind of the people of Ptolemais, he nevertheless sailed on, and landing at Sycamina, as it is called, there disembarked his force. The army with him, both foot and horse, numbered some thirty thousand in all, and this he led to the neighborhood of Ptolemais and encamped there; but as they would neither admit his envoys nor listen to his proposals he was in great anxiety.

However, when Zoilus and the people of Gaza came to him with the request that he would aid them, as their territory was being ravaged by the Jews under Alexander, Alexander in the fear of Ptolemy raised the siege and led his army home again, and thereafter resorted to cunning; for while secretly sending for Cleopatra to attack Ptolemy, he openly proposed a friendly alliance to him, thus acting a part. He also promised to give him four hundred talents of silver, asking him to return to put the local ruler Zoilus out of the way and to assign his territory to the Jews. And so Ptolemy at that time gladly formed a friendship with Alexander, and laid hands on Zoilus. But later, when he heard that Alexander had secretly sent to his mother Cleopatra, he broke the sworn agreements he had made with him, and attacked Ptolemais, and when he refused to admit him, besieged it. Then leaving his generals and a part of his force to carry on the siege, he set out with the rest of his army to subdue Judaea. But when Alexander learned of Ptolemy's intention, he also collected an army, consisting of about fifty thousand natives, or eighty thousand, as some writers state, and taking this force went out to meet Ptolemy. Ptolemy, however, made a sudden attack on Asochis, a city of Galilee, on the Sabbath, and taking it by storm, captured about ten thousand persons and a great deal of booty besides.

He also made an attempt on Sepphoris at a little distance from the city which had just been sacked, but lost many of his men, and went on to fight Alexander. Alexander met him in the neighborhood of the river Jordan, at a place called Asophon, not far from the river Jordan, and pitched his camp close to the enemy. He had, moreover, eight thousand front-line fighters, whom he called "hundred-fighters" carrying long shields covered with bronze. Now Ptolemy's front-line fighters also had round shields covered with bronze, but as his troops were inferior to the enemy in other respects, they were more cautious about risking an engagement. However they were not a little encouraged by the tactician Philostephanus, who told them to cross the river, which was between their camp and the enemy's. And Alexander decided not to prevent their crossing thinking that he would the more easily take the enemy if they had the river behind them and so were unable to flee. And at first both sides equally performed deeds of prowess and daring, and great was the slaughter in both armies;

but as Alexander's men were getting the upper hand, Philostephanus divided his force and skillfully came to the relief of those who were giving ground. And as no one came to aid that part of the Jewish force which was falling back, it had to flee; and not even those near them helped them, but joined in their fight. Ptolemy's men, however, did just the opposite, for they followed the Jews and killed them, until finally, when they were completely routed, they tracked them down to slaughter them until their swords became blunted with killing, and their hands were utterly tired. It was said, in fact, that thirty thousand of them perished – Timagenes says there were fifty thousand –, while as for the rest, some were taken captive, and others escaped to their native places.

After this victory Ptolemy overran other territory, and when evening fell, halted in some villages of Judaea, which he found full of women and infants; he thereupon commanded his soldiers to cut their throats and chop them up and then to fling the pieces into boiling cauldrons and to taste of them. This order he gave that those who had escaped from the battle and had returned to their homes might get the notion that the enemy were eaters of human flesh, and so might be the more terrified by this sight. And both Strabo and Nicolas say that they treated the Jews in the manner which I have just mentioned. Ptolemy's men also took Ptolemais by storm, as we have shown elsewhere.

When Cleopatra saw her son growing in power, and ravaging Judaea with impunity and holding Gaza subject to him, she decided not to be idle and coveted the throne of Egypt; and so she at once set out against him with a sea and land force, appointing as leaders of her entire army the Jews Chelkias and Ananias. At the same time she sent the greater part of her wealth and her grandsons and her testament to Cos for safekeeping. Then she commanded her son Alexander to sail toward Phoenicia with a great fleet, while she herself came to Ptolemias with her entire force, and when the inhabitants refused to admit her, besieged the city. Thereupon Ptolemy left Syria and hastened to Egypt, thinking to get possession of it suddenly while it was left without an army, but he was disappointed of his hope. It was just at this time that Chelkias, one of Cleopatra's two commanders, died in Coele-Syria while in pursuit of Ptolemy.

When Cleopatra heard of her son's attempt and learned that his plans concerning Egypt had not prospered as he had expected, she sent a portion of her army against him and drove him out of the country. And so he left Egypt once more and spent the winter at Gaza. Meanwhile, Cleopatra besieged the garrison in Prolemais and took it and the city itself. And when Alexander came to her with gifts and such marks of attention as were to be expected after the harsh treatment he had suffered at the hands of Ptolemy – for he had no other course of safety than this –, some of her friends advised her to take these things and at the same time invade his country and occupy it, and not suffer such an abundance of resources to belong to one man, who was a Jew. Ananias, however, gave the opposite advice, saying that she would commit an injustice if she deprived an ally of his own possessions, "especially one who is our kinsman. For I would have you know that an injustice done to this man will make all us Jews your enemies." By this exhortation of Ananias Cleopatra was persuaded not to do Alexander any wrong, but instead she made an alliance with him at Scythopolis in Coele-Syria (*Ant.* 13. 324–55).

In this detailed account of the events of 103 B.C.E., Josephus notes that Ptolemy Lathyrus arrived with his army in Palestine following a request for help from the people of Acre. Ptolemy Lathyrus' fleet was anchored at Shiqmona from where he and his army marched to Acre. After a brief negotiation, Ptolemy Lathyrus clashed with Alexander Jannaeus and proceeded to invade the Galilee. He went on to defeat Alexander Jannaeus' army in a battle that took place near Zafon, a town near the Jordan River, before moving on to invade Judaea. Concerned by Ptolemy's success, his mother, Cleopatra III, the Queen of Egypt, rushed to Syria. Because of the advance of the Egyptian army toward Philistia, Ptolemy interrupted his campaign in Judaea before conquering Jerusalem.

This description in *Jewish Antiquities* XIII is based on Hellenistic sources from which Josephus drew the name of one of the leaders of Acre—Demaentus, as well as the name of Ptolemy Lathyrus' commander, Philostephanos. The account is written from a point of view hostile to Alexander Jannaeus, who treated Ptolemy Lathyrus treacherously and breached the treaty between them.[3] The Judaean army did not succeed in the battle along the Jordan because the soldiers did not work together as a fighting unit. In contrast, Ptolemy's army defeated its enemies by fighting as a cohesive force.

---

3   Menahem Stern suggested that the description of Jannaeus' insincerity originated in a Hellenistic composition which was influenced by Ptolemy Lathyrus' propaganda, and noted that such behavior was condemned in Hellenistic literature; see M. Stern, "Judaea and Her Neighbors in the Days of Alexander Jannaeus," in *The Jerusalem Cathedra I* (ed. L. I. Levine; Jerusalem: Ben-Zvi, 1982) 36, n. 66.

Josephus mentioned the sources on which he relied to describe this battle: Timagenes, Strabo, and Nicholaus.[4]

While we only have Josephus' accounts for events that occurred in Syria between 103–101 B.C.E.,[5] there are several inscriptions and papyri discovered in Egypt relating to various details of Cleopatra III's campaign against her son Ptolemy Lathyrus during those years. Among these, there is a private letter written in September 103 B.C.E. by a soldier in Cleopatra's army. It was written in Ptolemais (Acre) and mentions that King Ptolemy Alexander (Cleopatra's son and her co-ruler) had left for Damascus. This testifies that Cleopatra had conquered Acre prior to September 103 B.C.E.[6] A Demotic inscription testifies that Cleopatra was in Peulsion with her son Ptolemy Alexander in 102 B.C.E.[7] Coins from Cyprus and the Galilee provide some additional evidence.[8]

In the *Pesher on Isaiah* A, (4Q161=4QpIsaᵃ), a paragraph commentating on Isa 10:24–34 is preserved. The remnants of this pesher are rather fragmentary, though it seems that this pesher should be associated with the events of 103–102 B.C.E. The second column of frgs. 2–6 reads as follows:[9]

21 [ ] "He has come to Aiath. He has passed [through Migron.] At

---

4 For an analysis of this battle and a discussion of the sources that served Josephus, see B. Bar-Kochva, "The Battle between Ptolemy Lathyrus and Alexander Jannaeus in the Jordan Valley and the Dating of the Scroll of the War of the Sons of Light," *Cathedra* 93 (1990) 7–56 (Hebrew).

5 For the events in Cyprus, see *The Judean-Syrian-Egyptian Conflict of 103–101 B.C.* (ed. E. Van 't Dack et al.; Collectanea Hellenistica 1; Brussel: Koninklijke Academie voor Wetenschappen, 1989) 27–28.

6 Ibid., 50–61. The reason for Ptolemy's departure to Damascus should be understood in the context of the struggle within the Seleucid dynasty. This struggle held mutual interests for Cleopatra and Antiochus VIII Grypos, since the latter fought Antiochus IX Kyzikenós who was supported by Ptolemy Lathyrus; see the discussion in ibid., 121–24.

7 Ibid., 83-84. This means that Cleopatra first conquered Acre and then returned to Egypt to fight Ptolemy Lathyrus, in contrast to the order of events described in *Ant.* 13. 350–53, where Acre falls into Cleopatra's control only after Ptolemy Lathyrus is defeated.

8 G. Barkay, "A Coin of Alexander Jannaeus from Cyprus," *IEJ* 27 (1977) 119–20; H. Gitler and A. Kushnir-Stein, "The Chronology of a Late Ptolemaic Bronze Coin-Type from Cyprus," *INJ*, 13 (1999) 46–53.

9 This pesher was published by John Allegro in 1956; see J. M. Allegro, "Further Messianic References in Qumran," *JBL* 75 (1956) 177–82. Allegro's readings were substantially improved by John Strugnell and other scholars. For details of the various emendations, see M. P. Horgan, *Pesharim: Qumran Interpretations of Biblical Books* (CBQ Monograph Series 8; Washington, D.C.: Catholic Biblical Association, 1975) 75. The text provided above is according to J. H. Charlesworth et al., ed., *The Dead Sea Scrolls: Hebrew, Aramaic, and Greek Texts with English Translations: Volume 6B, Pesharim, Other Commentaries, and Related Documents* (Tübingen: Mohr Siebeck / Louisville: Westminster John Knox, 2002) 90–91.

Michma[sh]

22 [he stores his baggage. They have crossed] over the pass. Geba is a
lodging place for them. [Ramah becomes] ill. [Gibeah of]

23 [Saul has fled. Cry] aloud, O daughter of Galim! Hearken [O Laishah!
Answer her, O Anathoth!]

24 Madmenah [is in flight.] The [in]habitants of Gebim flee for safety.
This very [day he will halt at Nob.]

25 [He will shake] his fist at the mount of the daughters of Zion, the hill
of Jerusalem." [...]

26 [The interpretation of the] matter with regard to the end of days
concerns the coming of [...]

27 [   ]*rh* when he goes up from the Valley of Acco to fight against
Phil[istia...]

28 [   ]*dh*, and there is one like it, and among all the cities of *h*[...]

29 and even up to the boundary of Jerusalem [...]

This pesher is written in the Herodian script which is characteristic of the second
half of the first century B.C.E.[10] Isaiah 10:24–34 vividly describes a sequence of
events: how an enemy will rise against Judaea, conquer settlements along the
road northeast of Jerusalem, when it will approach Jerusalem itself and how the
enemy will be able to shake his hand towards the mountain of Zion, God will
smite him and deliver Jerusalem.[11] In 1974, Joseph Amusin proposed connecting
this pesher to Ptolemy Lathyrus' campaign against Alexander Jannaeus.[12] This
view is based primarily on line 27: "when he goes up from the Valley of Acco to
fight against Phil[istia]." John Allegro read the letter before the tear in line 27 as a
yod. Scholars have suggested reconstructing the text as "when he goes up to fight
J[udea]" or "I[srael]" or " J[erusalem]".[13] John Strugnell read the same letter as

---

10 See Horgan, *Pesharim*, 71, 138.

11 It is commonly accepted that this prophecy refers to the campaign of Sennacherib, King
of Assyria, to Jerusalem in 701 B.C.E. See, for example, O. Kaiser, *Isaiah 1-12* (OTL; Philadelphia:
Westminster Press, 1972) 150.

12 See J. D. Amoussine, "A propos de l'interprétation de 4Q161 (fragments 5-6 et 8)," *RQ*
8 (1974) 381–92; J. D. Amusin, "The Reflection of Historical Events of the First Century B.C. in
Qumran Commentaries (4Q161; 4Q169; 4Q166)," *HUCA* 48 (1977) 123–34.

13 The reconstruction of 'J[erusalem]' was suggested by Y. Yadin, "Recent Developments
in the Dead Sea Scrolls Research," in *Studies in the Dead Sea Scrolls* (ed. J. Liver; Jerusalem: Kiryat
Sepher, 1957) 52 (Hebrew). "I[srael]" was proposed by Adam van der Woude, Andre Dupont-Sommer and Joseph Fitzmyer; see A. S. van der Woude, *Bijbelcommentaren en Bijbelse verhalren* (Am-
sterdam: Proost en Brandt, 1958) 176–78; A. Dupont-Sommer, *The Essene Writings from Qumran*

pe, and argued that prior to the tear there are remnants of a *lamed*. He suggests the reading: "when he goes up to war against Phil[istia]."[14] In my opinion, this reading seems to be correct. If we accept the connection of the *Pesher on Isaiah* to Ptolemy Lathyrus' campaign, it seems that the mention of "Phil[istia]" refers to the first stage of Ptolemy Lathyrus' campaign, when Zoilus, the Ruler of Dor, and the people of Gaza approached him to request his help to fight Alexander Jannaeus' army and end its corrupt influence on the country (*Ant.* 13.334). It is improbable that the author of the pesher is referring to Ptolemy's retreat from Judaea and to his stay in Gaza in line 27 (*Ant.* 13.352) since it is only in line 29 that "unto the boundary of Jerusalem" is written. Line 29 goes on to describe the arrival of the enemy forces to the perimeter of Mount Zion. It may be that the pesher followed with an account of Ptolemy's retreat from Jerusalem, without conquering the city.[15]

Since the relation of the pesher to the events of 103–101 B.C.E. seems clear, it is appropriate at this juncture to cite the two reasons that led J. D. Amusin to be the first to make the link between the pesher and Ptolemy Lathyrus' campaign.[16] The first reason was Allegro's contention connecting the Valley of Acco in the pesher to the tradition of the apocalyptic war near Megiddo at the End of Days

---

(Gloucester and New York: World Publishing Company, 1962) 274, n. 2; J. A. Fitzmyer, "Review of J. M. Allegro, *Qumran Cave 4.I (4Q158–4Q186) DJD 5*," *CBQ* 31 (1969) 237. The reconstruction "against J[udea]" was suggested by Amusin, "Reflection of Historical Events," 125.

14 J. Strugnell, "Notes en marge du volume V des *Discoveries in the Judaean Desert of Jordan*," *RQ* 7 (1970), 184.

15 On Jannaeus' attempt to conquer Gaza during the time he was fighting Acre, see Stern, "Alexander Jannaeus," 33.

16 Even after Amusin's articles were published, most scholars overlooked his suggestion to link *Pesher on Isaiah* A and the campaign of Ptolemy Lathyrus. Thus, for example, Stern "Alexander Jannaeus," 32–39, did not mention the *Pesher on Isaiah*, and referred to Amusin's article only in his discussion of the *Pesher on Nahum* and the war against Demetrius III (ibid., n. 97). Van 't Dack, ("The Conflict," 3–35) collected all the historical sources concerning the war between Cleopatra and Ptolemy Lathyrus and quoted Getzel Cohen's suggestion to associate the description of the Kittim in the *Pesher on Habakkuk* (6:10–12) as relentless warriors who have no mercy on the elderly, women, and children with the description provided by Josephus (*Ant.* 13.345–47) of Ptolemy Lathyrus' soldiers who boiled women and children to scare the Jews. However, 4QpIsa^a, which indeed refers to the events of 103–101 B.C.E., is not discussed in Van 't Dack's book at all. Lately this tendency has changed, and it seems that Amusin's suggestion is now more favorably received; see M. Stern, *Hasmonean Judaea in the Hellenistic World: Chapters in Political History* (ed. D. R. Schwartz; Jerusalem: Shazar, 1995) 181, n. 12 (Hebrew); Bar-Kochva, "The Battle," 8, n. 2; J. C. Charlesworth, *The Pesharim and Qumran History* (Grand Rapids and Cambridge: Eerdmans, 2002) 102–3.

(Rev 16:16). Allegro went on to propose that 4QpIsa[a] describes the prospective journey of the Messiah from the Galilee to Jerusalem after the apocalypse.[17] Since the pesher is based on the description of the campaign of the King of Assyria against Jerusalem, it is implausible that this description would refer to the journey of the Messiah. Therefore some scholars have suggested that the pesher describes the campaign of Gog and Magog (the Antichrist) to Jerusalem.[18] In any case, Allegro's proposal led several scholars to the opinion that this pesher relates to eschatological times rather than actual historical events. The second reason that deterred scholars from accepting the association of the pesher with Ptolemy Lathyrus' campaign was the mention of the Kittim in the third column of the *Pesher on Isaiah* A, which provides the remainder of the pesher on Isaiah chapter 10 (col. 3):[19]

6   [... "and the th]ickets of [the forest will be hacked down] with an axe, and the Lebanon together with a mighty one

7   [will fall." They are the Kittim, wh[o] will fa[ll] by the hand of Israel. And the Poor Ones of

8   [...] all the nations, and the mighty ones will be filled with terror, and [their] cour[age] will dissolve

9   [... "and those who are lofty] in stature will be cut down." They are the mighty ones of the Kitt[im]

10   [...] "and the thickets of the forest will be hacked down with an axe". Th[ey are]

11   [...] for the battle of the Kittim [*vacat*] "And Lebanon (together) with a mi[ghty one]

---

17   Allegro posited that the pesher is based on a similar tradition to the one in Revelation whose roots can be found in Zech 12:11. In his view, the author of the pesher described the journey of the Messiah from the battleground to Jerusalem after defeating the kings of the Kittim; see Allegro, "Further Messianic," 177–82, and also idem, "Addendum to Professor Millar Burrow's Note on the Ascent from Acco in 4QpIsa[a]," *VT* 7 (1957) 183.

18   For criticisms of Allegro's argument that 4QpIsa[a] refers to the journey of the Messiah, see: Y. Yadin, "New Developments," 51–52; M. Burrows, "The Ascent from Acco in 4QpIsa[a]," *VT* 7 (1957) 104–5. Millar Burrows suggested that the pesher refers to the campaign of Gog and Magog.

19   This fragment is provided according to Charlesworth, *Pesharim*, 92–93. There seems to be a connection between this description and the one in *Sefer ha-Milhamah* (4Q285), frgs. 4 and 5. *Sefer ha-Milhamah* provides another explanation of Isa 10:34 where the slain Kittim are mentioned. Apparently, *Sefer ha-Milhamah* speaks of a King of the Kittim who will be slain by the Prince of the Congregation; see G. Vermes, "The Oxford Forum for Qumran Research: Seminar on the Rule of War from Cave 4 (4Q285)," *JJS* 43 (1992) 85–94. This subject will be discussed in chapter 9.

12 [will fall". They are the] Kittim, who will be giv[en] into the hand of
     his great ones [...]
13 [...]ym when he flees befo[re Is[rael [....]

The mention of the Kittim in 4QpIsaᵃ led a few scholars to suppose that the
pesher describes events related to the Roman period, and they did not associate
the pesher with Ptolemy Lathyrus. But as I will show in chapter 9, the Kittim in
the Dead Sea Scrolls are at times identified with the Seleucids and at other times
with the Romans. Therefore, there is no reason to reject the hypothesis that the
Kittim mentioned in 4QpIsaᵃ are the Seleucids, just as they are in the *War Scroll*.

The author of 4QpIsaᵃ interpreted the verses describing the King of Assyria,
the enemy who conquered Judaea and reached the gates of Jerusalem, as a figure
coming from the Valley of Acco. Based on *Jewish Antiquities* XIII, it seems that
this enemy should be identified with Ptolemy Lathyrus, as proposed by Amusin.
This hypothesis is based on the mention of the Valley of Acco in the pesher,
as well as on the similarity between Isaiah 10 and the account given in *Jewish
Antiquities* XIII. In both Isaiah 10 and Josephus' account in *Jewish Antiquities,*
the enemy is described as advancing toward Jerusalem from the northeast,
almost reaching the city, but then retreating, explaining that it was some kind
of a Divine intervention that miraculously saved Jerusalem. According to *Jewish
Antiquities* XIII, after the battle by the Jordan River Alexander Jannaeus was no
match for Ptolemy Lathyrus' forces, and Jerusalem was only saved because of
Cleopatra's campaign against her son in Palestine. The author of the pesher on
Isaiah 10 seems to have interpreted these events as evidence of God's intervention
to spare Jerusalem.

If Amusin's approach is correct and 4QpIsaᵃ indeed refers to the events
of 103 B.C.E., then the pesher was composed after Ptolemy Lathyrus' retreat
from Syria, but before 88 B.C.E. In that year, Demetrius III campaigned against
Jerusalem from Shechem, passing through the sites mentioned in Isaiah 10, and
like Ptolemy Lathyrus, left Judaea without conquering the city. Had 4QpIsaᵃ
been composed after 88 B.C.E., one would have expected the author to have
used Isaiah 10 to refer to Demetrius III rather than Ptolemy Lathyrus. However,
with the reference to the Valley of Acco, one can assume that 4QpIsaᵃ relates to
Ptolemy Lathyrus and not to Demetrius III, so that it was most likely composed
between 103 and 88 B.C.E. In chapter 6, I will further elucidate and connect these
sources, documents, and events, including Demetrius' war against Alexander
Jannaeus. In chapter 5, however, I will discuss another scroll which also likely
refers to Alexander Jannaeus' war against Ptolemy Lathyrus.

CHAPTER FIVE

A Prayer for the Welfare of King Jonathan

In this chapter I will consider another scroll, 4Q448, which I believe is also associated with the war of Alexander Jannaeus against Ptolemy Lathyrus.[1] Unlike the scrolls discussed in the previous three chapters, this scroll is not sectarian in nature, and it should therefore be assumed that it was brought to Qumran by one of the people who joined the sect. This scroll documents a composition by a Hasmonean supporter, which stands in contrast to the pesharim which reflect opposition to the Hasmoneans. 4Q448 preserves fragments of three columns, an upper column and two lower columns that mention the name of King Jonathan twice.[2] A square piece of leather was attached to the right margin of the scroll, used for inserting a strap that was wrapped around the scroll. Similar reinforcing tabs were attached to many scrolls.[3] The last six lines of col. A include parts of

1   E. Eshel, H. Eshel, and A. Yardeni, "A Qumran Composition Containing Part of Ps 154 and a Prayer for the Welfare of King Jonathan and his Kingdom," *IEJ* 42 (1992) 199–229.

2   Despite the cursive script of 4Q448 which is hard to decipher, the words "King Jonathan" in line 2 of col. B and in line 8 of col. C are clear and indisputable. Thus there is no grounds for Philip Alexander's doubt and his desire to revert back to Strugnell's original proposal of the reading of the second line in the right column as עליצת המלך ("The king's joy"; Strugnell himself retracted the reading); see P. S. Alexander, "A Note on the Syntax of 4Q448," *JJS* 44 (1993) 301–2. Even Puech, who impeded the progress of deciphering this text rather than advancing it, agreed on the reading "King Jonathan" in those two lines; see E. Puech, "Jonathan le Prêtre impie et les débuts de la Communauté de Qumrân: 4QJonathan (4Q523) et 4QPsAp (4Q448)," *RQ* 17 (1996) 241–70.

3   Some 200 similar leather squares and straps were found in caves 4 and 8 of Qumran, most of which were detached from the scrolls they originally sealed. Only 4Q448 and a copy of the Damascus Document (4Q266) were preserved with the reinforcing tabs attached to them. On those tabs, see J. Carswell, "Fastenings on the Qumran Manuscripts," in *Qumran Grotte 4, II*

Psalm 154 which is known from the *Psalms Scroll* from Cave 11 (11QPs[a]) as well as from several Syriac manuscripts and which facilitated its reconstruction.[4] 4Q448 can therefore be read as follows:[5]

Column A

1 Halleluyah, a song of [
2 You loved as a fat[her
3 You Ruled over [
4 *vacat*
5 They were terrified of Senna[cherib and cried out: With a loud voice glorify God, in the congregation]
6 of the many procl[aim His majesty. Bind your souls to the good ones,]
7 and to the pure ones [to glorify the Most High. Behold the eyes of the Lord are compassionate over the good ones,]
8 And upon those who glorify Him He [increases His mercy. From an evil time He will deliver their soul, (He) who redeems]
9 the humble from the hand of adversaries. [And He delivers the perfect from the power of the wicked. He who desires]
10 His habitation in Zion, ch[ooses Jerusalem forever]

Column B

1 Keep guard, O Holy One
2 over King Jonathan
3 and over all the congregation of your people
4 Israel
5 who are in the four
6 corners of heaven
7 Let them all be at peace

Column C

by Your love *atys*[
in the day and until the evening *m*[
to approach to be *b*[
remember them for blessing *l*[
for Your name, which is called [
kingdom to be blessed [
for the day of war *y*[

(4Q128–4Q157), (ed. R. de Vaux and J. T. Milik; DJD 6; Oxford: Clarendon, 1977) 23–28.

4 Esther Eshel has shown that the last three lines of column A are parallel to the end of Psalm 154; see Eshel, Eshel, and Yardeni, "A Qumran Composition," 204–7. André Lemaire identified lines 5–7 of the same column as parallel to the beginning of Psalm 154; see A. Lemaire, "Attestation textuelle et critique littéraire: 4Q448 col. A et Psaume 154," in *The Dead Sea Scrolls: Fifty Years after Their Discovery* (ed. L. H. Schiffman, E. Tov, and J. C. VanderKam; Jerusalem: The Israel Exploration Society, 2000) 12–18.

5 E. Eshel, H. Eshel, and A. Yardeni, "448. 4QApocryphal Psalm and Prayer," in *Qumran Cave 4. VI: Poetic and Liturgical Texts, I* (ed. E. Eshel et al.; DJD 11; Oxford: Clarendon, 1998) 403–25; H. Eshel and E. Eshel, "4Q448, Psalm 154 (Syriac), Sirach 48:20 and 4QpIsa[a]," *JBL* 119 (2000) 645–59.

8	and upon Your kingdom	to king Jonathan[
9	May your name be blessed	*mt*[

Column A is a hymn in praise of God, while cols. B–C are a prayer for the welfare of King Jonathan. Column B is narrow and has been preserved in full. Column C is apparently the continuation of col. B, and appears to have been narrower than col. A. There are some differences in the paleography of col. A from that of cols. B–C, so it is probable that two different scribes are responsible for col. A and cols. B–C, though the possibility that the same scribe wrote all three columns with some time lapse between cols. A and B–C cannot be disregarded completely.[6]

I begin with a discussion of the *Prayer for the Welfare of King Jonathan*. The opening words of the prayer, at the top of col. B are difficult to interpret, since the combination of עור על—"rise upon"—usually means "rise against" in most of its occurrences in the Hebrew Bible. It has been suggested by a few scholars that the prayer opens with a call to God asking him to act against King Jonathan.[7] Since King Jonathan is paired with "all the congregation of your people Israel," Frank Cross assumed that the opening of the prayer should be understood as a plea to the Lord to rise against the enemies of King Jonathan. In his view, the opening of the prayer should be interpreted as: "Rise, O Holy One, to war on behalf of King Jonathan and all the congregation of your people Israel".[8] Elisha Qimron noted that the first two words in col. B should be compared with two verses where the verb עור is used in the sense of guarding, necessitating the preposition "on" (על): "… he will protect (יעיר) you and grant well-being on your righteous home" (Job 8:6); "Like an eagle who rouses (יעיר) his nestlings, gliding down to his young" (Deut 32:11). He proposed the meaning of the beginning of the prayer to be: "Keep guard, O Holy One, over King Jonathan and over all the

---

6   See Ada Yardeni's discussion in Eshel, Eshel, and Yardeni, "A Qumran Composition," 219–29. It is therefore difficult to accept Kister's proposal that that the scribe of 4Q448 deliberately omitted the words: "Who establishes a horn out of Jacob" (verse 19) which appear in 11QPs[a] and in the Syriac manuscripts, since he was an adherent of the Hasmoneans and wished to avoid an association with the Davidic dynasty; see M. Kister, "Notes on Some New Texts from Qumran," *JJS* 44 (1993) 289–90.

7   In the preliminary publication, we were wondering whether the first word of col. B should be read as "city" (עיר) or "rise" (עור—see Eshel, Eshel, and Yardeni, "A Qumran Composition," 208), but it seems that the middle letter of this word is indeed a *waw*, requiring the reading provided here.

8   See E. Eshel, H. Eshel, and A. Yardeni, "Rare DSS Text Mentions King Jonathan," *BAR* 20/1 (1994) 76.

congregation of your people Israel...."[9] The use of the root עוּר as guardianship, was well known at Qumran, because the title of the Watchers (עירין, עירים), used for angels, was derived from it.[10] This title (עירין) appears in the Book of Daniel, the Books of *Enoch*, the *Genesis Apocryphon*, a *Pseudo-Jubilees* work (4Q227) and in a fragment of the *Damascus Document* (4Q266).[11] Based on the context and the two occurrences mentioned above, it seems that though the usual meaning of עוּר על is "rise against," it is not to be understood as a call to rise against King Jonathan, but rather a plea for his welfare. The suggestion that the author is imploring God to act against King Jonathan is unacceptable, since immediately after, in lines 3–4, the author adds "and all the congregation of your people Israel." As there is no reason to assume that the author of the prayer would wish God to rise against the entire congregation of Israel who are in the "four corners of heaven," it seems more reasonable to posit that the author of the prayer in 4Q448 was a proponent of King Jonathan.[12]

9   E. Qimron, "On the Blessing for King Jonathan," *Tarbiz* 61 (1992) 565–66 (Hebrew); see also E. Dhorme, *A Commentary on the Book of Job* (trns. H. Knight; 2d ed; Nashville: T. Nelson, 1984) 114–15.

10   See J. J. Collins, "Watcher עיר," in *Dictionary of Deities and Demons in the Bible*, (ed. K. van der Toorn, B. Becking, and P.W. van der Horst; Leiden, New York, and Köln: Brill, 1995) 1681–85.

11   Dan 4:10, 14, 20; see J. T. Milik, *The Books of Enoch* (Oxford: Clarendon, 1976) 387; J. A. Fitzmyer, *The Genesis Apocryphon of Qumran Cave 1 (1Q20)* (3d ed.; Rome: Editrice Pontificio Istituto Rome, 2004) 68–69. 76–79; J. C. VanderKam, "227. 4Qpseudo-Jubilees,"in *Qumran Cave 4. VIII: Parabiblical Texts, I* (*DJD* 13; Oxford: Clarendon, 1994) 173; J. M. Baumgarten, "266. 4QDamascus Document^a," in *Qumran Cave 4, XIII: The Damascus Document (4Q266–273)* (DJD 18; Oxford: Clarendon, 1996) 37.

12   The suggestion that the author opposed King Jonathan was cautiously raised by John Strugnell and Daniel Harrington; see D. J. Harrington and J. Strugnell, "Qumran Cave 4 Texts: A New Publication," *JBL* 112 (1993) 498. André Lemaire and Emmanuelle Main also adopted this idea. See A. Lemaire, "Le Roi Jonathan à Qoumran (4Q448 B-C)," in *Qoumran et les manuscrits de la Mer Morte: Un Cinquantenaire* (ed. E. M. Laperrosaz; Paris: Cerf, 1997) 57–70; E. Main, "For King Jonathan or Against? The Use of the Bible in 4Q448," in *Biblical Perspectives: Early Use of and Interpretation of the Bible in Light of the Dead Sea Scrolls* (ed. M. E. Stone and E. G. Chazon; STDJ 28; Leiden: Brill, 1998) 113–35. This reading is based on the understanding of עוּר על in col. B, line 1, as "rise against" and the *waw* of וכל in line 3 as adversative. Thus the meaning of this column would be "Rise up, O Holy one, against King Jonathan, [but let] all the congregation of your people Israel … be in Peace." However, this reading is unacceptable, for if the author had wanted to ask God to attack King Jonathan he would have started the positive sentence concerning Israel with "Let them all be in peace" and would have written "Rise, O Holy one against King Jonathan, that there may be peace (יהו שלום) on all the congregation of your people Israel." Some additional details in Main's article need correction as well. For example, the discussion that in Judg 9 the tribe of

The author of the prayer has implied that the kingdom of God is the kingdom of Jonathan. Although it is possible to understand the plea "and upon your kingdom may Your name be blessed" (col. B, lines 8–9) as referring to the whole world, the proximity between "King Jonathan" and "the Kingdom of God" in these columns indicates that the Hasmonean kingdom was understood as the Kingdom of God. The plea for God's name to be blessed upon his kingdom may signify that God is blessed when His deeds are manifested in His kingdom (the world), but the author may have also meant that God's name shall be blessed by the people in His kingdom.[13] Since it is not entirely clear to whose kingdom, either God's or Jonathan's, the author was referring (in col. B, line 8), it seems that such ambiguity was deliberate.[14]

In col. B and the beginning of col. C, the author addressed God and asked him to guard King Jonathan, to bless him and Israel with peace. He expressed the fervent hope that the Kingdom of God would be blessed and that someone would be remembered and enabled to approach Jerusalem or the Temple. It seems that at the end of line 4 in col. C, the text shifts from being a plea to a thanksgiving prayer. God is praised for having placed his name upon Israel, and for delivering King Jonathan on the "Day of War."[15] If this approach is correct, then it follows that King Jonathan was assisted by God and achieved a military success on a "Day of War."

King Jonathan should be identified with Alexander Jannaeus. This identification is based on the fact that Jonathan son of Mattathias was a high priest but not a king.[16] Besides Alexander Jannaeus, no other kings of the

---

Judah fights the tribe of Benjamin and not the tribe of Ephraim (pp. 121–22) has nothing to do with the fact that the scribes of the Qumran sect called themselves "Judah" and the Pharisees "Ephraim." Since Alexander Jannaeus was a Sadducee, Main's whole reconstruction makes little sense.

13 Compare the phrase: "and on all shall Your name be blessed and exalted" in the eighteenth blessing of the *Amidah* prayer with the phrase "Your name will be blessed in the mouth of every living creature" in the second blessing after the meal.

14 In this context it should be noted that the *Prayer for Jonathan's Welfare* describes the people of Israel as dispersed to the four corners of heaven, without any plea for their ingathering; see D. Flusser, "Some Notes about the Prayer for King Jonathan," *Tarbiz* 61 (1992) 297–300 (Hebrew).

15 The *Prayer for the Welfare of King Jonathan* is patterned like several known Hebrew pleas and thanksgiving prayers which include a list of items that are presented with the preposition "on" (על) such as: "On Israel and on its rabbis and on their pupils" in the *Kaddish* or: "On the Righteous and on the Pious and on the proselytes" in the *Amidah* prayer; see Eshel, Eshel, and Yardeni, "A Qumran Composition," 214–16.

16 On the fact that Jonathan son of Mattathias was not a king, see *J.W.* 1.70 and *Ant.* 13.301, which mention that Aristobulus, the son of John Hyrcanus, was the first of the Hasmoneans to have

Second Temple period were named Jonathan.[17] Josephus described four battles in which it seems that Alexander Jannaeus was unexpectedly rescued. One of these battles may be intended in the phrase "Day of War" of 4Q448, in which Alexander Jannaeus was believed to have received God's help. The first of such battles is when, in 103/2 B.C.E., Ptolemy Lathyrus did not succeed in conquering Jerusalem. A second battle is the one in which Alexander Jannaeus escaped death when battling the army of the Nabataean king Obodas I in the Golan in 94 B.C.E. The third such instance took place in 88 B.C.E., when Demetrius III failed to conquer Jerusalem. Finally, in 86 B.C.E., Antiochus XII, Dionysus penetrated the fortifications built by Alexander Jannaeus between Kfar Saba and Jaffa, but nevertheless did not capture Jerusalem.[18] On the other hand, it cannot be completely dismissed that the author of the prayer was not referring to any one of the battles described by Josephus, but that he was expressing gratitude to God for strengthening Alexander Jannaeus in all his battles.[19]

In order to try and moderate between 4Q448 and Josephus, I now turn to col. A of the scroll. Lines 5–10 of col. A in 4Q448 preserve fragments of verses from Psalm 154, a psalm which had otherwise been preserved in Syriac, in a collection of five apocryphal psalms.[20] In 1930, Martin Noth published a

---

claimed being a king. Despite this, Vermes suggested that one of Jonathan's followers considered him to be a king, even though he only held the title of high priest; see G. Vermes, "The So-Called King Jonathan Fragment (4Q448)," *JJS* 44 (1993), 294–300.

17 Herod's wife, Mariamne, had a brother named Jonathan; see *J.W.* 1.435–37. This Jonathan Aristobulus was not a king. He was drowned in a pool in Jericho shortly after he was appointed high priest. It is hard for me to accept the hypothesis that one of Alexander Jannaeus' sons was called Jonathan, a suggestion that was made by several scholars based on Hasmonean coins that bear the inscription "Jonathan"; see Y. Meshorer, *A Treasury of Jewish Coins* (Jerusalem and New York: Ben-Zvi and Amphora, 2001) 26–27.

18 M. Stern, "Judea and her Neighbors in the Days of Alexander Jannaeus," in *The Jerusalem Cathedra I* (ed. L. I. Levine; Jerusalem: Ben-Zvi; 1981) 32–44.

19 Flusser suggested that the prayer was composed in the year 80 B.C.E. In that year Alexander Jannaeus returned to Jerusalem after conquering Gamla and was warmly accepted by the Jews of Jerusalem. He based this assumption on the account in the Book of *Josiphon*; see D. Flusser, "Some Notes," 298.

20 The first edition of the five apocryphal psalms in Syriac was published by William Wright; see W. Wright, "Some Apocryphal Psalms in Syriac," *Proceedings of the Society of Biblical Archaeology* 9 (1887) 257–66. For an updated version, see W. Baars, *The Old Testament in Syriac IV*, fascicle 6: *Apocryphal Psalms* (Leiden: Brill, 1972), and F. Van Rooy, "The Hebrew and Syriac Versions of Psalm 154," *Journal for Semitics* 5 (1993) 97–109. The apocryphal psalms were preserved in most manuscripts as an insertion between two parts of a *Book of Discipline* (*Ketaba dedurša*) written by the Nestorian Bishop Elijah of al-Anbar. In two manuscripts they are preserved as part of the Bible. In the earliest manuscript where these psalms are to be found (Mosul [12t4]) of the

reconstruction of the Hebrew text of three of these five psalms (152, 154, and 155).[21] In 1956 the *Psalms Scroll* of Cave 11 (11QPs[a]) was discovered, containing three of the five apocryphal psalms (151, 154, and 155).[22] A comparison of Noth's proposed Hebrew reconstructed text of Psalms 154 and 155 with those in 11QPs[a] shows how accurate his work was. Since three of the five psalms that were preserved in Syriac were found in the Qumran *Psalms Scroll*, some scholars have suggested a connection between the Syriac psalms and the accounts of the discovery of Hebrew manuscripts in a cave in the region of Jericho at the end of the eighth century or the beginning of the ninth century C.E.[23] In a letter written in Syriac sent by Timotheus I, the Nestorian Patriarch of Seleucia (near Baghdad; 726–819 C.E.) to a bishop named Sergeius residing in Elam, he describes how Jews who came to him for conversion told him that ten years previously an Arab huntsman chasing after his dog found Hebrew manuscripts in a cave near Jericho. When the Jews of Jerusalem became aware of this find, many went out to the area to dig. According to Timotheus, the Jews found biblical manuscripts and other books written in Hebrew. One of the Jews told Timotheus that the books included over two hundred psalms composed by King David. Timotheus wrote Christian clergy in Palestine and Syria, asking them to locate these books for him. The letter sent to Sergeius is apparently such a request. Since Timotheus wrote in Syriac and the Qumran caves yielded two of the four psalms preserved only in Syriac, some scholars have suggested that Timotheus' efforts to secure additional hymns were apparently successful, leading to his possession of four

---

twelfth century C.E.), these Psalms are appended to the Book of Psalms and are numbered Psalms 151 through 155.

21 M. Noth, "Die fünf syrisch überlieferten apokryphen Psalmen," *ZAW* 48 (1930) 1–23. The Hebrew reconstruction was done in the following manner: he found the words that appeared in the Syriac apocryphal psalms in other psalms in the Peshitta (the Syriac translation of the Bible), and chose one of the Hebrew equivalents from the canonical psalms and used it to reconstruct the apocryphal psalms.

22 Cave 11 and the *Psalms Scroll* were discovered in January or February 1956, but the *Psalms Scroll* was not opened until November 1961, when Elizabth Bechtel reimbursed the Jordanian Antiquity Authority for their original investment in buying it from the Bedouins. James Sanders published Psalm 151 in 1963; see J. A. Sanders, "Ps. 151 in 11QPss," *ZAW* 75 (1963) 73–86. Psalms 154 and 155 were published by Sanders in 1964; see idem, "Two Non-Canonical Psalms in 11QPs[a]," *ZAW* 76 (1964) 57–75.

23 On the hypothesis that the Syriac psalms originated from Qumran, see J. A. Sanders, "*Variorum* in the Psalms Scroll (11QPs[a])," *HTR* 59 (1966) 92; J. Strugnell, "Notes on the Text and Transmission of the Apocryphal Psalms, 151, 154 (=Syr. II) and 155 (=Syr. III)," *HTR* 59 (1966) 257–58, 278; A. S. van der Woude, "Die fünf syrischen Psalmen," in *Jüdische Schriften aus Hellenistic – römischer Zeit* (ed. W. G. Kümmel; Gütersloh: Mohn, 1974) 34.

psalms with a Qumran origin. These psalms would have then been translated into Syriac by Timotheus or one of his associates. The text of Psalm 154 in the Psalms Scroll and in the Syriac manuscripts reads as follows: [24]

1. [With a loud voice glorify God, in the congregation of the many proclaim His Majesty.]
2. [In the multitude of the upright glorify His name, and with the faithful recount His greatness.]
3. [Bind] your souls to the good ones, and to the pure ones to glorify the Most High.
4. Form an assembly to proclaim His salvation. And be not lax in making known His might and His majesty to all simple folk.

5. For to make known the glory of the Lord is wisdom given.
6. And for recounting His many deeds She was revealed to men.
7. To make known to the simple folk His might, and to explain to senseless folk His greatness.
8. Those far from Her gates, those who stray from Her portals.

9. For the Most High is the Lord of Jacob, and His majesty is over all His works.
10. And a man who glorifies the Most High, he accepts as one who brings a meal offering,
11. as one who offers he-goats and bullocks,
    as one who fattens the altar with many burnt offerings,
    as with a sweet-smelling fragrance from the hand of the righteous.

12. From the gates of the righteous Her voice is heard, and from the assembly of the pious Her song.

24 The missing words in 11QPs[a] were reconstructed based on the Syriac manuscripts and appear in parentheses; see J. A. Sanders *The Psalms Scroll from Cave 11* (DJD 4; Oxford: Clarendon, 1965) 64–70; idem, *The Dead Sea Psalms Scroll* (Ithaca: Clarendon, 1967) 103–9. When we published 4Q448, we suggested several emendations to Sanders' suggestions; see Eshel, Eshel, and Yardeni, "A Qumran Composition," 204–7, 212–14. Sanders accepted these suggestions; see J. A. Sanders, "Psalm 154 Revisited," in *Biblische Theologie und gesellschaftlicher Wandel* (ed. G. Braulik; Freiburg im Breisgau: Herder, 1993) 296–306; see also A. Lemaire, "Le Psaume 154: sagesse et site de Qoumran," in *From 4QMMT to Resurrection* (ed. F. García Martínez, A. Steudel, and E. Tigchelaar; STDJ 61; Leiden and Boston: Brill, 2006) 195–204.

13. When they eat with satiety She is cited, and when they drink in a community together.
14. Their meditation is on the Law of the Most High, their words on making known His might.
15. How far from the wicked is Her word, from the haughty men to know Her.

16. Behold the eyes of the Lord are compassionate over the good ones,
17. And upon those who glorify Him He increases His mercy. From an evil time will He deliver [their] soul.
18. [Bless] the Lord, who redeems the humble from the hand of adve[rsaries, and He delive]rs [the pure ones from the power of the wicked].
19. [Who establishes a horn out of Ja]cob, and a judge [of peoples out of Israel.]
20. [He who desires His habitation in Zion chooses Jerusalem forever.]

Psalm 154 is comprised of five loosely connected units. Noth remarked that the first unit (vv. 1–4) is related to the fifth unit (vv. 16–20), since both call for praising the Lord and mention "the pure ones." The second unit (vv. 5–8) and the fourth unit (vv. 12–15) speak of Lady Wisdom. The third unit (vv. 9–11) claims that one who praises God is as favorable to Him as one who offers sacrifices.[25] It seems likely that some of the verses, which are found in 11QPsᵃ and in the Syriac manuscripts, were added to Psalm 154 in a later stage, since some of them disturb the psalm's strophic structure and do not integrate into the larger context of the hymn. One such example is the expression "bless the Lord" in v. 18, which is not found in 4Q448.

These are the verses of Psalm 154 which are found in 4Q448:[26]

1. With a loud voice glorify God, in the congregation of the many proclaim His Majesty.
3. Bind your souls to the good ones, and to the pure ones to glorify the Most High.
16. Behold the eyes of the Lord are compassionate over the good ones,
17. And upon those who glorify Him He increases His mercy. From an evil time will He deliver their soul.

---

25 See Noth, "Apokryphen Psalmen," 18–19.
26 See Eshel and Eshel, "4Q448," 647–49.

18b-c. He redeems the humble from the hand of adversaries, and delivers the perfect from the power of the wicked.

20. He who desires His habitation in Zion chooses Jerusalem forever.

The parts of Psalm 154 that have been preserved in 4Q448 attest to the likely accuracy of Noth's analysis of the structure of the hymn. 4Q448 col. A preserves verses of the first and fifth units, which were later split by the redactor of Psalm 154. This redactor integrated the first part in the beginning of the psalm, and the second part in its conclusion. This proposal seems more plausible than the assumption that the author of 4Q448 had the full version of Psalm 154 in front of him and that he chose to copy only verses 1, 3, 16–18, and 20 from it.[27]

In the Syriac manuscripts, Psalm 154 bears the title: "The Prayer of Hezekiah, when the Assyrians were surrounding him; and he asked God for deliverance from them."[28] Since the surviving remnants of line 4 of column A of 4Q448 indicate that the beginning of the line was left empty, it can be assumed that line 5 was the opening of the unit that was later incorporated in Psalm 154. In line 5 we read: "They were terrified of *sn*[". As the words preserved in line 6 are part of verse 1 of Psalm 154, the beginning of the psalm should therefore be reconstructed in line 5. There is no room to reconstruct more than one additional word after the word that begins with "of *sn*[". Based on the title preserved in the Syriac manuscripts, one should consider the following reconstruction: "They were terrified of Senna[cherib and cried out]."[29] The reconstruction: "and cried out" is derived from the verse: "Then Hezekiah the king and Isaiah the prophet, the son of Amoz, prayed and cried out to Heaven" (2 Chr 32:20). This reconstruction is similar to Jonah 1:5: "And the sailors were terrified and they cried out." Though the combination "terrified of" (מ ויראו...) before a proper name is not found elsewhere in the Bible, there is one occurrence of such phrase

27 See n. 6 above.

28 According to the Syriac manuscripts, Psalms 154 and 155 share the same title, while in the most ancient manuscript of these psalms (12t4), the twelfth-century Mosul manuscript, Psalm 154 has a double title which attributes it both to Hezekiah and to the people who had received permission from Cyrus to return to their land. This fact, as well as the content of Psalm 154, led P. W. Skehan to suggest that the attribution of Psalm 154 to Hezekiah originally belonged to Psalm 155 ("Again the Syriac Apocryphal Psalms," *CBQ* 38 [1976]: 156). Our reconstruction of 4Q448 col. A line 5 testifies to the antiquity of the ascription to Hezekiah, dating it back to the Second Temple period. It should be noted that the version of Psalm 154 found in 4Q448 explicitly mentions distress (vv. 16–17).

29 The reconstruction "They were terrified of Senna[cherib" was proposed by Lemaire ("4Q448," 16).

in a scroll found in Qumran (4Q382): "he feared Jezebel and Ahab."[30] This proposed reconstruction suggests that the hymnic unit of 4Q448 was attributed to Hezekiah and Isaiah.

In 2 Kgs 19:4, the text relates how Hezekiah turned to Isaiah, asking him to "pray for the remnant that still survives." Yet Isaiah's subsequent prayer is not documented in the Book of Kings. Instead, in response to Hezekiah's request, 2 Kings provides a prophecy delivered by Isaiah that Sennacherib would not conquer Jerusalem. Evidently the chronicler did not feel comfortable with the absence of Isaiah's prayer for Sennacherib's retreat from Jerusalem, especially after Hezekiah specifically requested it. He therefore chose to add a description of Hezekiah and Isaiah praying and crying to Heaven for the salvation of Jerusalem (2 Chr 32:20). But since the Second Book of Chronicles still does not contain Hezekiah and Isaiah's actual prayer, a Second Temple author composed it in the form of a psalm, attributing it to Isaiah and Hezekiah. It is this prayer which eventually found its way into 4Q448.

It should be noted that 2 Chr 32:20 is preceded and followed by a closed *parasha* (a *vacat* between verses but within the same line) designating this verse as a separate unit. Since 1 Sam 16:12 has a *pisqah be'emsaʿ pasuq* (a *vacat* in the middle of the verse) which in all likelihood serves to point to Psalm 151, another apocryphal psalm which appears in the Qumran scroll,[31] it is possible that the closed *parasha* before and after 2 Chr 32:20 alludes to the Second Temple period psalm attributed to Isaiah and Hezekiah, the same one that was copied in col. A of 4Q448.

The relationship between Sennacherib's campaign against Jerusalem as described in the Book of Kings and the unit in 4Q448 may be better understood in light of 2 Kgs 18:28: "Then Rabshakeh stood and called out in a loud voice in Judean..." The prayer in 4Q448, however, opens with the words "With a loud voice glorify God." It seems probably, that the prayer of Hezekiah and Isaiah was a response to the words of Rabshakeh, which is why it concludes with a plea for God to deliver the blameless from the wicked, mentioning Jerusalem specifically. The psalm's content is certainly consistent with a prayer that was apparently recited while the Assyrian army was camping outside Jerusalem's walls.

---

30 S. Olyan, "4Qpap paraKings," in *Qumran Cave 4. VIII: Parabiblical Texts, I* (DJD 13; Oxford: Clarendon, 1994) 364.

31 See S. Talmon, "Hebrew Apocryphal Psalms from Qumran," *Tarbiz* 35 (1966), 228–34 (Hebrew); idem, "Pisqah Beʾemsaʿ Pasuq and 11QPsᵃ," *Textus* 5 (1996), 11–21. Shemaryahu Talmon documented a number of cases of *pisqah beʾemsaʿ pasuq* found in different biblical manuscripts, and the fact that sometimes a closed *parasha* replaced the *pisqah beʾemsaʿ pasuq*.

An allusion to the prayer attributed to Isaiah and Hezekiah is found in *Laus Patrum* (the "Praise of the Fathers") written by Ben Sira (Sir 48:17–21).[32] In the lines dedicated to Isaiah and Hezekiah, we are told:[33]

17 Hezekiah fortified his city	in that he brought water into it
With bronze tools he cut through the rocks	and dammed up a mountain site for a reservoir
18 During his reign Sennacherib led an invasion	and sent Rabshakeh (his adjutant)
He shook his fist at Zion	and blasphemed God in his pride
19 [Then] their hearts melted within them	and they were in anguish like that of childbirth
20 They called upon the Most High God	and lifted up their hands up to him
He heard the prayer they uttered	and saved them through Isaiah
21 [God struck the] camp of the Assyrians	and routed them with a plague.

In this passage Ben Sira used two puns based on the names of Hezekiah and Isaiah: in verse 17 "Hezekiah (חזקיה) fortified (חזק) his city" and in verse 20 "and saved them (ויושיעם) through Isaiah (ישעיהו)."[34] The whole statement refers to these two characters,[35] and it is consistent that the description in verse 20 refers to the prayer attributed to them: "They called upon the Most High God, and lifted up their hands up to him, He heard the prayer they uttered."[36] There is no way to determine whether Ben Sira knew of a specific prayer that was attributed to Hezekiah and Isaiah such as the excerpt found in col. A of 4Q448, or whether the description in the *Praise of the Fathers* is based on 2 Chr 32:20.

Josephus mentions a prayer uttered by Isaiah when the Assyrian army was camping by the walls of Jerusalem: "He (Hezekiah) also sent some of his friends, and some of the priests to the prophet Isaiah and asked him to pray to God and, when he had offered sacrifices for the common safety, to exhort Him to show His wrath upon the hopes of the enemy, but to take pity on His own people. And when the prophet had done these things he received an oracle from God..." (*Ant.*

32 See Eshel, Eshel, and Yardeni, "4Q448," 650–51.

33 The English translation is based on R. H. Charles (ed.), *The Apocrypha and Pseudepigrapha of the Old Testament in English* (2 vols.; Oxford: Clarendon Press, 1913), 1:502–3 and P. W. Skehan and A. A. Di Lella, *The Wisdom of Ben Sira* (AB; New York: Doubleday, 1987) 536.

34 This is why Isaiah is not mentioned in the beginning of the unit but only in verse 20.

35 P. C. Beentjes, "Hezekiah and Isaiah: A Study on Ben Sira xlviii 15–25," in *New Avenues in the Study of the Old Testament* (ed. A. S. van der Woude; OTS 25; Leiden: Brill, 1989) 81–84.

36 It is therefore hard to accept Skehan and Di Lella's suggestion that the people on the wall who heard the words of Rabshakeh are the ones who said the prayer; see Skehan and Di Lella, *Ben Sira*, 538.

10.12).[37] Thus, I suggest that lines 5–10 in col. A of 4Q448 include a complete literary unit, attributed to Isaiah and Hezekiah based on 2 Chr 32:20.[38]

Given this interpretation of col. A of 4Q448, the question that arises is, what is the relationship of this hymn with the *Prayer for the Welfare of King Jonathan* in cols. B–C? It is my view that the *Prayer for the Welfare of King Jonathan* ended up on the same scroll alongside the prayer attributed to Hezekiah and Isaiah from the time of Sennacherib's siege because of a link between Sennacherib's campaign (in 701 B.C.E.) and Ptolemy Lathyrus' invasion of Judaea (in 103 B.C.E.). This link was known at Qumran (based on 4QpIsaᵃ), as we have seen in the previous chapter.

It cannot be determined whether or not the psalm and the prayer are Qumranic compositions,[39] since it is possible that an author who knew that Sennacherib's campaign was interpreted as referring to events in the days of Alexander Jannaeus added the prayer to the scroll where Isaiah and Hezekiah's prayer was copied. This addition could have happened some time after col. A had been copied. Since there are indications that pesharim were composed during the Second-Temple period by authors who were not part of the Qumran sect,[40] it may therefore be possible that a link between Sennacherib's campaign and Ptolemy Lathyrus' campaign was also known outside of Qumran.

It is widely accepted that many compositions discovered at Qumran were brought to Qumran from elsewhere by new members of the sect. Several words and phrases in 4Q448 are not characteristic of the language of the sectarian scrolls discovered in Qumran. These include "Halleluyah," "You Ruled Over," "the congregation of your people Israel," "the four corners of heaven," and "in the day and until the evening." Accordingly, it is most likely that 4Q448 was brought

---

37 The translation is based on R. Marcus, *Jewish Antiquities, Books IX–XI* (Loeb Classical Library; Cambridge, MA: Harvard University Press, 1937) 163.

38 The length of the prayer in lines 5–10 of col. A in 4Q448 is close to that of Hezekiah's prayer in 2 Kgs 19:15–19.

39 See the discussion by Yardeni in Eshel, Eshel, and Yardeni, "A Qumran Composition," 219–29.

40 See for example the integration of a pesher in the Masoretic text of Isa 9:13–14; M. H. Goshen-Gottstein, "Hebrew Syntax and the History of the Bible Text: A Pesher in the MT of Isaiah," *Textus* 8 (1973) 100–106. The end of Ben Sira (Sir 50:37–38) includes a pesher on Deut 32:21–22; see M. Kister, "A Common Heritage: Biblical Interpretation at Qumran and Its Implications," in *Biblical Perspectives: Early Use and Interpretation of the Bible in Light of the Dead Sea Scrolls* (ed. M.E. Stone and E.G. Chazon; STDJ 28; Leiden, Boston, and Köln, 1998) 104. The New Testament also includes pesharim, such as Acts 4:25–27 which includes a pesher on Ps 2:1–2; see D. Flusser, *Judaism and the Origins of Christianity* (Jerusalem, 1988) 376; Eshel and Eshel, "4Q448," 655–56.

to Qumran from outside.[41] The reference to King Jonathan by name is additional evidence for a non-sectarian origin of the scroll, since Qumran authors do not normally mention the Hasmonean rulers by name.[42] It therefore follows that the *Prayer for the Welfare of King Jonathan* was composed in Sadducean circles that supported Alexander Jannaeus.[43] The fact that the psalm copied in col. A of 4Q448 relates to Sennacherib's campaign, along with the discovery of a relevant pesher among the fragments of cave 4 that links Sennacherib's campaign to the campaign of Ptolemy Lathyrus, indicates that the *Prayer for the Welfare of King Jonathan* was composed just after 103 B.C.E.[44] The author of the *Prayer*

41 Eshel, Eshel, and Yardeni, "A Qumran Composition," 219, n. 85; J. H. Charlesworth, *The Pesharim and Qumran History*, (Grand Rapids: Wm. B. Eerdmans, 2002) 103–5. A different view was put forward by Hartmut Stegemann who suggested that 4Q448 was composed at Qumran. According to him, this scroll was composed as an epistle to Alexander Jannaeus, but that later the sectarians retracted and decided not to send it; see H. Stegemann, *Die Essener, Qumran, Johannes der Täufer und Jesus* (Freiburg, Basel, and Wien: Herber, 1993) 187–88 (= idem, *The Library of Qumran: On the Essenes, Qumran, John the Baptist and Jesus*, [Leiden, New York and Köln: Brill, 1998] 133–34). Baumgarten also assumed that this scroll was composed at Qumran, but does not explain why; see J. M. Baumgarten, *Qumran Cave 4.XIII: The Damascus Document: 4Q266-273* (DJD 18; Oxford: Clarendon Press, 1996) 2.

42 E. Eshel, "Personal Names in the Qumran Sect," in *These Are The Names: Studies in Jewish Onomastics* (ed. A. Demsky, J. A. Reif, and J. Tabory; Ramat Gan: Bar Ilan University Press, 1997) 39–52. It has been suggested that the name Jonathan (=Yehonatan) appears in another scroll (4Q523). This scroll is very fragmentary, and its editor, E. Puech, did not succeed in reconstructing a very coherent reading. In line 2, he read the name Jonathan. Line 5 mentions Gog and Magog. In line 4, he suggested reading "[They stol]e the flesh-hooks and[" (ו המזלגות גנ[בו). This meaning-less reading does not seem likely. Instead, it may be that the phrase should be read as "[will fa]ll the *mwlgdt*" (נפ[לו המולגדת), a scribal error for "the towers will fall" (נפלו המגדלות), based on Ezek 38:20. This verse, which relates the Gog and Magog war, is as follows in the Masoretic text: "The mountains will topple, the cliff will fall, and every wall will fall to the ground." The Syriac version (as quoted in *BHS*), however, reads "the towers will fall" instead of "the cliff will fall." Whatever the case may be, the reading "Jonathan" is doubtful, since the upper parts of the last two letters are missing. Even if one accepts it, one would then need to explain why an author wished to associate Jonathan with the Gog and Magog war. On 4Q523; see E. Puech, "4QJonathan", in *Qumran Grotte 4, XVIII: Textes Hébreux* (DJD 25; Oxford: Clarendon Press, 1998) 78–81.

43 See Eshel, Eshel, and Yardeni, "A Qumran Composition," 219; Eshel and Eshel, "4Q448," 654.

44 Recently, Annette Steudel suggested that 4Q448 was the beginning of *Miqsat Ma'asé Ha-Torah* (4QMMT); see A. Steudel, "4Q448 The Lost Beginning of MMT?" in *From 4QMMT to Resurrection* (ed. F. García Martínez, A. Steudel, and E. Tigchlaar; STDJ 61, Leiden and Boston: Brill, 2006) 247–63. In her article she ignores our proposal about the connection between col. A of 4Q448 and the *Prayer for the Welfare of King Jonathan* in cols. B–C. Neither does she discuss 4Q448's vocabulary, though it points to the composition being non-sectarian. Even if one accepts

for the Welfare of King Jonathan was apparently thanking the Lord for being on Alexander Jannaeus' side on the "Day of War" when Ptolemy Lathyrus failed to conquer Jerusalem. In other words, the author of the prayer was aware that prophecies related to Sennacherib's campaign were being interpreted as relating to the campaign of Ptolemy Lathyrus. Thus, the *Prayer for the Welfare of Alexander Jannaeus* was most likely composed in the early days of his reign, before the civil war and the execution of the Pharisees in 88 B.C.E., an event which will be discussed in the next chapter.

---

her assumption that the beginning of 4QMMT was lost, it is hard to assume that the letter would have opened with the words: "Halleluyah, a song of." Furthermore, any study of 4Q448 must deal with the connection between the hymn in col. A to the prayer in cols. B and C. Therefore, I still believe that 4QMMT should be dated to the middle of the second century B.C.E., while 4Q448 was composed after 103 B.C.E.

Fig. 1: Absalom's Tomb in the Kidron Valley in Jerusalem, mentioned in the Copper Scroll and may be connected with the House of Absalom (chap. 2). *Photo:* Z. Radovan

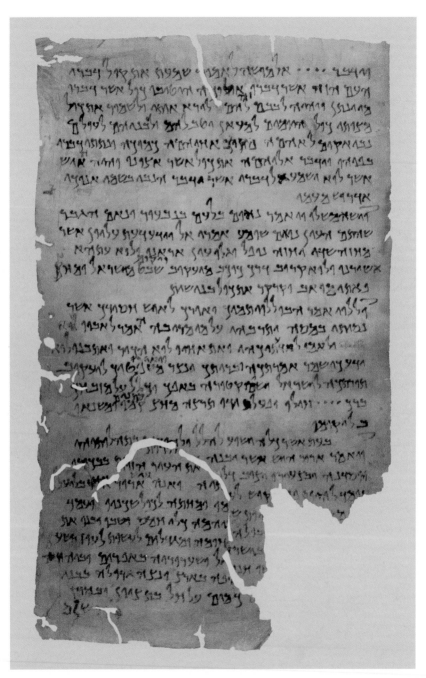

Fig. 2: 4QTest: one page containing biblical passages relating to prophecy, leadership, and priesthood. It ends with a passage recounting Joshua's curse against the builder of Jericho (chap. 3). *Photo:* B. and K. Zuckerman

Fig. 3: The siege system around the fortress of Doq, the arrows pointing to the two siege towers (chap. 3). *Photo:* Z. Radovan

Fig. 4: The fortress of Doq from the west (chap. 3). *Photo:* Z.H. Erlich

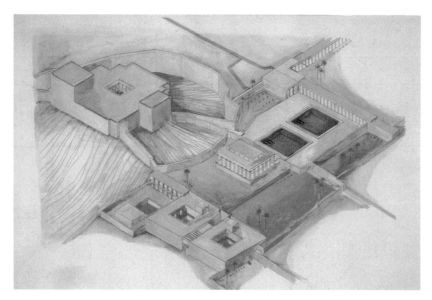

Fig. 5: Reconstructed view of the Hasmonean winter palace in Jericho by E. Netzer (chap. 3)

Fig. 6: Shiqmona, from the west. Here Ptolemy Lathyrus' fleet anchored and then marched to Acre (chap. 4). *Photo:* Z. Radovan

Fig. 7: 4Q448: prayer for the welfare of King Jonathan (chap. 5). *Photo:* Israel Antiquities Authority

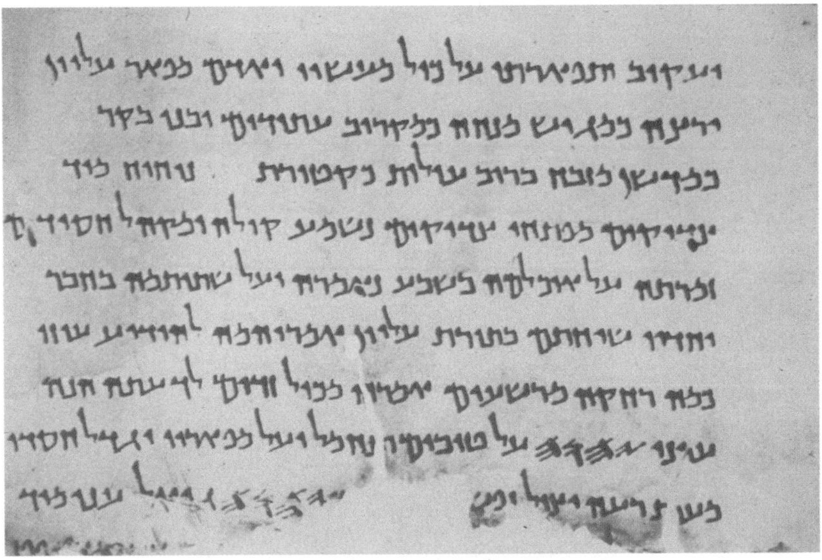

Fig. 8: Psalm 154 in 11QPs[a] (chap. 5). *Photo:* Israel Antiquities Authority

Fig. 9: Fragments 3–4 of Pesher Nahum (4QpNah) (chap. 6). *Photo:* Israel Antiquities Authority

Fig. 10: The Yarmuk River near Gadara; in this area the Nabatean King Obodas I ambushed the Hasmonean army of Alexander Jannaeus (chap. 6).
Photo: Z. Radovan

Fig. 11: Columns 56–58 of the Temple Scroll (chap. 6). *Photo:* Israel Museum, Jerusalem

Fig. 12: Large iron nail in the heel bone of a young Jew named Yehohanan who was crucified and buried in an ossuary in Jerusalem (chap. 6). *Photo:* Z. Radovan

Fig. 13: Columns 11–12 of the War Scroll (1QM) (chap. 9). *Photo:* Israel Museum, Jerusalem

The Pharisees' Conflict with Alexander Jannaeus and Demetrius' Invasion of Judaea

At the end of an extended yearlong campaign which ended in a protracted siege, Alexander Jannaeus conquered Gaza around 99 B.C.E.[1] Despite their alliance with the Nabateans, the people of Gaza waited in vain for the Nabateans to come to their rescue. With Alexander Jannaeus' conquest of Gaza, the Nabateans lost their main access to the Mediterranean Sea, since Gaza had served as their port. Further conquests of Alexander Jannaeus in northern Transjordan, and especially his gaining control of Gadara, led the Nabataean king Obodas I to launch a campaign against him, since Judaea's expansion endangered the main roads of commerce which connected the Nabatean kingdom to Rome and Damascus.[2]

The pivotal battle between Obodas I and Alexander Jannaeus took place in the Golan. According to Josephus, the Hasmonean army was trapped in an ambush, having been forced into a narrow valley (this may refer to the slopes along the Yarmuk River) where they were then beaten by a camel-mounted Nabatean army.[3] Alexander Jannaeus himself barely managed to escape to Jerusalem. The events that followed the battle are described by Josephus as follows:[4]

---

1   For the dating of Gaza's conquest by Alexander Jannaeus, see G. Fuks, "On the Reliability of a Reference in Josephus," in *Josephus Flavius: Historian of Eretz-Israel in the Hellenistic-Roman Period* (ed. U. Rappaport; Jerusalem: Ben-Zvi, 1982) 133–35 (Hebrew).
2   M. Stern, "Judaea and her Neighbors in the Days of Alexander Jannaeus," in *The Jerusalem Cathedra I* (ed. L. I. Levine; Jerusalem: Ben-Zvi, 1981) 40–42.
3   On the location of the battlefield, see A. Kasher, *Jews, Idumaeans, and Ancient Arabs* (Tübingen: Mohr, 1988) 92–95.
4   The translation is based on R. Marcus, *Josephus, Jewish Antiquities Books XII–XIV* (Loeb Classical Library; Cambridge, MA: Harvard University Press, 1933) 413–19.

As for Alexander, his own people were revolting against him – for the nation was aroused against him – at the celebration of the festival, and as he stood beside the altar and was about to sacrifice, they pelted him with citrons, it being a custom among the Jews that at the festival of Tabernacles everyone holds wands made of palm branches and citrons – these we have described elsewhere; and they added insult to injury by saying that he was descended from captives and he was unfit to hold office and to sacrifice; and being enraged at this, he killed some six thousand of them, and also placed a wooden barrier about the altar and the temple as far as that coping (of the court) which the priests alone were permitted to enter, and by this means blocked the people's way to him.[5] He also maintained foreign troops of Pisidians and Cilicians, for he could not use Syrians, being at war with them. And after subduing the Arabs of Moab and Galaaditis, whom he forced to pay tribute, he demolished Amathus, as Theodorus did not venture to meet him in the field. Then he engaged in a battle with Obedas, the king of the Arabs, and falling into an ambush in a rough and difficult region, he was pushed by a multitude of camels into a deep ravine near Gadara, a village of Gaulanis, and barely escaped with his own life, and fleeing from there, came to Jerusalem. But when the nation attacked him upon this misfortune, he made war on it and within six years slew no fewer than fifty thousand Jews. And so when he urged them to make an end to their hostility toward him, they only hated him more on account of what had happened. And when he asked what he ought to do and what they wanted of him, they all cried out, "to die"; and they sent to Demetrius Akairos, asking him to come to their assistance.

Thereupon Demetrius came with his army, and taking alone those who had summoned him, encamped near the city of Shechem. And Alexander on his side took six thousand two hundred mercenaries and about twenty thousand Jews who favored his cause, and went out to meet Demetrius, who had three thousand horse and forty thousand foot soldiers. Now there was much activity in both camps, the one side attempting to cause Alexander's mercenaries to desert because they were Greeks, while the other made the same appeal to the Jews who were with Demetrius. But as neither side could persuade the other, they engaged in battle, and

---

5   On the possibility that the *Megillat Ta'anit* implies that Alexander Jannaeus built a confinement in the temple, see U. Liebner, "The 23rd Day of Heshvan in *Megillat Ta'anit*," *Tarbiz* 71 (2002) 5–17 (Hebrew).

Demetrius was victorious, while all the mercenaries of Alexander met death after giving proof of their loyalty and courage. Many of Demetrius' soldiers, however, also died.

Alexander thereupon fled to the mountains, where out of pity for him at this reverse six thousand Jews gathered to his side. And at this Demetrius withdrew in alarm. But later on the Jews fought against Alexander, and were defeated, many of them dying in battle. The most powerful of them, however, he shut up and besieged in the city of Bethoma,[6] and after taking the city and getting them into his power, he brought them back to Jerusalem, and there he did a thing that was as cruel as could be: while he was feasted with his concubines in a conspicuous place, he ordered some eight hundred of the Jews to be crucified, and slaughtered their children and wives before the eyes of the still living wretches. This was the revenge he took for the injuries he had suffered; but the penalty he exacted was inhuman for all that, even though he had, as was natural, gone through very great hardships in the wars he had fought against them, and had finally found himself in danger of losing both his life and throne, for they were not satisfied to carry on the struggle by themselves but brought foreigners as well, and at last reduced him to the necessity of surrendering to the king of the Arabs the territory which he had conquered in Moab and Galaaditis and the stronghold therein, in order that he might not aid the Jews in the war against him; and they committed countless other insulting and abusive acts against him. But still he seems to have done this thing unnecessarily, and as a result of his excessive cruelty he was nicknamed Thrakidas (the "Cossack") by the Jews. Then his opponents, numbering in all about eight thousand, fled by night and remained in exile so long as Alexander lived. And he, being rid of trouble they had caused him, reigned thereafter in complete tranquility. (*Ant.* 13.372–83).

A similar account is given in *The Jewish War* (1.90–98), but according to this account the Jews revolted against Alexander Jannaeus only after he had been beaten by Obodas. Another difference between the two accounts can be noted in the number of soldiers that participated in the battle between Alexander and Demetrius. In *Jewish Antiquities* the number is higher (26,200 of Alexander and

---

6   For the location of Bethoma, see A. Zertal and N. Mikron, *The Manasseh Hill Country Survey: From Nahal 'Iron to Nahal Shechem* (3 vols.; Tel Aviv: Ministry of Defence Pub. House, 2000) 3.77, 188–91 (Hebrew).

43,000 of Demetrius) than in *The Jewish War* (19,000 of Alexander and 17,000 of Demetrius).

There is no doubt that these accounts are written from a point of view hostile towards Alexander Jannaeus. For example, *Jewish Antiquities* emphasizes the loyalty of the Hellenic mercenaries, but does not mention the performance of the Jewish soldiers who made up most of Alexander's army. Since this account is based on a Hellenistic source, there are scholars who have doubted that a Hasmonean king could have actually executed his Jewish opponents as described by Josephus. This point of view is vigorously expressed by Joseph Klausner: [7]

> The stories of Josephus concerning Jannaeus' cruel deeds are nothing but legends. First of all, the figure 800 for those who were crucified (all of them leading rebels) and the figure of 8,000 who fled are enough to arouse suspicion (the number of those fleeing being exactly ten times the number crucified). Secondly, crucifixion was not a Jewish form of punishment, and until the period of Roman rule in Judaea this cruel type of death is not found in Judaea at all. Thirdly, the name "Thracian," with which the Jews dubbed Jannaeus seems strange coming from Jews… Josephus obtained his information on Jannaeus from Pharisees and Greek sources. The former hated him for his Sadducaism; the latter had an aversion to Jews in general and Jannaeus in particular for having conquered idolatrous, Hellenistic cities in Palestine, as related above. For this reason they invented all sorts of lies about Jannaeus and attributed to him the cruelest of acts, which he did not do. There is no doubt that he avenged himself on the Pharisees, who embittered his life and caused him to lose the fruit of his great victories in Transjordan and refused to make peace with him under any condition save his death. But it may be said with certainty that he did not commit the acts of cruelty which Josephus ascribes to him.

Joshua Efron adopted a similar position, arguing that this account was an invention of Nicolaus of Damascus and has no historical ground: [8]

> That story was not invented by Sadducees or born of any Jewish conception, sect, or sectarian view, but created in the same Damascene

---

7   J. Klausner, "Judah Aristobulus and Jannaeus Alexander," in *The World History of the Jewish People: The Hellenistic Age* (ed. A. Schalit; London: Allen, 1972) 234.

8   J. Efron, *Studies on the Hasmonean Period* (Leiden, New York, Københaven, and Köln: Brill, 1987) 173.

work that heaped abuse upon the entire people of Israel, their Hasmonean leaders and their spiritual mentors. Such aspersions were cast throughout the whole Hasmonean period, and the position comes from the same Herodian historiography.

In 1956, however, a fragment of a scroll from Cave 4, containing a commentary (a pesher) to Nahum was published, substantiating the historicity of these accounts.[9]

The pesher has been preserved in five fragments: frgs. 1 and 2 belong to the first two columns of the composition; frg. 4, the largest of the five, includes almost four full columns; frg. 3 belongs to the right bottom edge of the first column in fragment 4; the last, frg. 5, is a small fragment belonging to another column and includes remnants of a pesher to Nah 3:13. The first column of frg. 4, includes a commentary on the prophecy in Nahum 2, associating it with events that took place in Judaea in the first century B.C.E. The author of this pesher mentions two Seleucid kings who were not given a sobriquet by the sectarians, and accordingly were mentioned by name.[10]

The *Pesher on Nahum* is the only pesher among the 18 "Continuous Pesharim" found in Qumran that mentions personal names of historical figures.[11] The first column of frg. 4 is not fully preserved and the first third of most its lines is missing, except for several words preserved in frg. 3. Nevertheless, the size of the missing part can be determined based on a reconstruction of the biblical verses quoted in the pesher:[12]

1. [The interpretation of it concerns Jerusalem, which has become] a dwelling for the wicked ones of the nations. "Where the lion went to enter, the lion's cub [

9   J. M. Allegro, "Further Light on the History of the Qumran Sect," *JBL* 75 (1956) 89–95.

10   Another scroll which may include a name of a foreign ruler is 4Q578. This scroll is preserved in a small fragment of four lines. Line 2 probably reads "Ptolemy," a name which can be reconstructed in lines 3 and 4 as well. The editor of this scroll was not able to conclude whether this title was a reference to the Greek name of the city of Acco or to one of the Ptolemaic kings. This scroll is very fragmentary and it is impossible to draw any historical details from it; see E. Puech, *Qumran Grotte 4. XVIII: Textes Hébreux* (DJD 25; Oxford: Clarendon, 1998) 205–8.

11   See E. Eshel, "Personal Names in the Qumran Sect," in *These are The Names: Studies in Jewish Onomastics* (ed. A. Demsky, J. A. Reif, and J. Tabory; Ramat Gan: Bar Ilan, 1997) 39–52.

12   The translation of the pesher is quoted here according to M. P. Horgan, *Pesharim: Qumran Interpretations of Biblical Books* (CBQ Monograph Series 8; Washington DC: The Catholic Biblical Association of America, 1979) 163, with some emendations.

2. [and no one to disturb." The interpretation of it concerns Deme]trius, king of Greece, who sought to enter Jerusalem on the advice of the Seekers-After-Smooth-Things,

3. [but God did not give Jerusalem] into the power of the kings of Greece from Antiochus until the rise of the rulers of the Kittim; but afterwards [the city] will be trampled

4. [and will be given into the hand of the rulers of the Kittim.] "The lion tears enough for his cubs and strangles prey for his lionesses."

5. [The interpretation of it concerns Demetrius who made war] against the Lion of Wrath, who would strike with his great ones and the men of his counsel

6. [but they fled before him "And he fills up] his cave [with prey] and his den with torn flesh." Its interpretation concerns the Lion of Wrath,

7. [which will bring ven]geance on the Seekers-After-Smooth-Things; he would hang men up alive

8. [upon the tree]in Israel before, for regarding one hanged alive upon the tree [it] reads ... "Behold I am against [you]

9. say[s the Lord of hosts. I shall burn up yo]ur [abundance in smoke,] and the sword will devour your lions. And [I] shall cut off its [p]rey [from the earth,]

10. And [the voice of your messengers] will no [longer be heard."] The [interpre]tation of it: "your abundance"—they are the detachments of his army th[at are in Jerusal]em; and "his lions"—they are

11. his great ones [and his partisans, who banished by the sword]and "his prey"—that is the wealth that the [prie]sts of Jerusalem have amas[sed,] which

12. they [will] give [E]phraim, Israel will be given [   ]

Since Demetrius is mentioned in this passage, it is widely accepted that the author of the pesher associated Nahum's prophecy with the events of 88 B.C.E.,[13]

13 The only two scholars who did not associate the *Pesher on Nahum* with the events of 88 B.C.E. are Harold Rowley and Isaac Rabinowitz; see H. H. Rowley, "4QpNahum and the Teacher of Righteousness," *JBL* 75 (1956) 188–93; I. Rabinowitz, "The Meaning of the Key ("Demetrius")-Passage of the Qumran Nahum-Pesher," *JAOS* 98 (1978) 394–99. In their view the pesher relates to events in the time of Demetrius I and not Demetrius III. They argue that the pesher should be associated with the description in 1 Macc 7:1–25 of Alcimus' appointment as High Priest by Demetrius I, and how he and his party subsequently took revenge against the Maccabees. Rowley considered the mention of those hung alive in the *Pesher on Nahum* to be a reference to those crucified in the

which leads to the identification of the Lion of Wrath as Alexander Jannaeus.[14] This passage differentiates between "the kings of Greece," referring to the Seleucid kings, and "the rulers of the Kittim," who are the Romans. There is no doubt that the pesher was composed after Jerusalem's conquest by Pompey in 63 B.C.E., since the author of the pesher already knew that Jerusalem had not been conquered by the Seleucid kings from the times of Antiochus and until the Roman conquest, while after that the city had been ransacked by the Romans.[15] It is difficult to determine definitively to which Antiochus the pesher is referring, since it could be Antiochus IV, who reigned during the outbreak of the Hasmonean revolt, or it could be Antiochus V, who reigned

---

times of Antioch IV. Rabinowitz argued that the phrase "the advice of the Seekers-After-Smooth-Things" refers to a council of those seekers, and that the phrase "to enter Jerusalem" indicates that Demetrius I wished to consign Jerusalem in the hands of the council of the "Seekers-After-Smooth Things", whom he identified with the Hellenized Jews. The identification of Demetrius mentioned in the *Pesher on Nahum* with Demetrius III is better than Rowley's and Rabinowitz's proposal, since Demetrius I ruled Jerusalem to which he sent Nicanor and Bacchides. The sentence "who sought to enter Jerusalem" will therefore become senseless when read in reference to Demetrius I. With respect to hanging people alive, it is also suitable to Alexander Jannaeus' action after the retreat of Demetrius III; see F. M. Cross, *The Ancient Library of Qumran and Modern Biblical Studies* (Garden City, NY: Doubleday, 1961) 93, n. 29. The mention of the Romans (the Kittim) in the pesher indicates that it relates the events of the first century B.C.E. and not the second century B.C.E.; see Y. Yadin, "Recent Developments in Dead Sea Scrolls Research," in *Studies in the Dead Sea Scrolls* (ed. J. Liver; Jerusalem: Kiryat Sepher, 1957) 45 (Hebrew). Regarding Rabinowitz's suggestions, it should be noted that there is no evidence that Judas Maccabeus or his brothers hung or crucified Hellenized Jews.

14 G. Doudna is the only scholar who did not identify the Lion of Wrath as Alexander Jannaeus, since for him the lion cannot be a Jewish leader; see G. L. Doudna, *4QPesher Nahum: A Critical Edition* (JSPSup, 55; Sheffield: Sheffield Academic Press, 2001) 507–73.

15 Jerusalem neither fell nor was under foreign rule from the death of Antiochus IV in 163 B.C.E. until the conquest of Pompey in 63 B.C.E., this in spite of the fact that during that period several rulers, both Seleucids and Ptolemaic, tried to conquer Jerusalem. Tryphon invaded Judaea after the capture of Jonathan in 143 B.C.E., but did not succeed in conquering Jerusalem due to a blizzard (1Macc 13:20–23). Antiochus VII Sidetes led a campaign against Judaea during the reign of Simeon (1Macc 15:38–41), and charged up to Jerusalem after Simeon was murdered by his son-in-law, in order to capture John Hyrcanus. At the end of a long siege which lasted from 134 B.C.E. to 132 B.C.E., Antiochus VII and John Hyrcanus reached a settlement, in which John Hyrcanus became a vassal of Antiochus and some of Jerusalem's fortifications were destroyed (*Ant.* 13.236–47). With Alexander Jannaeus' succession to the throne, Ptolemy Lathyrus invaded Judaea, but again without success in conquering Jerusalem. Demetrius III defeated Alexander Jannaeus in a battle near Shechem, but did not conquer Jerusalem. Antiochus XII Dionysos and Aretas III, the Nabatean king, invaded Judaea during the reign of Alexander Jannaeus, but neither did they succeed in conquering Jerusalem (*J.W.* 1.99–103; *Ant.* 13.389–92).

when the Temple was purged, or Antiochus VII, who besieged Jerusalem in 134 B.C.E.[16]

Dead Sea Scrolls scholars have paid attention to three questions pertaining to the understanding of lines 7 and 8 in this column of the *Pesher on Nahum*. The first question is: what is the meaning of the phrases "he would hang men up alive" and "one hanged alive"? In particular, what is the meaning of the word "alive" in such a context? The second is, how ought line 8 be reconstructed? And the third, how does one understand the sentence: "for regarding one hanged alive upon the tree [it] reads ..."? With respect to the first question, the meaning of the word "alive" in the pesher is commonly thought to be a description of a particular manner of execution, namely crucifixion.[17] With respect to the second question, line 8 has been reconstructed, in three ways, "[which was never done] before in Israel,"[18] or "[which no one ever did] before in Israel,"[19] or "[which never happened] in Israel before."[20] In 1971 Yadin published a section of the *Temple Scroll* dealing with transgressions similar to those committed by the people who invited Demetrius to invade Judaea.[21] In light of this parallel, Yadin called for a reconsideration of the common reconstructions of lines 7–8

16   Most scholars accept Allegro's proposal, who assumed it was Antiochus IV; see Allegro, "Further Light," 93. Still, it cannot be dismissed that the pesher may be referring to Antiochus V who reigned during the purge of the Temple, or to Antiochus VII who tried to conquer Jerusalem after the death of Simeon in 134 B.C.E.; see Yadin, "Recent Developments," 44.

17   J. M. Baumgarten, "Does TLH in the Temple Scroll Refer to Crucifixion?," *JBL* 91 (1972) 472–81; M. Hengel, *Crucifixion in the Ancient World and the Folly of the Message of the Cross* (Philadelphia: Fortress, 1977) 85; J. A. Fitzmyer, "Crucifixion in Ancient Palestine, Qumran Literature, and the New Testament," *CBQ* 40 (1978) 498–507; D. J. Halperin, "Crucifixion, the Nahum Pesher, and the Rabbinic Penalty of Strangulation," *JJS* 32 (1981) 32–34; O. Betz, "The Death of Choni-Onias in the Light of the Temple Scroll from Qumran," in *Jerusalem in the Second Temple Period, Abraham Schalit Memorial Volume* (ed. A. Oppenheimer, U. Rappaport, and M. Stern; Jerusalem: Ben-Zvi, 1980) 91–92 (Hebrew); M. Wilcox, " 'Upon the Tree': Deuteronomy 21:22–23 in the New Testament," *JBL* 96 (1977) 88.

18   This reconstruction was offered by Allegro, "Further Light," and it was followed by most translators; see J. Carmignac, E. Cothenet, and H. Lignée, *Les textes de Qumran traduits et annotées* (2 vols.; Paris: Letouzey et Ané, 1963) 2.86; T. H. Gaster, *The Dead Sea Scriptures* (Garden City, NY: Doubleday, 1956) 243; G. Vermes, *The Dead Sea Scrolls in English* (Baltimore: Penguin, 1962) 232.

19   A. Dupont-Sommer, "Le Commentaire de Nahum découvert près de la Mer Morte (4Q p Nah): Traduction et notes," *Semitica* 13 (1963) 55–88; D. Flusser, "Pharisäer, Sadduzäer und Essener im Pescheer Nahum," in *Qumran: Wege der Forschung* (ed. K. E. Grözinger; Darmstadt: Wissenschaftliche Buchgesellschaft, 1981) 134.

20   A. M. Haberman, *The Scrolls from the Judean Desert* (Tel Aviv: Mahbaroth Lesifruth, 1959) 153 (Hebrew).

21   Y. Yadin, "Pesher Nahum (4Q pNahum) Reconsidered," *IEJ* 21 (1971) 1–12.

in this column of the *Pesher on Nahum*. In col. 64 of the *Temple Scroll*, there is a paragraph dealing with hanging which includes the following laws:[22]

6.   .... If
7. a man informs against his people, and delivers his people up to a foreign nation, and does harm to his people,
8. you shall hang him on the tree, and he shall die. On the evidence of two witnesses and on the evidence of three witnesses
9. he shall be put to death, and they shall hang him on the tree. *vacat* And if a man has committed a crime punishable by death, and has defected into
10. the midst of the nations, and has cursed his people and the children of Israel, you shall hang him also on the tree,
11. and he shall die. And their body shall not remain upon the tree all night, but you shall bury them the same day, for
12. those hanged on the tree are accursed by God and men; you shall not defile the land which I
13. give you for an inheritance ...

According to the *Temple Scroll*, hanging is the punishment of those who inform against their people, deliver them to a foreign nation, or harm them. Yadin suggested that the Lion of Wrath, who executed his enemies for inviting Demetrius, acted in accordance with the law of the *Temple Scroll*. Therefore, Yadin argued that the *Pesher on Nahum* should not be read as being critical of Alexander Jannaeus and consequently proposed to reconstruct line 8 of frgs. 3–4 of the *Pesher on Nahum* as follows: "[for this is the law] in Israel before", suggesting either תורה or משפט for "law".[23] Joseph Fitzmyer, accepting Yadin's contention, offered the following alternative reconstruction: "[for so it was done] in Israel before."[24] In summary, most posit that the author of the *Pesher*

---

22 The following quotation is from the translation of Y. Yadin, *The Temple Scroll* (3 vols.; Jerusalem: Israel Exploration Society, 1977–83) 2.288–91. For improved readings, see E. Qimron, "Further New Readings in the Temple Scroll," *IEJ* 37 (1987) 34–35 [=E. Qimron, *The Temple Scroll*, (Beer Sheva and Jerusalem: Israel Exploration Society, 1996) 89]. On the interpretation of Deut 21:22–23 in the *Temple Scroll*, see M. J. Bernstein, "*Midrash Halakha* at Qumran? 11QTemple 64:6–13 and Deuteronomy 21:22–23," *Gesher* 7 (1979) 145–66.

23 Yadin, "Pesher Nahum."

24 Fitzmyer, "Crucifixion," 502. Martin Hengel also accepted Yadin's proposal; see Hengel, *Crucifixion*, 84.

on Nahum criticized the Lion of Wrath, while according to the reconstructions of Yadin and Fitzmyer the author of the pesher was justifying the actions of the Lion of Wrath, claiming he had acted according to the customary law in Israel, as documented in the *Temple Scroll.*

In light of the similarities between the *Pesher on Nahum*, the descriptions of Josephus, and the law quoted in the *Temple Scroll*, it can be assumed that Alexander Jannaeus believed he was acting in accordance with the law when he executed the people who had invited Demetrius to wage war on Judaea, since they had delivered their own people into the hands of a foreign nation. Despite this, it cannot be ascertained that the people of Qumran also considered Alexander to have acted in accordance with the law when he ordered the execution of his opponents. In order to determine which reconstruction in the *Pesher on Nahum* is correct, one must first answer the third question at hand, concerning the meaning of the end of line 8, "for regarding one hanged alive upon the tree [it] reads..." This phrase is followed by a quotation from Nah 2:14: "Behold I am against thee says the Lord of Hosts, and I will burn in smoke thine abundance, and thy young lions the sword shall devour. And I will cut [off from the land] his [p]rey. And the voice of thy messengers shall no more be heard." The relation between the phrase "for regarding one hanged alive upon the tree [it] reads..." and the verse following it has been explained in three different ways. Allegro suggested associating the phrase with the verse, in the sense that the one hanged alive will have it read of him: "Behold I am against thee..." Accordingly, the verse in which Nahum describes God burning and devouring is to be interpreted as relating to the one being hanged alive.[25] It is hard to accept this view, however, because the quotation from Nah 2:14 is in fact the beginning of a new section in the commentary.[26] The second interpretation was offered by Yadin, who considered the sentence to be an explanation provided by the author of the pesher, clarifying that the one hanged alive should be compared to the man in Deut 21:22–23. Yadin contended that there was a debate in Judaea as to

25 This suggestion was brought forth in the preliminary edition of the *Pesher on Nahum*; see J. M. Allegro, *Qumran Cave 4, 1 (4Q158–4Q186)* (DJD 5; Oxford: Clarendon, 1968) 39.

26 See Fitzmyer, "Crucifixion," 500, n. 26. Baumgarten proposed that the word "hanged" be read in an active sense, so that it is in reference to the one who hangs people on the tree that it will be said: "Behold, I am against thee..."; see J. M. Baumgarten, "Hanging and Treason in Qumran and Roman Law," *Eretz-Israel* 16 (1982) 14*. On the active sense to the phrase "accursed by God and men" in the *Temple Scroll*, see D. R. Schwartz, "The Condemners of Judges and Men (11QTemple 64:12)," idem, *Studies in the Jewish Background of Christianity* (Tübingen: Mohr, 1992) 81–88. On the difficulties raised by such an interpretation, see M. J. Bernstein, "כי קללת אלהים תלוי" (Deut. 21:23): A Study in Early Jewish Exegesis," *JQR* 74 (1983) 33–34, n. 25.

whether or not a convict should be hung while he is still alive or only after he is already dead. According to this approach, the author of the *Pesher on Nahum* was explaining to its readers what was customary prior to its era.[27] This is a difficult interpretation to accept, for if the author of the pesher had wanted to emphasize that the Lion of Wrath had acted in accordance with Deuteronomy 21, he would not have stressed that the people were hung alive, a specification not found in Deuteronomy. In order to prove that Alexander's deeds were in accordance with the law, his main task would have been to convince his readers that the people who invited Demetrius were indeed culpable and should have been executed as stated in the first half of v. 22.[28] It therefore seems that the third interpretation of the three is the most plausible. It suggests that the author did not want to quote Deut 21:23 to explain that "the one hanged upon a tree" is cursed, because the verse can be read in such a way that it implies that it is God who is cursed. It is the author's religious sensitivities, therefore, that precluded him from citing the verse when it could lead to such an offensive misunderstanding. Therefore, instead of citing the passage (Deut 21:22–23), the author preferred alluding to it, assuming that the allusion alone would be enough for his readers to recall the passage and understand that "the one hanged upon a tree" is cursed.[29]

It therefore seems that the author of the *Pesher on Nahum* was not a supporter of Alexander Jannaeus, nor that he considered the actions of the Lion of Wrath to be in accordance with the law when he hanged alive the Seekers-After-Smooth-Things, all the more so since the pesher to Nahum's prophecy alluded to the passage from Deuteronomy as a proof text. Hence the author of the pesher

27 Yadin, "Pesher Nahum," 11.

28 There are two more scrolls which record a discussion of people who should be executed. Puech published a copy of the *Temple Scroll* from Cave 4 (4Q524) which he believes to preserve an older version of the *Temple Scroll*. This copy preserves the law under debate; see E. Puech, "Fragments du plus ancien exemplaire du *Rouleau de Temple (4Q524)*," in *Legal Texts and Legal Issues* (ed. M. J. Bernstein, F. García Martínez, and J. Kampen; STDJ 23; Leiden, New York and Köln: Brill, 1997) 35–39; idem, "Notes sur 11Q19 LXIV 6–13 et 4Q524 14, 2–4: À propos de la crucifixion dans le Rouleau du Temple et dans le Judaïsme ancien," *RQ* 18 (1997) 109–24. Furthermore, a copy of the Damascus Document from Cave 4 (4Q270) has been published, which includes a list of transgressions similar to the one which appears in the Temple Scroll; see J. M. Baumgarten, *Qumran Cave 4, XIII: The Damascus Document* (DJD 18; Oxford: Clarendon, 1996) 144–45. For slightly different reconstructions than those of Puech of 4Q524 and for a discussion of the connection between these laws and their relation to the Pesher on Nahum, see H. Eshel, "Alexander Jannaeus in the Pesharim: Two Notes on 4QpNah and 4QpHos^b," in *Fifty Years of Dead Sea Scrolls Research: Studies in Memory of Jacob Licht* (ed. G. Brin and B. Nitzan; Jerusalem: Ben-Zvi, 2001) 220–30 (Hebrew).

29 As suggested by Frank Moore Cross and David Noel Freedman, as quoted by Allegro, "Further Light," 91, n. 0-0.

believed that Alexander transgressed the law in the Book of Deuteronomy when he hung the Seekers-After-Smooth-Things while they were alive.[30] This being the case, the reconstructions offered by Yadin and Fitzmyer for line 8, "[for this is the law] in Israel before" or "[for so it was done] in Israel before," are no longer relevant. Rather, I agree with the reconstruction that was commonly accepted prior to Yadin's publication of the *Temple Scroll*: "[which was never done] before in Israel."[31] Furthermore, the law in the *Temple Scroll* sheds light on the legal concept that lies behind Alexander Jannaeus' controversial punishment. While some regarded the execution of such opponents as being consistent with the law that is documented in the *Temple Scroll*, the author of the *Pesher on Nahum* did not agree that the Lion of Wrath had acted in accordance with the law. Instead, he emphasized that the Lion of Wrath acted against the laws and practices of Israel and that the Lion of Wrath had transgressed a specific command in the Book of Deuteronomy when he did not bury the executed men on the day they were hung. The presumption that this was Alexander's sin depends on whether the law in the *Temple Scroll* relates to a hanging or a crucifixion. Some scholars assume that the similarity between the transgressions mentioned in the *Temple Scroll* and the actions of the men who invited Demetrius indicates that the Temple Scroll, like the *Pesher on Nahum*, deals with crucifixion.[32] However, it should be noted that the *Pesher on Nahum* emphasizes that these men were hung alive, while in the *Temple Scroll* no such specification is made. This led Joseph Baumgarten to argue that the people at Qumran indeed considered the Seekers-After-Smooth-Things culpable and deserving of execution, but they thought that Alexander Jannaeus should have sentenced them to hanging rather than crucifixion.[33] The author of the *Pesher on Nahum* stressed the fact that the

30 But see the well-balanced discussion by Berrin, who did not accept such a proposal, S.L. Berrin, *The Pesher Nahum Scroll from Qumran*, (STDJ 53; Leiden and Boston: Brill, 2004) 184–92.

31 Doudna suggested that the scribe who copied the *Pesher on Nahum* accidentally omitted the words "cursed by God" following the phrase "for regarding one hanged alive upon the tree, he will be called"; see Doudna, *Pesher Nahum*, 758. The weakness of this proposal lies in the fact that he assumes this is merely a mistake of a scribe, demanding no further explanation.

32 See Fitzmyer, "Crucifixion," 505–7; Halperin, "Crucifixion," 46; Betz, "Death of Choni-Onias," 91; Wilcox, "Upon the Tree," 89; and the summary of the various opinions in Berrin, *Pesher Nahum*, 184–92.

33 See Baumgarten, "TLH." Baumgarten suggested to distinguish between "hang" which is a type of strangling and "hang alive" which indicates crucifixion. A different view was expressed by David Halperin ("crucifixion"), who noted that in the *Pesher on Nahum* the words "hang alive" are interpreting the words "strangle for his lionesses" (Nah 2:13). Hence the author of the pesher assumed a connection between hanging alive and strangling. Despite this observation, Halperin con-

Lion of Wrath hung the individuals alive, thus transgressing the written law of Deuteronomy.[34]

Death on the cross was slow and prolonged and in order to be certain that the crucified had died, their bodies were left on the cross for a long period of time.[35] Philo of Alexandria relates his own eyewitness account of cases in which people were put on the cross and their bodies were removed only several days later on the occasion of a festival such as the emperor's birthday (*Flaccus*, 83).[36] Josephus states that: "Jews are so careful about funeral rites that even malefactors who have been sentenced to crucifixion are taken down and buried before sunset" (*J.W.* 4.317). This statement supports the fact that the Jewish custom was different from other contemporaneous practices. Josephus also relates that after the conquest of Jerusalem in 70 c.e. he was sent to a village named Thekoa, and that when he returned from his assignment back to Jerusalem, he identified three of his associates who had been crucified and were still hanging on their crosses. After Josephus appealed to Titus for mercy, they were taken off the cross and one even survived (*Life* 420–21).[37] The Gospel according to John states that "the Jews did not want the bodies should remain upon the crosses during the Sabbath" (19:31). It seems that the accusation by the author of the *Pesher on Nahum* that the bodies were left hanging is consistent with the statement that the rebels were crucified, since execution by crucifixion required leaving the bodies on the cross at least overnight.

---

tended that both in the *Pesher on Nahum* and in the *Temple Scroll* the reference is to crucifixion. It seems that Halperin's correct observation is not enough to dismiss Baumgarten's proposal that "hang alive" refers to crucifixion while "hang" denotes a strangling. For the author of the *Pesher on Nahum*, who wished to interpret these verses on the events of 88 b.c.e., the words "strangle for his lion-esses" were associated with the execution of the Pharisees even if they were crucified and not hung.

34 Deuteronomy states as follows: "And if a man has committed a crime punishable by death and he is put to death, and you hang him on a tree" (21:22). According to the order of events recorded in the verse, the Rabbis concluded that one must first put to death and only then hang the body; see *Sifri Deut* 221, 22 (Finkelstein edition, 254); *b. Sanhedrin* 46b. Occasionally people were hung or crucified after they were put to death in some other manner; see Hengel, *Crucifixion*, 24. On the other hand, the *Temple Scroll* states: "you shall hang him on the tree, and he shall die" (64:8). It is possible that this reordering of the actions in relation to Deuteronomy is connected with the debate mentioned by Yadin and Baumgarten.

35 For descriptions testifying that death on the cross was slow, see Hengel, *Crucifixion*, 29; and also, V. Tzaferis, "Crucifixion: the Archaeological Evidence," *BAR* 11/1 (1985) 49–50.

36 F. M. Colson, *Philo* (10 vols.; Loeb Classical Library, Cambridge, MA: Harvard University Press, 1941) 9.346–47.

37 S. Mason, *Life of Josephus: Translation and Commentary* (Leiden, Boston, and Köln: Brill, 2001) 167.

The *Pesher on Hosea* B (4QpHos^b=4Q167) also describes how the Lion of Wrath punished the Pharisees. This pesher enables us to understand why Alexander Jannaeus was named the Lion of Wrath.[38] One of the remaining paragraphs includes fragments of a commentary on Hos 5:13–14: "When Ephraim saw his sickness, and Judah his wound, then Ephraim went to Assyria, and sent envoys to the great king. But he is not able to cure you or heal your wound. For I will be like a lion to Ephraim, and like a young lion to the house of Judah." Only a few words have survived from this part (fragment 2) of the *Pesher on Hosea*:[39]

1. ["...nor can he heal yo]ur sore." The in[terpretation...]
2. [   ] the Lion of Wrath. "For I am like a young l[ion to E]ph[rai]m, [and like a lion]
3. [to the house of Judah." The interpretation of it con]cerns the last priest who will stretch out his hand to smite Ephraim

Despite the extremely fragmentary nature of the pesher, it is easy to follow the exegetical method of its author.[40] The author's view is that Ephraim refers to the Pharisees and Judah refers to the members of the sect. He interprets Hos 5:13, "then Ephraim went to Assyria," as referring to the invitation the Pharisees extended to Demetrius III, king of Syria, asking him to come to their aid, even though ultimately he could not cure them, nor heal their wounds. Since in the Second Temple period Syria was usually called Assyria, the author of the pesher identified Assyria with the Seleucids.[41] Based on Hos 5:14, "For I will be like a lion to Ephraim, and like a young lion to the house of Judah," the author of the *Pesher on Hosea* refers to Alexander Jannaeus as the Lion of

---

38 See Eshel, "Pesher Hosea," 228–29.

39 The pesher is quoted here on the basis of Horgan's edition, *Pesharim*, 149.

40 G. Doudna does not accept this reconstruction of this section of the *Pesher on Hosea* B because he thinks that those lines were much longer. Since the exegetical method of the author is obvious, I believe that my conclusions are correct, even if there were more words at the beginning of line 3; see G. L. Doudna, "4Q Pesher Hosea^b : Reconstruction of Fragments 4, 5, 18 and 24," *DSD* 10 (2003) 338–58.

41 See Y. Yadin, *The Scroll of the War of the Sons of Light against the Sons of Darkness* (Oxford: Oxford University Press, 1962) n. 4; D. Flusser, "Apocalyptic Elements in the War Scroll," in *Jerusalem in the Second Temple Period: Abraham Schalit Memorial Volume* (ed. A. Oppenheimer, U. Rappaport, and M. Stern; Jerusalem: Yad Ben-Zvi, 1980) 443 (Hebrew); M. Stern, *Greek and Latin Authors on Jews and Judaism* (3 vols.; Jerusalem: The Israel Academy of Sciences and Humanities, 1974–84) 2.345–36.

Wrath.[42] I conclude, therefore, that the title the Lion of Wrath as a designation for Alexander Jannaeus is based on this verse in Hosea. I further believe that the *Pesher on Hosea* was composed before the *Pesher on Nahum*, and that by the time the latter was composed, it had become well known that the epithet "the Lion of Wrath" referred to Alexander Jannaeus. The authors of both the *Pesher on Nahum* and the *Pesher on Hosea* criticized the actions of Alexander Jannaeus in 88 B.C.E. for the manner in which he punished his enemies, that is, an agonizingly slow death in public. I reject the interpretation of Yadin and Fitzmyer that the Lion of Wrath in the *Pesher on Nahum* was intended to indicate a protagonist. Since there is no doubt that the *Pesher on Nahum* was composed after the conquest of Pompey in 63 B.C.E., it seems that the events of 88 B.C.E. were so dramatic, that their impact was remembered and discussed 25 years after Alexander Jannaeus had executed the people who had invited Demetrius to Judaea.

In the first chapter of this book, I discussed a scroll known today as 4Q390 that was most likely brought to Qumran from outside the community. This scroll contemporized the 490-year prophecy of Daniel 9:24 and divided the 490 years into four sub-periods: a) 70 years of the Babylonian exile; 343 years in which those who returned from the exile behaved properly; 7 years in the days of Antiochus IV; and 70 years of Hasmonean rule. There is no doubt that the author of 4Q390 believed that at the end of these 490 years the final redemption would come. It is important to note the critical detail, that this author predicted that the Hasmoneans would rule 70 years. Whether the author of 4Q390 began his count from the purge of the Temple by Judah Maccabeus in 164 B.C.E., or from 160 B.C.E., seven years after the statue of Zeus was placed in the Temple, the 70 years came to an end close to the time of the rebellion of the Pharisees against Alexander Jannaeus. It therefore seems that the composition found in 4Q390 was written by an opponent of Alexander Jannaeus. The author of 4Q390 tried to encourage the opponents of Alexander Jannaeus to rise against the Hasmonean king, and this led to a composition which called for the end of the Hasmonean's priestly succession and control.[43]

---

42   Charlesworth was inclined to accept my proposal that this pesher relates the events of 88 B.C.E., but for the sake of scientific caution he remarked that the pesher is so fragmentary that it is difficult to draw any historical details from it; see Charlesworth, *Pesharim and Qumran History*, 101.

43   I am grateful to Prof. Albert Baumgarten for this suggestion.

CHAPTER SEVEN

The Successors of Alexander Jannaeus and the Conquest of Judaea by Pompey

Following the death of Alexander Jannaeus in 76 B.C.E., his wife Salamzion Alexandra assumed power in Judaea. During her reign, the Pharisees regained their influential political and religious standing. Since Alexandra was not eligible to serve as High Priest in the Temple, the position was entrusted to her eldest son, Hyrcanus II. This aroused intense jealousy from Aristobulus II, the younger son of Alexander Jannaeus and Salamzion Alexandra, who wished to seize power (*J. W.* 1.107–19; *Ant.* 13.408–33). The tension between Hyrcanus and Aristobulus turned into a fraternal war after the death of Alexandra in 67 B.C.E. During the struggle, Aristobulus succeeded in winning control over both Judaea and the High Priesthood. Hyrcanus and his aggressive advisor Antipater were not willing to concede power and continued to struggle against Aristobulus, enlisting the aid of the Nabateans. When Pompey's messengers arrived in Syria in 65 B.C.E., the two Hasmonean rivals approached them in the hopes of gaining Roman support for their own side of the dispute (*Ant.* 13.118–29; 14.1–23).

Some of the scrolls found at Qumran throw some light onto this turbulent period.[1] The political and religious situation documented in the *Pesher on Nahum* (4QpNah) reflects the period of Alexandra's reign, during which the Pharisees returned to a position of power in Judaea. In the second and third columns of the large fragment of the *Pesher on Nahum*, the author interpreted

---

1 See T. Ilan, "Shelamzion in Qumran: New Insights," in *Historical Perspectives: From the Hasmoneans to Bar Kokhba in Light of the Dead Sea Scrolls* (ed. D. Goodblatt, A. Pinick, and D. R. Schwartz; STDJ 37; Leiden and Boston: Brill, 2001) 57–68. For an interesting article on the early days and the name of Salamzion Alexandra, see idem, "Queen Salamzion Alexandra and Judas Aristobulus I's Widow," *JSJ* 24 (1993) 181–90.

Nahum's prophecy on Nineveh as a reference to the Pharisees. He describes a reality in which Jerusalem is governed by the Seekers-After-Smooth-Things, a pseudonym for the Pharisees. He predicts that "the simple ones of Ephraim," who were "misled" into following the Pharisees, will recognize the error of their ways and join "Judah," that is, the members of the Qumran sect. Such a description is most suitable to the state of affairs in Judaea during the reign of Alexandra, when the Pharisees were at the peak of their strength and influence.[2] After the author of the pesher mentions "Ephraim," another reference to the Pharisees, he interpreted the prophecy of Nahum on Egypt in connection to "Manasseh," meaning the Sadducees. At the end of col. 3 and the beginning of col. 4 of the *Pesher on Nahum* we read:[3]

8. ... "Will you do better than Am[on, situated by] the rivers?"

9. The interpretation of it: "Amon" – they are Manasseh, and "the rivers" – they are the gr[ea]t ones of Manasseh, the honoured ones of the [city who suppo]rt M[annaseh]

10. "Waters surrounding her, whose power is (the) sea and (the) water, her walls."

11. [The in]terpretation of it: they are the men of her [ar]my, her warrior[s]. "Ethiopia is her strength [and Egypt (too), without limit."]

12. [... "P]ut and the [Libyans are your help"]

1. The interpretation of it: they are the wicked one[s of Manasse]h, the House of Peleg who are joined to Manasseh. "Yet she too w[ent] into exile, [into captivity. Even]

2. her children, too, are dashed to pieces on every street corner, and for her honored ones they will cast lots, and all [her] g[rea]t [ones were bound]

3. in fetters." The interpretation of it concerns Manasseh at the last time, whose reign over Is[rael] will be brought down [ ]

 2 See J. D. Amoussine, "Ephraim et Manassé dans le Péshèr de Nahum (4 Q p Nahum)," *RQ* 4 (1963) 392–96; J. D. Amusin, "The Reflection of Historical Events of the First Century B.C. in Qumran Commentaries (4Q161; 4Q169; 4Q166)," *HUCA* 48 (1977) 134–46; D. Flusser, "Pharisäer, Sadduzäer und Essener im Pescher Nahum," in *Qumran: Wege der Forschung* (ed. K. E. Grözinger; Darmstadt: Wissenschaftliche Buchgesellschaft, 1981) 146–49; Ilan, "Shelamzion in Qumran," 58–61. In contrast, see S. L. Berrin, *The Pesher Nahum Scroll from Qumran* (STDJ 53; Leiden and Boston: Brill, 2004) 220–22.

 3 Following the edition of M. P. Horgan, *Pesharim: Qumran Interpretations of Biblical Books* (CBQ Monograph Series 8; Washington DC: The Catholic Biblical Association of America, 1979) 165.

4. his wives, his children, and his infants will go into captivity. His warriors and his honored ones [will perish] by the sword

The author of the *Pesher on Nahum* identifies the warriors as belonging to Manasseh, and remarks that in the end of days the rule of the Sadducees over Israel will collapse. It appears that the author of the pesher is referring to the conquest of Jerusalem by Pompey in 63 B.C.E., and to the humiliation of Aristobulus who had received Sadducean support.[4] There is no doubt that the *Pesher on Nahum* was composed after the Roman conquest, since the first column states that Jerusalem was not conquered by the kings of Greece until the rise of "the rulers of the Kittim," after which the city was ransacked.[5]

A reference to the fall of the Sadducees, the supporters of Aristobulus, at the time of the Roman conquest of Judaea by Pompey, is further documented in a polemic composition (4Q471a):[6]

1.]when you were commanded not to
2.] And you violated His covenant
3. You] said, "We shall fight His battles, because He redeemed us"
4.] your [   ] will be brought low, and they did not know that He despised
5.] ... you become mighty for battle, and you were accounted
6.] among those who hope for him (?) *vacat* You seek righteous judgment and service of
7.] you are arrogant *vacat*

The author of this passage attacks those who argue that the accomplishments of the Hasmonean state were proof that God had delivered Israel. The Hasmonean supporters breached the covenant of God, which is why they were eventually defeated, even though they were mighty in battle. It seems that the criticism of this passage was addressed to the Sadducees soon after Pompey's conquest of Judaea.[7] The author of this passage taunts those who prior to the Roman conquest argued that their safety and independence were signs of God's power and support. This small passage refers to the degradation of the Hasmonean

4   Amusin, "Reflection," 142–46.
5   See the discussion in the previous chapter, and also Berrin, *Pesher Nahum*, 101–4.
6   E. Eshel and M. Kister, "471a. 4QPolemical Text," in *Qumran Cave 4, XXVI: Miscellanea, Part 1* (ed. P. Alexander et al.; DJD 36; Oxford: Clarendon, 2000) 446–49.
7   Idem, "A Polemical Qumran Fragment," *JJS* 43 (1992) 277–81.

elite in a fashion which is reminiscent of the description in the *Pesher on Nahum*.

References to the rule of Alexandra and her sons are also found in three scrolls (4Q331–4Q333) which mention the priestly courses and some historical events. These scrolls are extremely fragmentary and it is impossible to ascertain their precise intent or purpose. Joseph Milik posited that the list included dates which were celebrated annually like *Megillat Ta'anit*.[8] Michael Wise labeled this list an "Annalistic Calendar," and claimed it was a composition which listed historical personages and events.[9] Shemaryahu Talmon and Jonathan Ben-Dov considered it to be a list of historical events, and that the courses were mentioned only because this was a customary way to record dates.[10] Although what remains of the texts is very fragmentary, I will discuss three fragments which mention historical figures. Column 1 of the first fragment of 4Q331 mentions Yohanan, probably John Hyrcanus I, and col. 2 mentions Salamzion:[11]

Col. 1
6. [...the] priest who all
7. [...] Yohanan to bring to

Col. 2
5. a human being[...]
6. [...]
7. Salamzio[n ...]

8 J. T. Milik, *Ten Years of Discovery in the Judean Desert* (Studies in Biblical Theology 26; London: SCM Press, 1959) 73.

9 M. O. Wise, "*Primo Annales Fuere*: An Annalistic Calendar from Qumran," in *Thunder in Gemin and Other Essays on the History, Language and Literature of Second Temple Palestine* (JSP-Sup 15; Sheffield: Sheffield Academic Press, 1994) 186–221. Since personal names are mentioned in those texts, and since the scribes of the Qumran sect sought to avoid mentioning them (see E. Eshel, "Personal Names in the Qumran Sect," in *These Are the Names: Studies in Jewish Onomastics* [ed. A. Demsky, J. A. Reif, and J. Tabory; Ramat Gan: Bar Ilan University Press, 1997] 39–52), and since the Babylonian month (Shebat) is mentioned in 4Q332, while the Qumran sect never used the Babylonian names of the months it seems that those texts were brought to Qumran rather than having been composed by the sectarians. For a different view, see K. Atkinson, "Representations of History in 4Q331, 4Q332, 4Q333 and 4Q468e: An Annalistic Calendar Documenting Portentous Events?" *DSD* 14 (2007), 125-51.

10 See S. Talmon and J. Ben-Dov, *Qumran Cave 4, XVI: Calendrical Texts* (DJD 21; Oxford: Clarendon, 2001) 12–13.

11 The translation of this fragment is quoted from its *editio princeps*: J. A. Fitzmyer, "331. 4QpapHistorical Text C," in *Qumran Cave 4, XXVI: Miscellanea, Part 1* (ed. P. Alexander et al.; DJD 36; Oxford: Clarendon, 2000) 276–77.

Since line 7 of col. 1 mentions Yohanan, and line 6 preserves the word "priest," Geza Vermes suggested the individual should be identified as Hyrcanus II, the eldest son of Alexander Jannaeus and Alexandra.[12] However, another copy of the same list mentions "Hyrcanus" explicitly, and if we are to assume that the two names refer to the same historical figure, it is hard to explain why this man was mentioned in the same composition by both his Hebrew and Hellenic name. Accordingly, Wise proposed that the "Yohanan" named in this text should be identified as John Hyrcanus I.[13] Yet all the other names which appear in the *Annalistic List* are individuals who were active during the first century B.C.E., so it is difficult to accept this suggestion. The second fragment of 4Q332 in which Hyrcanus is mentioned should be read as follows:[14]

1. [... to]give him honor among the Arab[s
2. [... on the n]inth of Shebat, this (is)[
3. [...] which is the [tw]entieth in the month[of
4. [...]with secret counsel Salamzion came [ ]
5. [...] to confront the[
6. [...]Hyrcanus rebelled [against Aristobulus]
7. [...]to confront[

It is difficult to determine who is the subject of the first line of the fragment, but it is possible that the meaning of the line is to distinguish one individual from among the "Arabs." Proceeding from this point, the "Arabs" can be understood as a designation for the Nabateans.[15] Line 4 mentions Salamzion, but it is hard to gather any historical information from this reference. Line 6 states that "Hyrcanus rebelled," and Michael Wise and Joseph Fitzmyer reconstructed the end of the phrase to be "[against Aristobulus]."[16] If one adopts such a reconstruction, it may

---

12 G. Vermes, "Qumran Forum Miscellanea," *JJS* 43 (1992) 304–5.

13 Wise, "Annalistic Calendar," 196.

14 The translation of this fragment is quoted from its *editio princeps*: J. A. Fitzmyer, "332. 4QHistorical Text D," in *Qumran Cave 4, XXVI: Miscellanea, Part 1* (ed. P. Alexander et al.; DJD 36; Oxford: Clarendon, 2000) 283–85.

15 According to Wise's suggestion; see Wise, "Annalistic Calendar," 206. Fitzmyer accepted this proposal in his edition ("4QHistorical Text D").

16 This reconstruction led the editor of 4Q322a to suggest the construction of "Ar[istobulus]" in another fragment of the *Annalistic Text*; see E. J. C. Tigchelaar, "322a. 4QHistorical Text H?" in *Wadi Daliyeh II: The Samaria Papyri and Qumran Cave 4, XXVIII: Miscellanea, II* (ed. D. M. Gropp et al.; DJD 28; Oxford: Clarendon, 2001) 125–28. Doudna claimed it should be reconstructed as "Hyrcanus the King"; see G. L. Doudna, *4Q Pesher Nahum: A Critical Edition*

be that this line is a reference to the time during which Hyrcanus and Antipater tried to regain their power after Aristobulus usurped the reign and the High Priesthood.

The third fragment (4Q333) includes another reference to the period following the death of Alexandra:[17]

1. [...] twenty
2. [...]
3. [... in Je]hezkel, which is
4. [...]Aemilius killed
5. [... in] the seventh [mon]th
6. [... the en]tr[ance of] Gamul
7. [... which] is
8. [...]Aemilius killed

Aemilius should be identified with the Roman general Marcus Aemilius Scaurus, whom Pompey appointed as the governor of Syria in 66 B.C.E.[18] Josephus mentions the actions of Aemilius Scaurus in Judaea, when he recorded the events of 65/64 B.C.E. In *The Jewish War*, Josephus writes the following:[19]

> Aristobulus was unable to resist this force (the Nabataeans). Defeated in the first encounter he was driven into Jerusalem, and would there have been speedily captured through the storming of the city, had not Scaurus the Roman general, intervening at this critical moment, raised the siege. The latter had been sent into Syria from Armenia by Pompey the Great, then at war with Tigranes. On reaching Damascus, which had recently been captured by Metellus and Lollius, he superseded those officers, and then, hearing of the state of affairs in Judaea, rushed there to snatch what seemed a heaven-sent opportunity.

(JSPSup 35; Sheffield: Sheffield University Press, 2001) 651, n. 749.

17 The fragment is quoted from its *editio princeps*: J. A. Fitzmyer, "333. 4QHistorical Text E," in *Qumran Cave 4, XXVI: Miscellanea, Part 1* (ed. P. Alexander et al.; DJD 36; Oxford: Clarendon, 2000) 288–89. See also Wise ("Annalistic Calendar," 190), who reconstructed considerable parts of the text.

18 D. R. Schwartz, "Aemilius Scaurus, Marcus," in *Encyclopedia of the Dead Sea Scrolls* (ed. L. H. Schiffman and J. C. VanderKam; Oxford: Oxford University Press, 2000) 9–10.

19 This translation is based on H. St .J. Thackeray, *Josephus, The Jewish War, Books I–III* (The Loeb Classical Library; Cambridge, MA: Harvard University Press, 1927) 60–63.

As soon as he entered Jewish territory he received deputations from the brothers, each imploring his assistance. Three hundred talents offered by Aristobulus outweighed considerations of justice; Scaurus, having obtained that sum, dispatched a herald to Hyrcanus and the Arabs, threatening them with a visitation from the Romans and Pompey if they did not raise the siege. Aretas, terror-stricken, retired from Judaea to Philadelphia, and Scaurus returned to Damascus. Aristobulus, however, not content with eluding capture, mustered all his forces, pursued the enemy, fought them in the neighborhood of a place called Papyron, and killed upwards of six thousand. Among the slain was Phallion, Antipater's brother.

Deprived of their Arab allies, Hyrcanus and Antipater turned their hopes to the opposite party, and when Pompey entered Syria and reached Damascus, they took refuge with him. Coming without presents and resorting to the same pleas which they had used with Aretas, they implored him to show his detest for the violence of Aristobulus, and to restore to the throne the man whose character and seniority entitled him to it. Nor was Aristobulus behindhand; relying on the fact that Scaurus was open to bribery, he too appeared, arrayed in the most regal style imaginable (*J.W.* 1.126–32).

An account of these events can also be found in *Jewish Antiquities*:[20]

Meanwhile Pompey sent Scaurus to Syria, as he himself was in Armenia, still making war on Tigranes. And when Scaurus came to Damascus, he found that Lollius and Metellus had just taken the city, and so he hurried on to Judaea. On his arrival, envoys came from both Aristobulus and Hyrcanus, each of whom asked him to come to his aid. Aristobulus offered to give him four hundred talents; and though Hyrcanus promised him no less a sum, he accepted Aristobulus' offer, because he was both wealthy and generous and asked for more moderate terms, whereas Hyrcanus was poor and niggardly and held out untrustworthy promises for greater concessions. It would not be easy to forcibly take control of a city which was among the most strongly fortified and powerful, in order to drive out the fugitives and their allies, the Nabateans, although they were not well prepared for warfare. Scaurus took Aristobulus' side and accepted

20 This translation is based on R. Marcus, *Josephus, Jewish Antiquities, Books XII–XIV* (The Loeb Classical Library; Cambridge, MA: Harvard University Press, 1933) 462–65.

the money and put an end to the siege by commands to withdraw or be declared an enemy of the Romans. Then he withdrew to Damascus, while Aristobulus marched a large force against Aretas and Hyrcanus, engaged them in battle at a place called Papyron, defeated them and killed some six thousand of the enemy. Notable among the fallen was Phallion, Antipater's brother (*Ant.* 14.29–33).

Subsequently Josephus describes how Hyrcanus and Aristobulus sent delegations to Pompey who was in Damascus:[21]

And not long afterward envoys again came to him, Antipater, on behalf of Hyrcanus, and, Nicodemus, on behalf of Aristobulus; the latter, indeed, also accused Gabinius and Scaurus of taking money from him, Gabinius first getting three hundred talents, and Scaurus four hundred talents; and so Aristobulus made these men his enemies in addition to the others he had (*Ant.* 14.37).

Josephus summarizes the events of 63 B.C.E.,[22] in which Pompey conquered Jerusalem:[23]

For this misfortune which befell Jerusalem Hyrcanus and Aristobulus were responsible, because of their dissension. For we lost our freedom and became subject to the Romans, and the territory which we had gained by our arms and taken from the Syrians we were compelled to give back to them, and in addition the Romans exacted of us in a short space of time more than ten thousand talents; and the royal power which had formerly been bestowed on those who were high priests by birth became the privilege of commoners. But of this we shall speak in the proper places. Now Pompey gave over to Scaurus Coele-Syria and the rest of Syria as far as the Euphrates river and Egypt, and two Roman legions (*Ant.* 14.77–79).

We have only few details concerning the actions of Aemilius Scaurus as the

---

21 Marcus, *Jewish Antiquities*, 466–67.

22 Concerning these events, see E. Schürer, *The History of the Jewish People in the Age of Jesus Christ,*(3 vols.; rev. and ed. by G. Vermes, F. Millar, and M. Black; Edinburgh: T & T Clark, 1973) 1.232–42.

23 Marcus, *Jewish Antiquities*, 486–89.

governor of Syria, primarily from a single account which Josephus repeats in both of his works. Josephus reports that Aemilius Scaurus waged war against the Nabateans in 62 B.C.E. The report of this battle in *The Jewish War* is as follows:[24]

> Meanwhile Scaurus had invaded Arabia. Being held up at Petra by the difficulties of the ground, he proceeded to lay waste to the surrounding country, but here again suffered severely, his army being reduced to starvation. To relieve his wants Hyrcanus sent Antipater with supplies. Antipater being on intimate terms with Aretas, Scaurus dispatched him to the king to induce him to purchase release from hostilities. The Arab monarch consenting to pay three hundred talents, Scaurus on these conditions withdrew his troops from the country (*J.W.* 1.159).

The account of this battle of Aemilius Scaurus against the Nabateans in *Jewish Antiquities* is similar:[25]

> Scaurus then marched against Petra in Arabia, and because it was difficult to access, ravaged the country round about it, but as his army suffered from hunger, Antipater, at the command of Hyrcanus, furnished him with grain from Judaea and whatever other provisions he needed. And when Antipater was sent by Scaurus as an envoy to Aretas because of their friendly relations, he persuaded him to pay a sum of money to save his country from being ravaged, and himself became surety for three hundred talents. And on these terms Scaurus ended the war, being no less eager to have this come about than was Aretas (*Ant.* 14.80–81).

In 61 B.C.E. Aemilius Scaurus was replaced as governor of Syria by Marcus Philipus.[26]

From the list of events recorded in 4Q333 frg. 1 (quoted above), it seems that Aemilius Scaurus killed Jews on two separate occasions: the first in the Hebrew month of Elul and the second in the month of Tishri (the sixth and seventh months of the year).[27] Josephus does not record that Aemilius Scaurus

---

24 Thackeray, *Jewish War*, 74–75.

25 Marcus, *Jewish Antiquities*, 489–91.

26 See Schwartz, "Aemilius," 9.

27 According to the reconstruction offered by Wise ("Annalistic Calendar," 190), the second occasion was on the fifteenth day of the seventh month, meaning during the festival of Tabernacles.

executed Hyrcanus' men when he forced them to retreat from Jerusalem in 65 B.C.E., nor that he slaughtered the men of Aristobulus when Pompey conquered the temple in 63 B.C.E. Even so, it seems there is no reason to doubt the evidence of the fragment found in Qumran, and there is no reason not to assume that on other occasions Aemilius could have killed the Jews who opposed him. Wise suggested that the killings mentioned in the text from Qumran took place in 63 B.C.E. with Pompey's conquest of the Temple Mount. In Wise's view, it is possible to deduce from the Qumran text that Pompey conquered Jerusalem in the fall.[28] A different possibility was suggested by Daniel Schwartz, who argued that the Qumran text explains why Nicodemus, Aristobulus' messenger, accused Aemilius Scaurus (*Ant.* 14.37). He contends that the slaughters occurred before Pompey conquered the temple.[29] Unfortunately, because of the highly fragmentary form of the *Annalistic Text* from Qumran, we are unable to learn any additional historical details to confirm either view.

I believe that the tiny fragment 4Q468e is also related to the *Annalistic Texts* (4Q331-4Q333). It includes the following lines:[30]

2. ki]lling the multitude of me[n
3.]Potlais and the people that [

Magen Broshi suggested identifying Potlais with Ptollas, a friend of Archelaus, who is mentioned in *Ant.* 17.219, immediately after the report on the Passover riots of 4 B.C.E. which led Archelaus to send his troops to quell the disturbance, resulting in the death of some 3,000 people (*Ant.* 17.213–18). Based on this text from Qumran, Broshi proposed that it was Ptollas who was responsible for the

---

28 Ibid, 212–18. For a discussion of the conquest of the temple by Pompeius, see E. Regev, "How Did the Temple Mount Fall to Pompey?" *JJS* 48 (1997) 276–89. Wise deduced from this passage in 4Q333 that the members of the sect at Qumran supported Aristobulus ("Annalistic Calendar," 219), but the text is so fragmentary that it is impossible to know whether it is referring to the men of Hyrcanus or of Aristobulus. Furthermore, it seems that the text is not a Qumranic composition, because it mentions the personal names of historical figures. Perhaps one should accept Schwartz's proposal ("Aemilius," 10), that the sectarians of Qumran mentioned Aemilius' cruelty not because they were supporters of Aristobulus, but as an example of the Roman cruelty which is also expressed in the *Pesher on Habakkuk*. See also D. Flusser, "The Kingdom of Rome in the Eyes of the Hasmoneans and as Seen by the Essenees," *Zion* 48 (1983) 149–76 (Hebrew).

29 Schwartz, "Aemilius."

30 The translation of this fragment is from its *editio princeps* in M. Broshi, "468e. 4QHistorical Text F," in *Qumran Cave 4, XXVI: Miscellanea, Part 1* (ed. P. Alexander et al.; DJD 36; Oxford: Clarendon, 2000) 406–11.

slaughter.[31] However, there are four arguments which make it hard to accept this identification: (a) if indeed it were the same name, it should have been written with a *waw* after the *taw* (Ptolais and not Potlais); (b) the Greek letter *theta* is usually transcribed as the Hebrew letter *tet* and not *taw*; (c) Archelaus' friend is called Poplas in *The Jewish War* (2.14), as in most of the manuscripts of *Jewish Antiquities*; (d) Josephus does not mention that it was Archelaus' friend who was responsible for the massacre at the Jerusalem Temple.[32]

It therefore seems that "Potlais" of the 4Q468e should be identified with Peitholaus, a Jewish officer who in 57 B.C.E. joined Gabinius (himself appointed by Pompey as governor of Syria) in his war against Alexander, the son of Aristobulus II. In this campaign, which took place near Jerusalem, some 3,000 people were killed (*J. W.* 1.162–63; *Ant.* 14.84–85). In 56 B.C.E. Aristobulus escaped from Rome. Subsequently, Peitholaus joined him with a thousand of his people, and in a battle that took place near Macherus in Transjordan, the Romans killed around 8,000 people, capturing Aristobulus and his son Mattathias Antigonus and bringing them to Gabinius, who promptly sent them back to Rome (*J. W.* 1.172; *Ant.* 14.93–95). In 53 B.C.E. Crassus (Gabinius' successor) executed Peitholaus. According to Josephus, Crassus was following Antipater's advice, since Peitholaus had been faithful to Aristobulus II (*J. W.* 1.180; *Ant.* 14.120).[33]

I believe that 4Q468e is related to the *Annalistic Texts* discussed above (4Q331–4Q333) in its content, referring mainly to executions, as well as by the period it describes, both of which can be linked to the turbulent years following the death of Alexander Jannaeus in 76 B.C.E. through the mid-first century

---

31 Idem., "Ptolas and the Archelaus Massacre (4Q468g-4QHistorical Text B)," *JJS* 49 (1998) 341–45.

32 D. R. Schwartz, "4Q468g: Ptollas?" *JJS* 50 (1999) 308–9; J. Strugnell, "The Historical Background to 4Q468g [=4Qhistorical text B]," *RQ* 19 (1999) 137–38.

33 See Schwartz, "4Q468g," 309; Strugnell, "Historical Background," 135; W. Horbury, "The proper Name in 4Q468g Peitholaus?" *JJS* 50 (1999) 310–11. These three scholars agreed that Potlais should be identified with Peitholaus. James Charlesworth also joined this view; see J. H. Charlesworth, *The Pesharim and Qumran History* (Grand Rapids, MI: Eerdman, 2002) 113. There still remains a debate, however, regarding which event is referred to in the fragment extant from Qumran. Schwartz suggested that this text refers to the events of 57 B.C.E., when Peitholaus helped Gabinius fight the Jews in the battle by Jerusalem (*J. W.* 1.162–63; *Ant.* 14.84–85). William Horbury believed the Qumran text to be referring to the events of 56 B.C.E., when Peitholaus participated in the battle near Macherus in Transjordan where Aristobulus and his son Antigonus were captured (*J. W.* 1.172; *Ant.* 14.93–95). In my opinion, the possibility that this text refers to the execution of Peitholaus in 53 B.C.E. should not be dismissed.

B.C.E.[34] It is possible to conclude that although the *Annalistic Text* was preserved in four different manuscripts which are all very fragmentary and consequently very hard to understand, that it is not sectarian and that it documents events, the majority of which occurred between 76 and 53 B.C.E.

Returning to Josephus' account of the siege laid by Hyrcanus and Aretas on Jerusalem in 65 B.C.E. before Aemilius Scaurus forced them to retreat, we read that after the Passover which occurred during the civil war there was such a heavy famine in Judaea that one *modius* of wheat was bought for eleven drachmas (*Ant.* 14.28; See also *Psalms of Solomon* 17:18–19). Before this, Josephus had already described how Hyrcanus' men had murdered Onias, "who, being a righteous man, and dear to God had once in a rainless period prayed to God to end the drought, and God had heard his prayer and sent rain" (*Ant.* 14.22).[35] The Babylonian Talmud tells of severe distress in Judaea during the civil war between Hyrcanus and Aristobulus, so that people had to go as far as the valley of Lod to bring the *omer* and the two loaves for the temple rituals (*b. Menahot* 64b and parallels).[36] Since this tradition mentions bringing the *omer* and the two loaves, it implies that the famine in Judaea must have lasted at least until the Festival of Weeks. The Mishna (*Ta'anit* 3,8) relates that Onias had made rain fall around the time of Passover, as can be implied from his request that the Passover ovens be brought in. The Babylonian Talmud states that he brought the rain towards the end of the month of Adar, the month prior to Passover (*b. Ta'anit* 23a). The Palestinian Talmud (*y. Ta'aniot* 3,10; 66,4) associates the tradition of Onias with a holiday set for the twentieth of Adar, marking the day on which the rain came after the drought, a tradition which appears in *Megillat Ta'anit*.[37] Therefore, the traditions of the drought, the miraculous rain brought by Onias, and the famine in Judaea during the civil war of 65 B.C.E. are all documented in Josephus' writings as well as in rabbinic literature.[38]

---

34 The latest recorded event that survived in this text seems to be related to Peitholaus, occurring some time between 57 and 53 B.C.E.

35 On the murder of Onias, see O. Betz, "The Death of Choni-Onias in the Light of the Temple Scroll from Qumran," in *Jerusalem in the Second Temple Period: Abraham Schalit Memorial Volume* (ed. A. Oppenheimer, U. Rappaport, and M. Stern; Jerusalem: Ben-Zvi, 1980) 84–97 (Hebrew).

36 See Z. Amar and A. Sasson, "Bringing the Omer from the Valley of Lod – A New Identification of the Site," *Judea and Samaria Research Studies* 6 (1996) 179–89 (Hebrew).

37 See V. Noam, *Megillat Ta'anit: Versions, Interpretation, History* (Jerusalem: Ben-Zvi, 2003) 309–11 (Hebrew).

38 Josephus' account of those events is similar to the account in the Rabbinic literature. Josephus wrote: "While the priests and Aristobulus were being besieged, there happened to come

We also find references to this famine in the *Pesher on Hosea* A (4QpHos^a), the *Pesher on Isaiah* B (4QpIsa^b) and twice in the *Pesher on Psalms* A (4QpPs^a). *Pesher on Hosea* A (4Q166), col. 2, reads:[39]

8. "Therefore, I shall take back my grain again in its time, and my wine [in its season,]
9. And I shall withdraw my wool and my flax from covering [her nakedness.]
10. I shall now uncover her private parts in the sight of [her] lo[vers and]
11. no [one] will withdraw her from my hand." *vacat*
12. The interpretation of it is that he smote them with famine and with nakedness so that they become a disgra[ce]

---

round the festival called *Phaska*, at which it is our custom to offer numerous sacrifices to God. But as Aristobulus and those with him lacked victims, they asked their countrymen to furnish them with these, and take as much money for the victims as they wished. And when these others demanded that they pay a thousand drachmas for each animal they wish to get, Aristobulus and the priests willingly accepted this price and gave them the money, which they let down from the walls by rope. Their countrymen, however, after receiving the money did not deliver the victims ..." (*Ant.* 14.25–27). The Babylonian Talmud quotes a *Beraita* in tractate *Menahot* which tells the following: "Our Rabbis taught: When the Kings of the Hasmonean house fought one another, Hyrcanus was outside and Aristobulus was within [the city wall]. Each day [those that were within] used to let down [to the other party] *denars* in a basket, and haul up [in return] animals for the Daily Offerings... On the morrow they let down *denars* in a basket and hauled up a pig. When it reached halfway up the wall, its stuck its claws in the wall, and the land of Israel was shaken" (*b. Menahot*, 64b. The English translation is quoted from I. Epstein [ed.], *The Babylonian Talmud. Seder Kodashim. Menahoth* [trans. E. Cashdan; London: Soncino Press, 1948] 381). As for the phenomenon of parallel historical traditions in Josephus and the rabbinic literature, see S .J. D. Cohen, "Parallel Historical Tradition in Josephus and Rabbinic Literature," *Proceedings of the Ninth World Congress of Jewish Studies* B/1 (1986) 7–14.

39 The following translation is based on Horgan, *Pesharim*, 141. Tal Ilan has suggested that the author of the *Pesher on Hosea* B had interpreted those verses as referring to Salamzion Alexandra since Hosea spoke about a prostitute in 2:6–7 and the author viewed Alexandra in a very negative way. Ilan also pointed to the fact that in the Rabbinic literature we find a tradition saying that in the days of Queen Salamzion rain was given in its season and the economic situation was ideal (*Sifre Deut.* 42). See Ilan, "Shelamzion in Qumran," 61–63. It is interesting to note that the author of the *Pesher on Hosea* B interpreted the famine of 65 B.C.E. as being a punishment for Alexandra's deeds, while the Rabbis emphasized that while she was alive the nation was blessed and that the troubles began only after she died. See also K. Atkinson, "Women in the Dead Sea Scrolls: Evidence for a Qumran Renaissance during the Reign of Queen Salome Alexandra," *The Qumran Chronicle* 11 (2003) 37–56.

13. and a reproach in the sight of the nations on whom they had leaned for support, but they
14. will not save them from their afflictions …

Joseph Amusin made the connection between the famine mentioned in the *Pesher on Hosea* A and the famine in 65 B.C.E., during the time that Hyrcanus and Aretas besieged Aristobulus in Jerusalem, two years before Pompey conquered Judaea.[40] A famine "in the time of the visitation of the land" is also mentioned in the *Pesher on Isaiah* B (4Q162), col. 2, which interprets verses from Isaiah 5:[41]

1. The interpretation of the passage with regard to the end of days concerns the condemnation of the land before the sword and the famine. And it will happen
2. in the time of the visitation of the land. "Woe to those who, when they rise early in the morning, run after strong drink, who are inflamed by wine when they stay late in the evening.
3. And there are zither and stringed instrument, tambourine and flute, the wine of their feasts; but the work of the Lord
4. they did not heed, and the works of his hands they did not regard. Therefore my people have gone into exile for lack of knowledge. Its honored ones are dying of hunger,
5. and its multitude is parched with thirst. So Sheol opened its throat and widened its mouth without limit.
6. And its splendor will go down, and its throngs, and its tumultuous crowd exulting in it." These are the men of Scoffing
7. who are in Jerusalem. They are the ones who "Rejected the law of the Lord, and the word of the Holy One of
8. Israel they treated without respect. So the anger of the Lord flared against his people and he stretched out his hand against it and smote it. The Mountains quaked

---

40 Amusin, "Reflection," 148–49. This opinion was accepted by Ilan, "Shelamzion in Qumran," 61–65. Flusser, on the other hand, contended that the famine mentioned in these pesharim is the famine which broke out in the days of Herod the Great in 25 B.C.E.; see D. Flusser, "Qumran and the Famine during the Reign of Herod," *Israel Museum Journal* 6 (1987) 7–16. As we shall show in the ninth chapter, there is evidence that no pesharim were composed after 31 B.C.E. This conclusion leads me to accept Amusin's and Ilan's suggestion that those pesharim relate to the famine that broke out during the civil war between Hyrcanus and Aristobulus.

41 The following translation is based on Horgan, *Pesharim*, 88.

9. and their corpse(s) became like offal in the midst of the streets. For all this [his anger] did not turn back
10. [and his hand is still stretched out.”] This is the congregation of Scoffers who are in Jerusalem.

Column 1 of the *Pesher on Isaiah* B is very fragmentary, and none of the verses that are interpreted at the top of col. 2 are extant.[42] Immediately after the pesher mentions the sword and the famine, vv. 11–14 of Isaiah 5 are quoted, referring to hunger and thirst. These verses are interpreted in lines 6–7, and associated to "the Men of Scoffing" who should be identified as the Pharisees, the supporters of Hyrcanus. Next, the author of the pesher quoted the second half of vv. 24 and 25.[43] These verses communicate the wrath of the Lord toward His people, how He will smite His people, and how their corpses will be found laying in the streets. These verses were interpreted as being about "the congregation of Scoffers who are in Jerusalem" (line 10). It therefore seems that the famine mentioned at the top of this column refers to the famine that struck Judaea in the spring of 65 B.C.E., before the conquest of Pompey in 63 B.C.E.[44] Two passages from the *Pesher on Psalms* A (4Q171) which interpret Psalm 37 refer to this same famine. The pesher on v. 7, in cols. 1–2 reads as follows:[45]

25. ["... Moa]n before [the Lord, and] writhe before him. Do not be angry with the one who makes his way prosperous, with the one

42 It can be assumed that the top of col. 2 is a commentary on vv. 8–10 of Isaiah 5, since the end of v. 8 has the word "earth" which is interpreted in the pesher, and v. 10 states that "a large vineyard will produce just a few gallons, and enough seed to yield several bushels will produce less than a bushel." This being the case, it would follow that the pesher is on a few consecutive verses of Isaiah 5.

43 It is interesting that the author of this pesher decided not to comment on Isa 5:20 – "Woe to those who call evil good and good evil are as good as dead, who turn darkness into light and light into darkness."

44 It seems that the author of the *Pesher on Isaiah* B alluded to the conquest of Pompey by using the phrases "condemnation of the land" and "visitation of the land," and by interpreting the verses that tell of the exile of the people (Isa 5:13) and the wrath of the Lord against his people and the corpses lying in the streets (v. 25). It is interesting to note that when John Allegro published this scroll he claimed that the phrase "condemnation of the land" was a scribal mistake, which should be read as "the dried land"; see J. M. Allegro, "More Isaiah Commentaries from Qumran's Fourth Cave," *JBL* 77 (1958) 216. Yigael Yadin contended that this phrase was not corrupt, and should be explained in light of Mishnaic Hebrew as meaning "the punishment of the earth"; see Y. Yadin, "Some Notes on Newly Published *Pesharim* of Isaiah," *IEJ* 9 (1959) 39.

45 The following translation is based on Horgan, *Pesharim*, 195.

26. [who carries] out evil plans." [The interpretation] of it concerns the Man of Lies who led many astray with deceitful words

27. for they chose empty words and did not lis[ten] to the Interpreter of Knowledge, so that

1. they will perish by the sword, by famine, and by plague. ...

This description reproaches the Man of Lies, who used his influence to mislead many not to follow the Interpreter of Knowledge (referring most likely to "the Teacher of Righteousness"), with the result that Israel was severely punished, with people dying by the sword, famine, and the plague.[46] This description, as well as those discussed above from the *Pesher on Hosea* B and the *Pesher on Isaiah* B, state that the wicked suffered famine but fails to describe how the righteous endured it. The pesher on Ps 37:18–20 in the *Pesher on Psalms* A states that while the wicked died of starvation, the penitents of the desert, meaning the members of the sect, did not suffer deprivation, but instead earned "all man's inheritance." The *Pesher on Psalms* A, cols. 2–3 reads:[47]

26. "... the[Lord knows the days of the blameless, and their inheritance will be for ever." The interpretation of it concerns the men of]

27. They [will] n[ot] be put to shame in [the time of evil." The interpretation of it concerns

1. those who return to the wilderness who will live for a thousand generations in saf[ety]; to them will belong all the inheritance of

2. Adam, and to their seed forever. "And in the days of famine they will be satisfied, for the wicked

3. will perish." The interpretation of it is th[at] he will keep them alive in famine, in the appointed time of fa[st]ing, but many

---

46 Another passage in the *Pesher on Psalms* A also expresses the idea that the conquest of Pompey was allowed because of the ill treatment of the Teacher of Righteousness. The next pesher in col. 2, lines 18–20, which was discussed in chapter 2, reads: "The interpretation of it concerns the wicked ones of Ephraim and Manasseh who will seek to lay their hands on the Priest and on the men of his counsel in the time of testing that is coming upon them. But God will redeem them from their hand and afterwards they will be given into the hand of the ruthless Gentiles for judgment." Such an interpretation is not very common among the authors of the pesharim, probably because of the time gap between the years during which the Teacher of Righteousness was active and Pompey's conquest; see H. Eshel, "The Two Historical Layers of Pesher Habakkuk," *Zion* 71 (2006) 143–52 (Hebrew).

47 The following translation is based Horgan, *Pesharim*, 197.

4. will perish on account of the famine and plague, all who do not go out
   [from there] to be [w]ith
5. the Congregation of his chosen ones. ...

This pesher calls the famine "the appointed time of fasting." It is possible that
the term for the famine reflects a fast-day that was set in response to the drought
of 65 B.C.E.[48] If we adopt the tradition preserved in the Palestinian Talmud and
in the *Scholion* (the "commentary") to *Megillat Ta'anit*, according to which the
date mentioned in *Megillat Ta'anit* is related to the day on which Onias made
the rain fall, it seems that this happened when the people were fasting in the
hopes of bringing an end to the drought.[49] This fast (and the holiday that was
fixed following the miracle of Onias) may have been the reason for the author of
the *Pesher on Psalms* A to label the famine of 65 B.C.E. as the "Appointed Time
of Fasting." According to the end of the passage, the people who did not join the
"Congregation of the Elects" perished from famine and plague. Based on this
sentence David Flusser suggested that people joined the sect during the famine
simply in order to survive.[50]

In conclusion, several scrolls found in Qumran include allusions to

48 The phrase "appointed time of fasting" is mentioned a second time in the *Pesher on
Psalms* A a few lines previously in the sentence: "The interpretation of it concerns the congregation
of the Poor Ones who will accept the appointed time of fasting and will be delivered from all the
snares of Belial" (col. 2, lines 9–11; see Horgan, *Pesharim*, 196). It seems that this phrase was used
twice in the *Pesher on Psalm* A, but each time with a different meaning. The "appointed time of
fasting" in the sentence just quoted refers to the Day of Atonement, as in the Damascus Document
(6:18–19) and several other scrolls; see N. Hacham, "Communal Fasts in the Judean Desert Scrolls,"
in *Historical Perspectives: From the Hasmoneans to Bar Kokhba in Light of the Dead Sea Scrolls* (ed.
D. Goodblatt, A. Pinnick, and D. R. Schwartz; STDJ 37; Leiden, Boston, and Köln: Brill, 2002)
127–45. On the other hand, one should consider the possibility that the phrase "he will keep them
alive in the famine in the appointed time of fasting" does not refer to the Day of Atonement, but
rather to the special fast fixed before the Passover of 65 B.C.E. on account of the famine; see Flusser,
"Famine," 11–12. Based on the distinction between the two fasts, and the assumption that the second fast was especially fixed due to the famine, it is possible that the second fast was observed by
all the people in Judea, and not only by the sect.

49 *Megillat Ta'anit* states that "On the twentieth of it (=Adar) the people fasted for rain,
and it rained for them." MS Parma of the *Scholion* reads: "Because there was famine and drought in
the Land of Israel and they didn't have rain for three consecutive years, until Onias passed in front
of the ark and prayed and it started raining. The day when it rained was fixed as a holiday" (Noam,
Ta'anit, 309–11).

50 Flusser, "Famine." See also C. M. Murphy, *Wealth in the Dead Sea Scrolls and in the
Qumran Community* (STDJ 40; Leiden, Boston, and Köln: Brill, 2002) 44.

historical events which occurred during the reign of Salamzion Alexandra (76–67 B.C.E.), the civil war between Hyrcanus and Aristobulus (67–63 B.C.E.) and the first ten years of the Roman rule in Judaea (63–54 B.C.E.). It is truly unfortunate that the scrolls which included the *Annalistic Text* are so fragmentary that it is very difficult to draw any historical details from them, but it seems that the pesharim still preserve allusions to the famine that struck Judaea in 65 B.C.E.

CHAPTER EIGHT

The Assassination of Pompey

In 1998, a scroll designated as 4Q386 was published. It documents an apocryphal composition based on the Book of Ezekiel, and has subsequently been entitled "Pseudo-Ezekiel." Its author freely used the Tetragrammaton, which is not found in the sectarian scrolls characteristic of Qumran. I believe that this text was brought to the community by a newcomer rather than composed by an author from the sect. At the beginning of col. 2 of the first fragment, one reads:[1]

1. " [...] and they shall know that I am the Lord." *vacat* And he said to me, "Look,
2. O son of man, at the land of Israel." And I said, "I have seen, Lord, and behold it lies waste,
3. and when will you gather them together?" And the Lord said, "A son of Belial will scheme to oppress My people
4. but I will not allow him; and his kin will not survive, nor will there be left from the impure one any seed;
5. and from the caperbush there shall be no wine, nor will a hornet make any honey. [*vacat*] And the
6. wicked one I will slay at Memphis but My children I will bring forth from Memphis, and their rem[na]nt I shall return.

---

1   The translation is based on D. Dimant, "4Q386 ii–iii, A Prophecy on Hellenistic King-doms?" *RQ* 18 (1998) 511–29; idem, *Qumran Cave 4, XXI, Parabiblical Texts, IV* (DJD 30; Oxford: Clarendon, 2001) 53–69.

7. As they shall say 'peace and tranquility have come,' and they shall say
   'the land sh[a]ll be
8. as it was in the days of [ ] old.'" …

A careful analysis reveals some interesting details. The meaning of the phrase
in line 4 "but I will not allow him" should be understood as "I will not leave
him in peace."[2] The word המן in that same line means "from," and is known
from Mishnaic Hebrew, but with a pronominal suffix, such as the word הימנו
("of it," "than it," etc.).[3] The first word in line 5, נצפה, is another word known
from Mishnaic Hebrew and should be identified as the caperbush.[4] The word
תזיז, which appears in the same line, seems to be contrasted with honey, and
should perhaps be understood as the product of insects that resemble bees,
probably hornets.[5] The word שדך in line 7 is an Aramaic word denoting quiet
or tranquility.[6] In this context, God speaks to the prophet and asks him to look
at the soil of the Land of Israel. After the prophet sees how dry and barren it is,
he asks God when the people of Israel will be permitted to return to their land.
In response, God tells the prophet of the son of Belial who has resolved to harm
Israel, but who would eventually be punished, with none of his relatives, nor

---

2 For this meaning, see Isa 14:3; Lam 5:5; Job 3:26.

3 See M. Bar-Asher, "המן (=מן) in a Fragment from Qumran," *Leshonenu* 55 (1991) 75
(Hebrew); S. Friedman, "Erasing Haman," *Leshonenu* 61 (1998) 259–63 (Hebrew); E. Qimron, "Dis-
missing המן", *Leshonenu* 64 (2002), 165–66 (Hebrew).

4 This word נצפה is mentioned in the Mishnah (*Demai* 1,1) as well as in other places in
the rabbinic literature. It is possible that the resemblance between the caperbush and the vine led
to contrasting the caper with the wine. These dual images also appear in a midrash in *Leviticus
Rabbah* (34,16): "It is told of a pious man who went for a stroll in his vineyard on the Sabbath to see
what it required, and he saw a breach, which he thought on the Sabbath that he should fence. When
Sabbath was over he said: 'Since I considered fencing it on the Sabbath, God forbid, I will never
repair it.' How did the Holy One, blessed be He, reward him? He conjured a caperbush (נצפה) to
grow in it (=the vineyard), and to fence it, and he earned a living from it for the rest of his life."
The same story is also told in a shorter version in the Babylonian Talmud, *Shabbat* 150b. The
Talmudic version mentions the more common Hebrew word צלף for caperbush, instead of נצפה;
see S. Friedman, "Lexicographic Enigmas in the Dead Sea Scrolls," *Leshonenu* 64 (2002) 168–69
(Hebrew).

5 See the comprehensive discussion of this word by Dimant, "4Q386," 516; Friedman,
"Lexicographic Enigmas," 169–70 (Hebrew); M. Bar-Asher, "Addition to S. Friedman's Note," *Leshonenu* 61 (1998) 265 (Hebrew).

6 Dimant, "4Q386," 517–18; M. Bar-Asher, "A Few Remarks on Mishnaic Hebrew and
Aramaic in Qumran Hebrew," in *Diggers at the Well* (ed. T. Muraoka and J. F. Elwolde; STDJ 36;
Leiden, Boston, and Köln: Brill, 2000) 17–19.

any of the seed of the impure, surviving, just as the caperbush cannot produce wine nor the hornet make honey.[7] The Wicked One is to be killed in Memphis, thereby allowing the people of Israel to depart from it. The text concludes with words of consolation, assuring that peace and tranquility will return to prevail in Israel, just as in the past.

It is important to consider further the passage which states that the Wicked One will be killed in Memphis. Memphis is the Greek name of the Egyptian town Moph (also called Noph in the Bible). Moph is the name used in this scroll to designate the city. Present-day Memphis, known as Saqqara, is situated some 13 miles south of Cairo.[8] Devorah Dimant, who published this text, noted that the mention of Memphis in this passage is based on Ezek 30:13: "Thus says the Lord God: I will destroy the idols and put an end to the images in Memphis; there shall no longer be a prince from the land of Egypt; so I will put fear in the land of Egypt." Regarding the historical background behind the passage, Dimant distinguished between the son of Belial mentioned in line 3, who set out to harm Israel, and the Wicked One, mentioned in line 6, who is to be killed in Memphis. According to Dimant, this passage refers to two antagonists, identifying the son of Belial of 4Q386 with Antiochus IV Epiphanes, who stayed in Memphis during his second campaign to Egypt in 168 B.C.E.[9] Dimant supposed that the emphatic wording that the Wicked One's kin would not survive supported the notion that the author of 4Q386 lived after Antiochus V had been assassinated in 162

7   Dimant, "4Q386," 516. Dimant stated that this description testifies to a harsh economic environment in the days of the Wicked One, but there is no certainty that this can be deduced from the contrasts of caper with wine and hornets with honey (line 5).

8   D. B. Redford, "Memphis," in *The Anchor Bible Dictionary* (6 vols.; ed. D. N. Freedman; Doubleday: New York, 1992) 4.689–91.

9   4Q386 was copied in the Herodian period. Dimant dated its composition to the second century B.C.E., following her view that this text , which she labeled as "pseudo-Ezekiel," was composed in its entirety in the second century B.C.E. This assumption is based on the fact that one of the scrolls which she considers to be part of "pseudo-Ezekiel" (4Q391) was copied at the end of the second century B.C.E.; see Dimant, *Qumran Cave 4*, 511–12. Though the text in frg. 1 of 4Q386 is parallel to fragments of 4Q385 and 4Q388, the relation between the various manuscripts of "pseudo-Ezekiel" is still not clear. There is no certainty that all the scrolls which include the non-biblical traditions based on the Book of Ezekiel are indeed all part of the same composition. This is especially true in regard to 4Q391. Its 77 fragments do not overlap with the other scrolls which document the apocryphal work based on the Book of Ezekiel. Therefore the date in which 4Q391 was copied cannot serve as evidence for the dating of 4Q386. Even if one does accept that 4Q391 is a copy of the same composition, implying that it would have been composed in the second century B.C.E., it may still be that "pseudo-Ezekiel" was updated during the first century B.C.E., appended with a passage relating to the assassination of Pompey.

B.C.E. Since she envisioned the son of Belial and the Wicked One as two different figures, she did not associate the account of the death of the Wicked One in Memphis in 4Q386 with the false rumors of Antiochus' death in Egypt (2 Macc 5:5) which were spread in Jerusalem during Antiochus IV's second campaign to Egypt.

Continuing in this vein, Dimant proposed connecting the son of Belial and the Wicked One mentioned in 4Q386, suggesting he is the governor Cleon whom Antiochus IV installed in Memphis. As an alternative, Dimant suggested that the Wicked One was one of the Egyptian priests who served in Memphis in the second century B.C.E. These priests were known for their hostility towards the Hellenist inhabitants and it is reasonable to assume that they also attacked Jews. Dimant also noted that if one does not assume that there is a connection between the son of Belial, who planned to harm the people of Israel, and the Wicked One who would die in Memphis, then it could be that the historical background of 4Q386 was the struggle and conflict within the Ptolemaic dynasty in which the Jews of Egypt and the priests of the Temple of Onias were engaged in the second century B.C.E.[10] In summary, Dimant has identified the son of Belial as being Antiochus IV, and the Wicked One as a historical figure active in Memphis during the reign of Antiochus IV or shortly thereafter. Accordingly, 4Q386 would reflect historical events which took place between 170–140 B.C.E.[11]

Although Dimant suggests that the author of 4Q386 was familiar with Egyptian geography and interested in its political events of the second century B.C.E., I believe that the author was more likely to have been an inhabitant of Judaea who was not immersed in Egypt's history. As with the authors of the pesharim, this author was interested in the eschatological significance of biblical

10 The "Temple of Onias" is a temple to the God of Israel, built in Leontopolis in Egypt by Onias III or IV in the second quarter of the second century B.C.E. (170–150 B.C.E.). This temple remained active until 74 C.E., when the Romans ordered it closed. It is mentioned in the writings of Josephus and in rabbinic literature. If one accepts Dimant's conclusion and assumes that the son of Belial and the Wicked One are two separate historical figures, the main argument to identify the son of Belial with Antiochus IV is nullified, since this identification is mainly based on the fact that Antiochus stayed in Memphis during his second campaign to Egypt. 4Q386 states that the Wicked One will be killed in Memphis, but it does not state that the son of Belial stayed in Memphis. Dimant assumed that the son of Belial was Antiochus IV, due to the negative depiction of this ruler in the Book of Daniel, in the Books of the Maccabees, in the Sibylline Oracles, in 4Q248, and perhaps in 4Q246.

11 Dimant, "4Q386," 523–28.

154

verses in the context of contemporary events in Judaea.[12] I contend that the designations "son of Belial" and "the Wicked One" refer to one figure rather than two,[13] and that the author of 4Q386 mentioned that the Wicked One would be killed in Memphis as an allusion to the following passage in Jeremiah:

> The word that the Lord spoke to Jeremiah the prophet about the coming of Nebuchadnezzar king of Babylon to strike the land of Egypt: Declare in Egypt, and proclaim in Migdol; proclaim in Memphis and Tahpanhes; Say: "Stand ready and be prepared, for the sword shall devour around you." Why are your stalwarts swept away? They do not stand because the Lord thrust them down. He made many stumble, and they fell, and they said one to another, "Arise, and let us go back to our own people and to the land of our birth, because of the sword of the oppressor" (46:13–16).

As I will show below, it is possible that the verse in Hos 9:6, "For behold, they are going away from destruction; but Egypt shall gather them; Memphis shall bury them," caused the author of 4Q386 to stress that the Wicked One would find his death in Memphis rather than in the other places mentioned in Jeremiah 46.[14] The phrase "Why are your stalwarts swept away?" in Jer 46:15 is probably what led the author of 4Q386 to associate the city of Memphis with the death of the Wicked One.

Chapter 46 in the book of Jeremiah begins the series of prophecies on the nations, including two prophecies on Egypt. The first one (vv. 2–12) was pronounced in 605 B.C.E., after the Babylonian army defeated the Egyptian army at Carchemish. The second one (vv. 13–26), however, cannot be as easily dated.[15] While scholars assume that the prophecy in vv. 15–16 speaks of a Babylonian victory over Egypt, they are uncertain as to the identity of the speakers in these verses.[16]

---

12 On the interest of the authors of the pesharim in the events which took place in the Land of Israel during the second and first centuries B.C.E., see J. H. Charlesworth, *The Pesharim and Qumran History* (Grand Rapids: Eerdmans, 2002) 116–18, and the discussions in chapters 2, 3, 4, 6, and 7 of this book.

13 Following Friedman's interpretation; see Friedman, "Erasing Haman," 261.

14 The connection between the verse in Hosea and 4Q386 was pointed out by Friedman, "Erasing Haman," 261.

15 For the claim that the two prophecies on Egypt belong to the same period of time, see J. Bright, *Jeremiah* (AB; Garden City, NY: Doubleday, 1984) 308; R. P. Carroll, *The Book of Jeremiah* (OTL; London: SCM, 1986) 765.

16 Scholars who asserted that Jeremiah's prophecy is related to the campaign in which

Nebuchadnezzar failed to conquer Egypt in 601 B.C.E. and did not succeed in this task until 568/7 B.C.E. There is no reason to assume that this prophecy was not uttered by Jeremiah, but it is difficult to accept that Jeremiah was alive twenty years after the destruction of Judaea. Consequently, I endorse the view that the second prophecy dates to 601 B.C.E., after Nebuchadnezzar failed to conquer Egypt.[17] The Babylonian Chronicles describe the 601 B.C.E. campaign as follows:[18]

> The fourth year (of Nebuchadnezzar): The king of Akkad mustered his army and marched to Hattu (Syria) [He marched about victoriously] in Hattu. In the month Kislev he took his army's lead and marched to Egypt. (When) the king of Egypt heard (the news) he mu[stered] his army. They fought one another in the battlefield and both sides suffered severe losses (lit. they inflicted a major defeated upon one another). The king of Akkad and his army turned and [when back] to Babylon.

Jehoiakim, the King of Judah appointed by the Egyptian King Necho II, was a partisan Egyptian supporter. When Nebuchadnezzar conquered Ashkelon in 604 B.C.E., Jehoiakim was compelled to subordinate his loyalties to Babylon, but after Nebuchadnezzar failed to conquer Egypt in 601 B.C.E., Jehoiakim decided to rebel against Babylon and to return to his pro-Egyptian stance.[19] I suggest Jer 46:13–26 is part of Jeremiah's polemic against the pro-Egyptian party in Jerusalem, which succeeded in persuading Jehoiakim to revolt against Babylon following Nebuchadnezzar's defeat. In this view, Jeremiah presented two arguments: first,

---

the Babylonian army succeeded in conquering Egypt also suggested that the speakers were either Egyptian soldiers who were sent to the Land of Israel in preparation for the Babylonian attack, or mercenaries who served in the Egyptian army and wished to return to their homelands after Egypt's defeat. For the former, see W. L. Holladay, *Jeremiah 2, A Commentary on Chapters 26–52* (Hermeneia; Minneapolis: Fortress Press, 1989) 328. For an assessment of both possibilities, see Y. Hoffman, *Jeremiah* (A Bible Commentary for Israel; Tel Aviv and Jerusalem: Am Oved and Magnes Press, 2001) 761–70 (Hebrew); J. R. Lunbom, *Jeremiah 37–52* (AB; New York: Doubleday, 2004) 212.

17 A. Malamat, *History of Biblical Israel* (Leiden, Boston, and Köln: Brill, 2001) 294–95

18 A. K. Grayson, *Assyrian and Babylonian Chronicles* (Locust Valley: Augustin, 1975) 99–102.

19 See 2 Kgs 24:1: "In his (=Jehoiakim's) days, Nebuchadnezzar king of Babylon came up, and Jehoiakim became his servant three years. Then he turned and rebelled against him." See the discussion in Malamat *History*, 307–8; and see I. Eph'al, "Nebuchadnezzar the Warrior: Remarks on his Military Achievements," *IEJ* 53 (2003) 178–91.

that it was the God of Israel, and not Necho II, who drove Nebuchadnezzar away from Egypt, and second, that despite Nebuchadnezzar's interim defeat, he would eventually conquer Egypt in the future and "Memphis shall become a waste" (v. 19).[20] According to this reading, vv. 15–16 are an account of Nebuchadnezzar's soldiers' disastrous defeat and their flight back to their homeland.

Whatever the original meaning of Jer 46:15–16 may have been, it is reasonable to consider that the author of 4Q386 regarded them to be a description of the defeat of an enemy who invaded Egypt. I contend that this author supposed that the words "Why are your stalwarts swept away? They do not stand because the Lord thrust them down" described events that occurred in his own time.

One should consider the possibility of identifying the son of Belial in 4Q386 with Pompey. After the battle of Pharsalus in Greece (on August 9th, 48 B.C.E.), Pompey fled from Julius Caesar's army to Egypt's shores. Cassius Dio (*Roman History* 42.3–5) mentions that when Pompey's ship arrived near the port of Pelusium (on September 28th, 48 B.C.E.), which is to be identified with Tell El-Farama (the name Baluza, a site next to Tell El-Farama, preserves the ancient name of Pelusium),[21] the ship remained offshore, while Pompey asked Ptolemy XIII to come out and see him. Lucius Septimus, a Roman official who was appointed by Gabinius to be in charge of the relations between Rome and Egypt, and Achileas, Ptolemy's general, sailed out to Pompey's ship and convinced him that his ship was too big to enter the port of Pelusium. Lucius and Achileas consequently invited Pompey to come ashore in their own boat, only to assassinate him before they reached the shore.[22] Plutarch also records these events (*Lives, Pompey,* 79–80) and adds that Pompey boarded the boat accompanied by his freed slave, Philipus. Subsequent to the murder, Pompey was beheaded and his body was thrown into the sea. Philipus found the body after it washed ashore, and cremated him according to the Roman custom before

20 In this context it would be worthwhile to compare the usage of the phrase "As I live, declares the Lord" in Jer 22:24 and Jer 46:18. In chapter 22, Jeremiah proclaims that even though Jehoiakim was not defeated beyond the gates of Jerusalem in 597 B.C.E. (Jer 22:19), he will nevertheless go into exile. In chapter 46 Jeremiah emphasizes that despite Nebuchadnezzar's defeat in Egypt in 601 B.C.E., he will eventually succeed in conquering Egypt at some point in the future.

21 M. J. Cledat, "Le Temple de Zeus Cassios a Péluse," *Annales du Service des Antiquités de l'Egypte* 13 (1913) 79–85; H. Jaritz, et al., *Pelusium: Prospection archéologique et topographique de la région de Tell et Kanais 1993 et 1994* (Stuttgart: Franz Steiner, 1996).

22 E. Cary, *Dio's Roman History* (9 vols.; Loeb Classical Library; Cambridge, MA: Harvard University Press, 1916) 6.118–23.

burying him near Mount Casius (some 18 miles east of Pelusium).[23] In October 48 B.C.E. in Alexandria, Pompey's head was presented to Julius Caesar. He was shocked and ordered a proper burial together with the erection of a tombstone on Pompey's grave on Mt Casius.[24]

The details of Pompey's death were known in Judaea, since the author of the *Psalms of Solomon* described it in the second psalm of his collection:[25]

25. Do not delay, O God, to repay them on their heads; to turn the pride of the dragon into dishonor.

26. And I did not wait long until God showed me his insolence, pierced, on the mountains of Egypt, more despised than the smallest thing on land and sea.

23 B. Perrin, *Plutarch's Lives.* (11 vols.; Loeb Classical Library; Cambridge, MA: Harvard University Press, 1917) 5.321–25.

24 Pompey's grave on Mt Casius was first mentioned by Strabo (*Geography* 16.2.33); see H. L. Jones, *The Geography of Strabo* (8 vols.; Loeb Classical Library; Cambridge, MA: Harvard University Press, 1930) 7.278-79. Hadrian renovated and adorned the grave when he passed by it at the end of 130 C.E. (*Vita of Hadrian* 14. 4); see D. Magie, *The Scriptores Historiae Augustae* (3 vols.; Loeb Classical Library; New York: Putnam's Sons, 1922) 1.44–45. The grave is mentioned in several historical accounts down to the fourth century C.E. See, for example, the account given by Ammianus Marcellinus (*History* 22.16.3) when he describes the Egyptian provinces; see J. C. Rolfe, *Ammianus Marcellinus* (3 vols.; Loeb Classical Library; Cambridge, MA: Harvard University Press, 1940) 2.296–97. For a review of the historical sources mentioning Pompey's grave, see P. Figueras, *From Gaza to Pelusium* (Beer Sheva 14; Beer Sheva: Ben-Gurion University Press, 2000) 214–29.

25 The English translation is based on K. Atkinson, *I Cried to the Lord: A Study of the Psalms of Solomon's Historical Background and Social Setting* (Leiden and Boston: Brill, 2004) 17–18. See also R. B. Wright, "Psalms of Solomon," in *The Old Testament Pseudepigrapha* (2 vols.; ed. J. H. Charlesworth; New York: Doubleday, 1985) 2.653. The collection entitled "*Psalms of Solomon*" was originally written in Hebrew. The composition is a collection comprised of 18 psalms in a uniform style that describe the controversy in Judaea between the pious, the holy, the righteous, and the God-fearing, and the sinners and the impure. The psalms describe the conquest of Judaea and Jerusalem by an alien ruler who besieged Jerusalem, captured it, robbed and massacred its people, and maliciously trampled the temple. In the psalms, his success is believed to be divine punishment for the wickedness of the rulers of Jerusalem (most likely referring to the Hasmoneans). In 1847, Franz Karl Movers suggested identifying the conqueror as Pompey, based primarily on the descriptions in Ps Sol 2:26–27 and Ps Sol 8:15–20. This identification has been accepted by most scholars; see K. Atkinson, "On the Herodian Origin of Militant Davidic Messianism at Qumran: New Light from Psalm of Solomon 17," *JBL* 118 (1999) 436, n. 3. The *Psalms of Solomon* have been preserved in Greek and in Syriac. On the connection between *Psalm of Solomon* 2 and the *Pesher on Nahum*, see S. Berrin, "Pesher Nahum, Psalm of Solomon and Pompey," in *Reworking the Bible: Apocryphal and Related Texts at Qumran* (ed. E. G. Chazon, D. Dimant, and R. A. Clements; STDJ 58; Leiden and Boston: Brill, 2005) 65–84.

27   His body, was carried about on the waves in great shame, and there was
no one to bury (him), for he (God) had rejected him in dishonor.

Concerning the background of Pompey's conquest of Judaea in 63 B.C.E. and
his desecrating entry of the Holy of Holies,[26] the author of the second hymn
of the *Psalms of Solomon* believed that God had avenged the desecration of
the temple through Pompey's assassination on the shore of Egypt fifteen years
later: "his body was carried about on the waves in great shame." It appears that
the author of the text from Qumran (4Q386) chose to identify the place where
the assassination took place with Memphis and not with Migdol or Tahpanhes
(which are also mentioned in Jeremiah's prophecy), since Ezek 30:13 and Hos
9:6 mention Memphis only (the description in Hosea: "but Egypt shall gather
them; Memphis shall bury them" suited the exegetical purposes of the verses
in Jeremiah and it is possible that in the author viewed this verse as relating to
Pompey's death on the shore of Egypt).[27] Migdol, Tahpanhes, and Memphis are
listed in Jer 44:1 since they were places where Jews lived after the destruction
of the First Temple. After asserting that the Wicked One would be killed in
Memphis, the author of 4Q386 stated that God would take his children out of
Memphis. This is a somewhat surprising citation since there is currently no
evidence that Jews lived in Memphis after the third century B.C.E.[28] However, we
know that Jewish soldiers lived in Pelusium in the first century B.C.E. since in 55
B.C.E. they helped Gabinius cross the Egyptian border and assisted in bringing
Ptolemy XII (Auletes) to power.[29]

The hypothesis that the author of 4Q386 embedded allusions to Jer 46:13–

---

26   *J.W.* 1.133–54; *Ant.* 14.48–72.

27   It is possible that the identification of Pelusium with Memphis relies on the fact that
Migdol and Tahpanhes are two sites quite close to Pelusium. Migdol is identified with today's Tel
el-Her south of Pelusium and Tahpanhes is Taphne, today's Tel Dafanah, southwest of Pelusium;
see E. D. Oren, "Migdol: A New Fortress on the Edge of the Eastern Nile Delta," *BASOR* 256 (1984)
7–44. However, it is difficult to know whether the author of 4Q386 would have been aware of this.
On Migdol and Tahpanhes, see J. K. Lott, "Migdol," in *The Anchor Bible Dictionary* (6 vols; ed. D. N.
Freedman; New York: Doubleday, 1992) 4.828; R. N. Jones and Z. T. Frema, "Tahpanhes," in idem,
6.308–9. It seems that the author of 4Q386 did not know that the ancient name of Pelusium was
"Sin," and that this is "Sin, the Stronghold of Egypt," mentioned in Ezek 30:15.

28   V. Tcherikover, *Hellenistic Civilization and the Jews* (Philadelphia: Jewish Publication
Society, 1959) 285. Aryeh Kasher assumed that in Memphis, just as in Alexandria, there was a Jew-
ish Polytomy (a religious or ethnic group which enjoys some political rights); see A. Kasher, *The
Jews in Hellenistic and Roman Egypt* (Tübingen: Mohr, 1985) 185, n. 87.

29   *J.W.* 1.175; *Ant.* 14.98–99.

16 and Ezek 30:13 can be substantiated by the fact that lines 7–8 are based on Jeremiah. The phrase "'the land sh[a]ll be as it was in the days of old" can be traced to: "and afterwards it shall be inhabited, as in the days of old" (Jer 46:26). The description in line 6: "but my children I will bring forth from Memphis" is linked to the first part of v. 27 in Jeremiah 46: "for behold, I will save you from far away, and your offspring from the land of their captivity," while the phrase "peace and tranquility" in line 7 is based on the end of the very same verse: "Jacob shall return and have quiet and ease, and none shall make him afraid."[30]

It is therefore possible that the author of 4Q386 intended the son of Belial, who conquered Judaea and annexed it to the Roman Empire, the man who desecrated the temple in Jerusalem, to be identified as the Wicked One who was punished when his body was washed up upon Egypt's shores.[31] Most scholars who have studied the *Psalms of Solomon* tend to agree that the Wicked One (or "the lawless one" in the translation below) in Psalm 17 is Pompey:[32]

11. The lawless one laid waste our land so that no one inhabited it,
    they destroyed young and old and their children together.

30 I am grateful to Yossi Baruchi for turning my attention to this matter.

31 The root סחף (=to wash away) appears only once more in the Hebrew Bible in Prov 28:3, where it appears within the phrase "beating rain," meaning rain that washes away. This same root, however, is documented in Mishnaic Hebrew, carrying a similar meaning.

32 The translation is based on Atkinson, *I Cried*, 130; see also White, "Psalms of Solomon," 2.666. The Hebrew text of the Psalms of Solomon was reconstructed by W. Frankenberg, "Die Datierung der Psalmen Salomos," *BZAW* 1 (1896) 66–85. Two additional Hebrew reconstructions can be found in M. Stein, "Psalms of Solomon," in *The Apocryphal Books* (2 vols.; ed. A. Kahana; Tel Aviv: Meqoroth, 1937) 1.431–62 (Hebrew); A. S. Hartom, *The Apocryphal Books* (2 vols.; Tel Aviv: Yavne, 1969) 2.129–63 (Hebrew). These three reconstructions present almost identical texts. The reconstructed Hebrew versions read the designation in v. 11 as רשע, the exact word for the "Wicked One" in line 6 of the discussed passage of 4Q386. The assumption that the Wicked One in the psalm is Pompey was widely accepted by scholars. Recently Johannes Tromp and Kenneth Atkinson suggested associating Psalm 17 with the events of 40-37 B.C.E., that is, to the Roman response to the Parthian invasion of Judaea, Mattathias Antigonus' takeover of the Land of Israel, and Herod's return to Judaea. Accordingly, the "wicked" mentioned in Psalm 17 would not be Pompey. Tromp preferred to identify him with Rome rather than with a specific historical figure. Atkinson, on the other hand, suggested this figure should be identified with Herod; see J. Tromp, "Psalm of Solomon 17," *Novum Testamentum* 35 (1993) 344–61; K. Atkinson, "Herod the Great, Sosius and the Siege of Jerusalem (37 B.C.E.) in Psalm of Solomon 17," *Novum Testamentum* 38 (1996) 313–22; idem, "Toward a Redating of the Psalms of Solomon: Implications for Understanding the *Sitz im Leben* of an Unknown Jewish Sect," *JSP* 17 (1998) 95–112; Atkinson, *Davidic Messianism*, 440–44. Later, however, Atkinson accepted the common view that the Wicked One (the lawless one in his translation) in Psalm 17 is Pompey; see Atkinson, *I Cried*, 135–44.

12. In the wrath of his anger he expelled them to the west,
    And [he exposed] the rulers of the land to derision, and he did not
    spare them.
13. Being an alien the enemy acted arrogantly
    and his heart was alien for our God.
14. And everything that he did in Jerusalem
    was just as the nations do in their cities for their gods.

In summary, I have presented a contextualized view of 4Q386 as an allusion to the assassination of Pompey in 48 B.C.E. with a contemporized interpretation of Ezek 30:13, also reflects a reading of verses in Jer 46:15–16 and Hos 9:6. The author interpreted the verses in Ezekiel, Jeremiah, and Hosea as a reference to the death of the man who conquered Judaea and desecrated the temple in Jerusalem.[33] I suggest that the interpretation of this passage should be related to the assassination of Pompey rather than to the two separate events which took place in Egypt during the second century B.C.E., primarily because these events had no effect on what transpired in Judaea during the same period. If our assertion that this text refers to the assassination of Pompey is correct, we conclude that the author of 4Q386 shared similar views on historical events with the psalmist who composed the *Psalms of Solomon*.[34]

---

33 On the usage of historical events in order to attest to the reliability of apocalyptic compositions, see J. Licht, "Biblisches Geschichtsdenken und apokalyptische Spekulation," *Judaica* 46 (1990) 208–40; idem, "Time and Eschatology in Apocalyptic Literature and in Qumran," *JSJ* 16 (1966) 177–82. On contemporizing interpretations similar to the pesharim outside of the Qumran sect, see the discussion in the fifth chapter, n. 40.

34 On the similarity between the description of the messiah as a leader who takes revenge on the enemies of Israel in *Psalms of Solomon* 17, and the descriptions of the messiah in some of the scrolls found at Qumran, see Atkinson, "Davidic Messianism," 444–60; idem, *I Cried*, 144–75.

CHAPTER NINE

The Changing Notion of the Enemy
and Its Impact on the Pesharim

One consistent but ambiguous element of the biblical texts and the fragmentary scrolls is the allusion to the "Kittim" both as an agent and victim of destruction. The word is always referred to in the plural as a people rather than a place, either generalized as the outsider-enemy or contextualized as a contemporary enemy.

The Balaam Prophecies (Num 24:14–24) conclude with an ominous description: "Ships come from the quarter of Kittim, they subject Asshur, subject Eber. They too shall perish forever" (v. 24). First mentioned in the "Table of the Nations" (Gen 10:4), the Kittim are listed as the descendants of Japheth, Javan, and Tarshish. A second reference found in Jer 2:10 states: "Just cross over to the isles of Kittim and look; send to Kedar and observe carefully." Jeremiah construes the word Kittim as a general epithet for western nations.[1] Extending this reference, Josephus wrote, "The name Kittim (Χεθίμ) is given by the Hebrews to all the islands and to most of the countries near the sea" (*Ant.* 1.128). Based on Num 24:24, Jews of the Second Temple period seem to have applied the name Kittim to every nation that came to the Land of Israel by ships.

Balaam's prophecy was understood as eschatological—that the Kittim would rule over Asshur and Israel as well, but would eventually perish. Since this was understood as a description of the End of Days, the identification of the

---

1   On the connection between the Kittim and the city Kition (Κίτιον) in Cyprus, see D. W. Baker, "Kittim," *The Anchor Bible Dictionary* (6 vols.; ed. D. N. Freedman; New York: Doubleday, 1992) 4.93; P. E. Dion, "Les KTYM de Tel Arad: Grecs ou Phéniciens?" *RB* 99 (1992) 70–97; S. Segert, "Kition and Kittim," in *Periplus* (ed. P. Aström and D. Sürenhagen; Studies in Mediterranean Archaeology 127; Jonsered: P. Astroms Forlag, 2000) 165–72.

Kittim was of great significance to those who were waiting for the End of Days in the Second Temple period.

However, in the second century B.C.E. there was a dispute in Judaea about the identification of the Kittim. The author of 1 Maccabees, writing at the beginning of the reign of John Hyrcanus around the year 135 B.C.E., identified the Kittim as the Macedonians (1 Macc 1:1; 8:5).[2] This association was based on the assumption that Persia was to be understood as the Assyrian kingdom, on the ground of Ezra 6: 22: "They joyfully celebrated the Feast of Unleavened Bread for seven days, for the Lord had given them cause for joy by inclining the heart of the Assyrian king toward them so as to give them support in the work of the House of God, the God of Israel." In this verse, the so-called Assyrian king is actually a reference to the Persian monarch. After the conquest of the kingdom of Persia, or Assyria, by Alexander the Great, the Kittim were identified as the Macedonians.

Another reference to the Kittim can be found at the end of the Book of Daniel, edited about 165 B.C.E., in which the Kittim appear to be Romans: "At the appointed time, he will again invade the south, but the second time will not be like the first. Ships from Kittim will come against him. He will be checked, and will turn back, raging against the holy covenant" (Dan 11: 29–30).[3] These verses describe the two invasions of Egypt by Antiochus IV, the first in 170 B.C.E. and the second in 168 B.C.E. During the second invasion a delegation of the Roman Senate headed by Popilius Laenas was sent to force Antiochus to retreat. This identification of the Kittim in Dan 11:30 with the Romans is confirmed in the Old Greek translation of the Book of Daniel, as well as the Vulgate, where Kittim is actually translated as the Romans.[4] Some scholars have suggested an emendation to v. 30, to read "messengers of the Kittim" (ציירים כתים) instead of "ships of the Kittim" (ציים כתים).[5] Nevertheless, the resemblance between Dan 11:30 and Num 24:24 makes this emendation unnecessary, and one can assume that this was the way the author of Daniel understood Num 24:24.

The author of the *Book of Jubilees* appears to identify the Kittim as the

2   On dating of 1 Maccabees, see B. Bar-Kochva, *Judas Maccabaeus* (Cambridge: Cambridge University Press, 1989) 151–70. Other scholars suggested a somewhat later date; see, for example, G. A. Goldstein, *1 Maccabees* (AB; Garden City, NY: Doubleday, 1976) 270–71.

3   On dating the second part of Daniel (chapters 7–12), see L. F. Hartman and A. A. Di Lella, *The Book of Daniel* (AB; Garden City, NY: Doubleday, 1978) 253–54.

4   J. J. Collins, *Daniel* (Hermeneia; Minneapolis: Fortress, 1993) 384.

5   H. Winckler, *Altorientalische Forschungen* II (Leipzig: Pfeiffer, 1901) 422; Hartman and Di Lella, *Book of Daniel*, 270–71.

people who lived in the area of Greece rather than being the Romans. The Kittim are mentioned after the story of Abimelech, when Isaac cursed the Philistines that they be conquered by the Kittim, who would kill them by sword (*Jub.* 24:28–29). Although this reference does not help us to identify the Kittim, in *Jub.* 37:10 the Kittim are included among Esau's troops in the description of the army enlisted by him to fight Jacob.[6] Since mercenaries from the Greek Islands were deployed in the land of Israel from the late Bronze Age on, the link to the Greeks appears reasonable.[7] It should be noted that there is no evidence of Italian mercenaries in the western part of the Mediterranean in the First or Second Temple periods.

Another reference to Balaam's prophecy can be found in the *Testament of Simon*, where we read in a description of the End of Days: "And all the Cappadocians shall perish, and all the Kittim shall be utterly destroyed" (6:3). From this description, however, it is difficult to attribute a specific location or ethnicity to the Kittim.[8]

The Kittim are mentioned in seven different Qumran compositions,[9] six of which are sectarian and express the world view of scribes who were part of the Qumran sect. The seventh occurrence of the Kittim is found in 4Q247, which does not seem to be of sectarian origin. 4Q247 is a *Pesher on the Apocalypse of Weeks* (Enoch 93 and 91).[10] The fragment reads as follows:[11]

1. [A period en]graved [in the heavenly tablets ...]
2. [And after it shall co]me the fif[th] week [and at its end ...]

---

6   Y. Yadin assumed that the name Kittim was added to this discussion in the *Book of Jubilees* at a later stage since the number of mighty men of war from the Kittim is not specified; see Y. Yadin, *The Scroll of the War of the Sons of Light against the Sons of Darkness* (Oxford: Oxford University Press, 1962) 24, n. 8.

7   On Kittim as Greek or Cypriot mercenaries who served in the Judaean army at the end of the First Temple period, see Y. Aharoni, *Arad Inscriptions* (Jerusalem: Israel Exploration Society, 1981) 12–13.

8   M. De Jonge, *The Testaments of the Twelve Patriarchs* (Leiden: Brill, 1978) 21.

9   Some have also offered to reconstruct "Kittim" in 4Q332. This is one of copies of the *Annalistic List*. See the discussion in chapter seven, and also J. A. Fitzmyer, "332. 4QHistorical Text D," in *Qumran Cave 4, XXVI* (ed. P. Alexander, et al., DJD 36; Oxford: Clarendon, 2000) 285.

10   On the *Ten Week Apocalypse*, see S. B. Reid, "The Structure of the Ten Week Apocalypse and the Book of Dream Visions," *JSJ* 16 (1985) 189–201; H. Eshel, "*Dibre Hame'orot* and the Apocalypse of Weeks," in *Things Revealed: Studies in Early Jewish and Christian Literature in Honor of Michael E. Stone* (ed. E. G. Chazon, D. Satran, and R. A. Clements; Leiden and Boston: Brill, 2004) 149–54.

11   M. Broshi, "247. 4QPesher on the Apocalypse of Weeks," in *Qumran Cave 4, XXVI* (ed. P. Alexander, et al., DJD 36; Oxford: Clarendon, 2000) 187–89.

3. [Years eighty and] four hundred Solo[mon shall build the Temple ...]
4. [Zede]kiah king of Judah [shall go into exile ...]
5. [...] Sons of Levi and the people of the Lan[d ...]
6.] ki[ng] of the Kittim [

Józef Milik associated this text with the *Apocalypse of Weeks*.[12] According to 1 *Enoch* 93:7–8, the First Temple was built during the fifth week, while the sixth week is characterized by blindness and lack of the fear of God. Milik noted that line 3 of 4Q247 describes the temple being built by King Solomon four hundred and eighty years after the Exodus (see 1 Kgs 6:1), while line 4 refers to the destruction of the temple in the days of King Zedekiah. The term "people of the land" in line 5 appears to describe the Persian period, namely the people of the land mentioned in the books of Ezra and Nehemiah. According to Milik's understanding, the king of the Kittim mentioned in line 6 is part of a description of the Hellenistic period. Thus, the king of the Kittim should be identified in 4Q247 as one of the Hellenistic kings.

Of the six sectarian compositions mentioning the Kittim, the *War Scroll* (1QM) is the most significant. In this work the Kittim are described as the major enemy of the Sons of Light in the first stage of the eschatological war and are mentioned eighteen times.[13] According to the *War Scroll*, the war would last forty-nine years, during which the Sons of Light would fight the Kittim at the beginning of the first six years.[14] In 1QM 1:2, the phrase "Kittim of Asshur" is found, while "the Kittim in Egypt" are mentioned in 1:4. On the basis of these phrases, E. L. Sukenik remarked: "In my mind, the *terminus post quem* of the War Scroll can be determined by the phrase 'the Kittim of Asshur' and 'the Kittim in Egypt' found in column 1."[15] In his opinion, these phrases refer to the Seleucids and the Ptolemies. Nevertheless, Sukenik's son, Yigael Yadin, used the very same

12 J. T. Milik, *The Books of Enoch* (Oxford: Clarendon, 1976) 256.

13 Five times in the first column (lines 2, 4, 5, 9, 12), once in col. 11 (line 11), and once in col. 15 (line 2), four times in col. 16 (lines 2, 5, 7, 9), three times in col. 17 (lines 12, 14, 15), twice in col. 18 (lines 2, 4), and twice in col. 19 (lines 10, 13).

14 See Yadin, *Scroll of the War of the Sons of Light*, 21–26, 35–37. It seems that the chronology of the war in 1QM is as follows: At the beginning of the first six years the war against the Kittim will take place, and later the nine tribes of Israel will gather to Judaea. After the first Sabbatical year, there will be six years of preparations for the final war. Only after the second Sabbatical year will the thirty-five years of the War of the Divisions begin.

15 E. L. Sukenik, *The Dead Sea Scrolls of the Hebrew University* (Jerusalem: Magnes, 1955) 36 n. 14. This view was accepted by H. H. Rowley, "The Kittim and the Dead Sea Scrolls," *PEQ* 88 (1956) 95–97.

phrases to argue that, as in the *Pesher on Habakkuk*, the Kittim mentioned in the *War Scroll* should be identified as the Romans. He wrote that in the *War Scroll* we find, " 'Kittim in Egypt.' Not 'of Egypt,' as 'Kittim of Asshur.' This shows that the Kittim had an army in Egypt, not that they dwelt there."[16] Both Sukenik and Yadin understood the beginning of 1QM in a similar way. Yadin translated the beginning of 1QM 1 as follows:[17]

1. And th[is is the book of the disposition of] the war. The first engagement of the Sons of Light shall be to attack the lot of the Sons of Darkness, the army of Belial, the troop of Edom and Moab, and the sons of Ammon
2. and the army [of the dwellers of] Philistia and the troops of the Kittim of Asshur, and in league with them the offenders against the covenant. The sons of Levi, the sons of Judah, and the sons of Benjamin, the exiles
3. of the wilderness, they shall fight against them with [...], yea, against all their troops, when the exiles of the Sons of Light return from the Wilderness of the Nations to encamp in the Wilderness of Jerusalem.
4. After the battle they shall go up thence against [all the troops of] the Kittim in Egypt. In His appointed time He shall go forth with great wrath to fight against the kings of the north, and His anger shall be such as
5. to destroy utterly and to cut off the horn of Belial. That shall be] a time of deliverance for the People of God, an appointed time of dominion for all men of His lot, and eternal annihilation for all the lot of Belial.
6. There shall be [great] panic [amongst] the sons of Japheth, Asshur shall fall, and none shall help him, and the dominion of the Kittim shall depart, so that wickedness be subdued without a remnant,
7. and none shall escape of [all Sons of] Darkness.

Yadin noted that the author of the *War Scroll* had borrowed various phrases in col. 1 from Dan 11:40–12:2. He argued that this was a linguistic dependence rather than a contextual one.[18] The similarities between the beginning of the *War Scroll* and chapters 11 and 12 of the book of Daniel are summarized below:

16 Yadin, *Scroll of the War of the Sons of Light*, 258.
17 Ibid., 256–59.
18 Ibid., 258.

1QM Col. 1	The Book of Daniel
1. "…the troop of Edom and Moab, and the sons of Ammon" (line 1)	1. "…but these will escape his clutches: Edom, Moab and the chief part of the Ammonites" (11:41)
2. "with them the offenders against the covenant" (line 2)	2. "those who act wickedly toward the covenant" (11:32)
3. "He shall go forth with great wrath to fight against the kings of the north, and His anger shall be such as to destroy utterly" (lines 4-5)	3. "But report from east and north will alarm him, and he will march forth in a great fury to destroy and annihilate many" (11:44)
4. "Asshur shall fall, and none shall help him" (line 6)	4. "…and he will meet his doom with no one to help him" (11:45)
5. "…so that wickedness be subdued without a remnant, and none shall escape of [all Sons of] Darkness" (lines 6-7)	5. "He will lay his hands on lands; not even the land of Egypt will escape" (11:42)
6. "That is a time of mighty trouble for the people to be redeemed by God. In all their troubles there was none like it …" (lines 11-12)	6. "It will be a time of trouble, the like of which has never been since the nation came into being" (12:1)

In 1981 David Flusser published an important article concerning the apocalyptic elements found in the *War Scroll*.[19] Flusser argued that the author of the *War Scroll* was aware that the last part of the vision found in Daniel 11 and 12 did not take place. In other words, the author of the *War Scroll* knew that Dan 11:40–12:3 was an unfulfilled prophecy and he believed that its fulfillment would occur in the near future.[20] Comparing the Book of Daniel to the beginning of the *War Scroll*,[21] Flusser suggested a different reconstruction

19 D. Flusser, "Apocalyptic Elements in the War Scroll," in *Jerusalem in the Second Temple Period: Abraham Schalit Memorial Volume* (ed. A. Oppenheimer, U. Rappaport, and M. Stern; Jerusalem: Ben Zvi, 1980) 434–52 (Hebrew).

20 For a discussion of these verses, see A. S. van der Woude, "Prophetic Prediction, Political Prognostication, and Firm Belief: Reflections on Daniel 11:40–12:3," in *The Quest for Context and Meaning: Studies in Biblical Intertextuality in Honor of James A. Sanders* (ed. C. A. Evans and S. Talmon; BIS 28; Leiden: Brill, 1997) 63–73.

21 For a discussion of the connection between Daniel 11 and col. 1 of the *War Scroll*, see D. O. Wenthe, "The Use of the Hebrew Scriptures in 1QM," *DSD* 5 (1998) 296–98. Wenthe was not familiar with Flusser's article and did not reach any historical conclusions.

of col. 1 of 1QM. Based on these suggestions, we may translate the beginning of col. 1 as follows: [22]

1. For the Ma[skil (the instructor), Rule of] the war. The first attack of the Sons of Light shall be launched against the Sons of Darkness, the army of Belial, the troop of Edom and Moab, and the sons of Ammon

2. and the ar[my of the dwellers of] Philistia and the troops of the Kittim of Asshur, these being helped by those who violate the covenant, (from) the sons of Levi, the sons of Judah, and the sons of Benjamin.[23] The exiles of the wilderness shall fight against them

3. [...], according to all their troops, when the exiles, the Sons of Light, return from the Wilderness of the Nations to encamp in the Wilderness of Jerusalem. After the battle they shall go up from there.

4. [And the king] of the Kittim will [come] to Egypt. In his appointed time he shall go forth with great wrath to wage war against the kings of the north, and his anger shall be such as to destroy utterly and to cut off the horn

5. [of Israel. That shall be] the time of salvation for the People of God, an appointed time of dominion for all men of his lot, but of everlasting destruction for all the lot of Belial. There shall be [great] panic

22   Flusser, "Apocalyptic Elements," 449. The translation is based on J. Duhaime, "War Scroll (1QM, 1Q33)," in *The Dead Sea Scrolls: Hebrew, Aramaic, and Greek Texts with English Translations: Volume 2, Damascus Document, War Scroll, and Related Documents* (ed. J. H. Charlesworth et al.; Tübingen: Mohr Siebeck / Louisville: Westminster John Knox, 1995) 97, with some emendations. Yadin did not correctly decipher the first two letters, ל and מ, at the beginning of 1QM, so that he was not able to read [למ]שכיל "For the instructor." I wish to thank Prof. Frank Moore Cross who clarified this point for me.

23   Based on the Prayer of Joseph (4Q371–2), it seems that the sentence in line 2 ends following the words the sons of Levi, the sons of Judah, and the sons of Benjamin. This means that the offenders against the Sons of Light are from the three tribes who returned from the Babylonian exile, and not that the Sons of Light belong to these three tribes; see H. Eshel, "The Prayer of Joseph, a Papyrus from Masada and the Samaritan Temple on ΑΡΓΑΡΙΖΙΝ," *Zion* 56 (1991) 126, n. 2 (Hebrew). Therefore, Ed Sanders' assertion that the *War Scroll* manifests the idea that the members of the sect saw themselves as the true Israel while the offenders against the covenant were not considered by them as Israelites, cannot be accepted; see E. P. Sanders, *Paul and Palestinian Judaism* (Philadelphia: Fortress, 1977) 248–52. This idea is documented in a later stage in the intellectual history of the Qumran Sect, in the *Pesher on Nahum* frgs. 3–4 col. III:5. On this concept, see Y. Liebes, "The Ultra-Orthodox Community and the Dead Sea Sect," *Jerusalem Studies in Jewish Thought* 1 (1982) 137–52 (Hebrew).

6. [amongst] the sons of Japeth, Asshur shall fall down, and none shall help him, and the dominion of the Kittim shall come to an end, so that wickedness be subdued without a remnant, and none shall escape of

7. [all the Sons of] Darkness . . .

The major distinction between the reconstruction of Yadin and that of Flusser focuses on line 4 which says, according to Flusser's understanding, that the king of the Kittim will come to Egypt. Thus, there is no evidence of the Kittim of Egypt in 1QM. In addition, in line 5 it says that the king of the Kittim will "cut off the horn of Israel," and not "the horn of Belial." In 1982, only a few months after Flusser's article appeared, the publication of the fragments of the *War Scroll* from Cave 4 was released. Among the fragments was 4Q496, which includes part of the first column of the *War Scroll*. It reads:[24]

3. [he shall go forth with] great wrath to [wage war] against [the kings of the north and his anger shall be such as

4. [to destroy utterly and to cut off the horn of Is]rael. That shall be the time of [salvation for the people of God, but of

5. everlasting destruction for the lot of Belial. There shall be [great] pa[nic amongst the sons of Japheth, Asshur shall fall down and none

6. shall help him] and the dominion of the [Kittim] shall [come to an end ...

Line 4 of this fragment proves that Flusser's reconstruction of the beginning of line 5 of 1QM 1 is correct and strongly supports his reconstruction of the beginning of line 4 as well. Thus, the *War Scroll* seems to make no reference to the existence of the "Kittim of Egypt," and the only connection is between the Kittim and Asshur. In further support of this view, there are two other references in the *War Scroll*. In 1QM 11:11–12, the author interpreted Isa 31:8 as proof that God himself would fight the Kittim, as He did with Pharaoh: "From the time You had anno[unced to us the ti]me (appointed) for Your mighty hand against the Kittim, saying: Asshur shall fall down by a sword of no man, a sword of no human being, shall devour him."[25] A second reference in 1QM to the connection between the Kittim and Asshur appears in 18:2: "... When they pursue Asshur,

---

24 See M. Baillet, *Qumran Grotte 4, III (4Q282–4Q520)* (DJD 7; Oxford: Clarendon, 1982) 58. The translation is based on the translation of 1QM above.

25 Yadin, *Scroll of the War of the Sons of Light*, 312–13; Duhaime, "War Scroll," 119.

the sons of Japhet will be falling down without recovery, the Kittim shall be smashed to nothing."[26]

Since it was common to call Syria Asshur during the Second Temple period,[27] we propose that the phrase "Kittim of Asshur" must refer to the Seleucids. It is significant to note that the king of the Kittim is mentioned in 1QM 15: 23: "And all those [prepared] for the battle shall go and encamp against the king of the Kittim and against all the army of Belial gathered with him..."[28]

In light of the clear connection between the *War Scroll* and the end of the Book of Daniel, it is reasonable to assume that the *War Scroll* was composed at a time proximate enough to the sixties of the second century B.C.E. when the memories of the events of Daniel 11 were still fresh and the people could distinguish between that which had occurred and that which had not. In other words, enough time had passed that the difference between Dan 11:1–39 and 11:40–12:3 was by then obvious. Thus, updating of the last part of Daniel's prophecy had become necessary in order to persuade the audience that these verses were still relevant and would occur in the near future. Consequently, the *War Scroll* was composed during the third quarter of the second century B.C.E., and the Kittim mentioned in this scroll should be identified as the Seleucids.[29]

A composition related to the *War Scroll* that also mentions the Kittim is *Sefer ha-Milhamah* (4Q285).[30] In 4Q285, fragment 7, line 6 "the s[lai]n [of the]

26 Yadin, *Scroll of the War of the Sons of Light*, 342–44; Duhaime, "War Scroll," 135.

27 Yadin, *Scroll of the War of the Sons of Light*, 25, n. 4; Flusser, "Apocalyptic Elements," 443; M. Stern, "The Assyrian Jerusalem in a Fragment of the Work of Asinius Quadratus," *Zion* 42 (1977) 295–97 (Hebrew); M. Stern, *Greek and Latin Authors on Jews and Judaism* (3 vols.; Jerusalem: Israel Academy of Sciences and Humanities, 1976–84) 2.345–46.

28 Yadin, *Scroll of the War of the Sons of Light*, 331–32; Duhaime, "War Scroll," 129.

29 On dating the composition of the War Scroll to the third quarter of the second century B.C.E., see K. M. T. Atkinson, "The Historical Setting of the 'War of the Sons of Light and the Sons of Darkness,'" *Bulletin of the John Rylands Library* 40 (1957) 286; M. Treves, "The Date of the War of the Sons of Light," *VT* 8 (1958) 422; M. H. Segal, "The Qumran War Scroll and the Date of its Composition," *Aspects of the Dead Sea Scrolls* (ed. C. Rabin and Y. Yadin; Scripta Hierosolymitana 4; Jerusalem: Magnes, 1958) 138–43.

30 The similarity between the *War Scroll* and 4Q285 was pointed out by J. T. Milik, "Milki-ṣedeq et Milki-Reša' dans les anciens écrits juifs et chrétiens," *JJS* 23 (1972) 142–43. Milik noted that several fragments from 4Q285 describe the war and angelology in a fashion similar to the *War Scroll*. For studies addressing the question of the King of Kittim in *Sefer ha-Milhamah*, see G. Vermes, "The Oxford Forum for Qumran Research Seminar on the Rule of War from Cave 4," *JJS* 43 (1992) 85–94; J. D. Tabor, "A Pierced or Piercing Messiah? The Verdict is Still Out," *BAR* 18/6 (1992) 58–59; M. G. Abegg, "Messianic Hope and 4Q285: A Reassessment," *JBL* 113 (1994) 81–91.

Kittim" are mentioned. Furthermore, most scholars who have dealt with this document suggest reconstructing "the king of the Kittim" in line 4 of the same fragment. The passage is based on Isa 10:34–11:1 and reads as follows:[31]

1. [As it is written in the book of] Isaiah the Prophet: "Cut down shall be,
2. [the thickets of the forest with an axe, and Lebanon by a majestic one shall f]all. And there shall come forth a shoot from the stump of Jesse
3. [and out of his roots a sapling will grow"] the Branch of David, and they will enter into judgment with [all]
4. [the army of Belial. And the king of the Kittim will be judged] and the Prince of the Congregation, the Bra[nch of]
5. [David] will kill him [. . . and they will go out with timbrel]s and dances. And [the Chief] Priest shall command
6. [to purify their flesh of the blood of the s[lai]n [of the] Kittim. [And al]l [the people].

Some of the fragments of 4Q285 overlap with fragments of 11QBer (11Q14), so that today the latter is now designated as a Cave 11 copy of *Sefer ha-Milhamah*.[32] It even preserves text parallel to that which is quoted above.[33] Although the *War Scroll* and *Sefer ha-Milhamah* have similarities, there are some fundamental differences between them. Chief among these is the reference to the Prince of the Congregation in *Sefer ha-Milhamah*, while only the High Priest is noted in the *War Scroll*. The Kittim are mentioned in *Sefer ha-Milhamah* only in eschatological contexts. Thus, it is impossible to identify them in this text.

Returning to the connection between this fragment of *Sefer ha-Milhamah* and Isa 10:34, the same verse was interpreted in the *Pesher on Isaiah* A (4QpIs[a]; 4Q161), this time in connection to the Kittim. In this pesher the Kittim are

---

31 P. Alexander and G. Vermes, "4Q285. 4QSefer ha-Milhama," in *Qumran Cave 4, XXVI* (ed. P. Alexander, et al., DJD 36; Oxford: Clarendon, 2000) 238–41.

32 See F. García Martínez, E. J. C. Tigchelaar, and A. S. van der Woude (eds.), *Qumran Cave 11, II: 11Q2–18, 11Q20–31* (DJD 23; Oxford: Clarendon Press, 1998) 243–46. On the relation of this composition to *Sefer ha-Milhamah* of Cave 4, see B. Nitzan, "Benedictions and Instructions for the Eschatological Community (11QBer; 4Q285)," *RQ* 16 (1993) 77–90; Abegg, "Messianic Hope and 4Q285"; E. J. C. Tigchelaar, "Working with Few Data: The Relation between 4Q285 and 11Q14," *DSD* 7 (2000) 49–56.

33 See García Martínez, Tigchelaar, and van der Woude, *Qumran Cave 11, II*, 245–46. It is interesting that 11Q14 frg. 2 is based on Deut 32:6, as also Sir 50:26. On the pesher in Sir 50:26, see the discussion at the end of the chapter five.

mentioned only in the commentary to Isa 10:34. I therefore propose that the *Pesher on Isaiah* A was using *Sefer ha-Milhamah* as its source. In the second column of the *Pesher on Isaiah* A the commentary that hints to the events of 103–102 is found (discussed in chapter four). In the third column of this pesher one reads:[34]

6. ... "and the th]ickets of [the forest will be cut down] with an axe, and Lebanon together with the might one
7. will fall." ... They are the] Kittim, who will fa[ll] by the hand of Israel. And the poor ones of
8. [Judah will judge] all the nations, and the warriors will be filled with terror, and [their] cour[age] will dissolve
9. ... "and those who are lofty] in stature will be cut off." They are the warriors of the Kitt[im]
10. [who . . .] "And the thickets of [the] forest will be cut down with an axe." Th[ey are]
11. [. . .] for the battle of the Kittim. "And Lebanon together with the mi[ghty one]
12. [will fall." They are the] Kittim, who will be gi[ven] into the hand of his great ones. [. . .]
13. [. . .] when he flees befo[re Is]rael. [. . .]

In light of the link between the two columns of the *Pesher on Isaiah* A, I believe that the Kittim should be identified in this context as the Greeks. The *Pesher on Isaiah* A was most likely composed at the beginning of the first century B.C.E. (between 103 B.C.E. and 88 B.C.E., see the discussion in chapter four), when it was still reasonable for the author and his audience to associate the Kittim with the Hellenistic Kingdoms, in the hope that they would be defeated by Israel.

In the present review of the numerous references to the Kittim, their identification has ranged from the Hellenistic kingdoms in 1 Maccabees, 4Q247, the *War Scroll*, and the *Pesher on Isaiah* A,[35] to the Romans in two other pesharim found at Qumran.[36]

34 M. P. Horgan, *Pesharim: Qumran Interpretations of Biblical Books* (CBQ Monograph Series, 8; Washington DC: The Catholic Biblical Association of America, 1979) 75–76.

35 Some scholars suggest to reconstruct Kittim in 1QpPs (1Q16), frg. 9, lines 2, 4 as well; see Horgan, *Pesharim*, 67. This pesher is very fragmentary and does not allow us to draw any further conclusions about the Kittim from it.

36 Hartmut Stegemann was the first to suggest that the Kittim in the earlier Essene works

In the *Pesher on Habakkuk* from Cave 1, the Kittim are mentioned nine times and two additional times in reconstructions.[37] In this pesher the title "the rulers of the Kittim" can be found (4:5, 10), rather than the king of the Kittim as in 4Q247 and the *War Scroll*. In this pesher, therefore, the Kittim are clearly associated with the imperialism of the Romans. [38]

There is additional support for this Roman link in the *Pesher on Habakkuk* (1QpHab 6:1–5), where worship of standards attributed to the Roman army is cited.[39]

1. the Kittim, and they increase their wealth with all their booty
2. like the fish of the sea. And when it says, "Therefore he sacrifices to his net
3. and burns incense to his seine," the interpretation of it is that they
4. sacrifice to their standards, and their military arms are
5. the objects of their reverence ...

The *Pesher on Habakkuk* clearly referred to the conquering of Judaea by Pompey, in 9:4–7:[40]

4. *vacat* The interpretation of it concerns the last priests of Jerusalem,
5. who amass wealth and profit from the plunder of the peoples;
6. but at the end of days their wealth together with their booty will be given into the hand of
7. the army of the Kittim ...

---

were identified as the Seleucids and Ptolemies, but that in the *Pesher on Nahum* and the *Pesher on Habakkuk* they are the Romans; see H. Stegemann, *The Library of Qumran* (Grand Rapids: Eerdmans, 1998) 131.

37 The Kittim are mentioned in 1QpHab 2: 12, 14, [17]; 3: 4, 9, [15]; 4: 5, 10; 6: 1, 10; 9: 7. On the nature of the *Pesher on Habakkuk*; see H. Eshel, "The Two Historical Layers of Pesher Habakkuk," *Zion* 71 (2006) 143–52 (Hebrew).

38 See R. Goossens, "Les Kittim du Commentaire d'Habacuc," *La Nouvelle Clio* 4 (1952) 155–61. In light of these pesharim, some scholars identified the Kittim with the Romans in all the Scrolls; see G. J. Brooke, "The Kittim in the Qumran Pesharim," in *Images of Empire* (ed. L. Alexander; JSOTSup 122; Sheffield: Sheffield Academic Press, 1991) 135–59; P. S. Alexander, "The Evil Empire: The Qumran Eschatological War Cycle and the Origins of Jewish Opposition to Rome," in *Emanuel: Studies in Hebrew Bible, Septuagint and Dead Sea Scrolls in Honor of Emanuel Tov* (eds. S. M. Paul, R. A. Kraft, L. H. Schiffman, and W. W. Fields; VTSup 94; Leiden and Boston: Brill, 2003) 17–31.

39 See Horgan, *Pesharim*, 15–16.

40 Ibid., 18.

The Kittim mentioned in Pesher Nahum should also be identified with the Romans. At the beginning of col. 1 of the main surviving column (frgs. 3–4), which was discussed in chapter six,[41] there is a contrast between "the kings of Greece" and "the rulers of the Kittim:"[42]

1. [The interpretation of it concerns Jerusalem, which has become] a dwelling for the wicked ones of the nations. "Where the lion went to enter, the lion's cub
2. and no one to disturb." The interpretation of it concerns Demetrius, King of Greece, who sought to enter Jerusalem on the advice of the Seekers-After-Smooth-Things,
3. [but God did not give Jerusalem] into the power of the kings of Greece from Antiochus until the rise of the rulers of the Kittim; but afterwards [the city] will be trampled
4. [and will be given into the hands of rulers of the Kittim

The author of the *Pesher on Nahum* emphasized that although various invasions of Seleucid and Ptolemaic kings were launched to conquer Jerusalem, Jerusalem was not conquered by any Hellenistic king from the time of Antiochus (probably Antiochus IV, see the discussion in chapter six) until Pompey's conquest. In contrast to other excerpts mentioned above, in both the *Pesher on Habakkuk* and the *Pesher on Nahum* there is no reference to the fall of the Kittim. The best explanation for such a difference is to recognize that it reflects a change over time in the views of the Qumran community from the early compositions in which the Kittim are associated with the Hellenistic kingdoms in general, and the Seleucids in particular, to the beginning of the second third of the first century B.C.E., perhaps a little before the conquest of Judaea by Pompey, and definitely after this event, in which they associated the Kittim with the Romans.[43]

This does not refer to a new invasion of the first century B.C.E., since this was already declared in Daniel 11. The shift in the identification of the Kittim was not a simple change, because the Qumran community believed that they learned the true way to interpret the words of the prophets from the Teacher

41 Some scholars suggest reconstructing Kittim in frgs. 1 and 2 of 4QpNah as well; see Horgan, *Pesharim*, 162 . This column is fragmentary. Nevertheless, it seems that this pesher refers to the Roman conquest of Judaea as well.

42 Horgan, *Pesharim*, 163.

43 See Stegemann, *The Library*, 131.

of Righteousness, who learned it from God Himself. In 1QpHab Column 2 one reads:[44]

5. The interpretation of the passage [concerns the trai]tors at the End of

6. Days. They are the ruthless [ones of the coven]ant who will not believe

7. when they hear all that is going to co[me up]on the last generation from the mouth of

8. the priest into [whose heart] God put [understandi]ng to interpret all

9. the words of His servants the prophets . . .

And in 1QpHab Column 7 there is the following:[45]

3.   And when it says, "so that he can run who reads it,"

4. The interpretation of it concerns the Teacher of Righteousness, to whom God made known

5. all the mysteries of the words of His servants the prophets. . .

As part of the argument between Jeremiah and Hananiah son of Azzur, the prophet from Gibeon, concerning the date of the return of Jehoiakim's exile to Judah, Jeremiah made the following pronouncement:

> But just listen to this word which I address to you and to all the people: The prophets who lived before you and me from ancient times prophesied war, disaster, and pestilence against many lands and great kingdoms. So if a prophet prophesies good fortune, then only when the word of the prophet comes true can it be known that the Lord really sent him (Jer 28:7–9).

According to this, a prophet who prophesied a calamity which did not occur need not necessarily be a false prophet, for it could still be possible for the prophet's audience to repent, resulting in a change to their fate. In contrast, a prophet who prophesied peace, or who utters a consolation prophecy, would certainly be a false prophet should his prophecy not be realied. In other words,

---

44 Horgan, *Pesharim*, 13.
45 Horgan, *Pesharim*, 16.

it is the prophet who prophesies an unfulfilled prophecy of peace who is the prophet described in Deut 18:20–22:

> "But any prophet who presumes to speak in My name an oracle that I did not command him to utter, or who speaks in the name of other gods—that prophet shall die." And should you ask yourselves, "How can we know that the oracle was not spoken by the Lord?"—if the prophet speaks in the name of the Lords and the oracle does not come true, that oracle was not spoken by the Lord; the prophet has uttered it presumptuously: do not stand in dread of him.

As an integral element in Balaam's prophecy, the identification of the Kittim was crucial to determining the time of the redemption. Those who thought the Kittim to be the Seleucids, assumed that salvation was near, and it would have been difficult for them to admit that this identification was wrong. We contend that a hint of this problem may be found in one of the scrolls from cave four, a scroll which apparently was ascribed to Moses (4Q375). Column 1 of the scroll reads:[46]

1. [all] that]thy God will command thee by the mouth of the prophet, and thou shalt keep
2. [all] these [sta]tutes, and thou shalt return unto the Lord thy God with all
3. [thy heart and with al]l thy soul and [or: then] thy God will turn from the fury of His great anger
4. [so as to save th]ee from thy distresses. But the prophet who rises up and preaches among thee
5. [apostasy so as to make] thee turn away from thy God he shall be put to death. But, if there stands up the tribe
6. [which] he comes from, and says "Let him not be put to death, for he is truthful, a
7. [fai]thful prophet is he," then thou shalt come, with that tribe and thy elders and thy judges,
8. [t]o the place which thy God shall choose among one of [sc. the territories of] thy tribes, into the presence of

---

46 J. Strugnell, "375. 4QApocryphon of Moses[a]," in *Qumran Cave 4, XIV: Parabiblical Texts, II* (ed. M. Broshi, et al.; DJD 19; Oxford: Clarendon Press, 1995) 113–15.

9. [the] anointed priest, upon whose head will be poured the oil of anointing

The rest of this text is missing, but it seems that this was followed by laws pertaining to a ritual absolving a prophet who was known to be righteous by his tribe. The author of this text stresses that the prophet should not be executed, since he is "a faithful prophet." Scholars have noted the biblical passages which are used in this text, but the idea that the tribe of a prophet can testify to his faithfulness in order to prevent his execution has no precedence in the Hebrew Bible.[47] Although the scroll in discussion has a clear legalistic orientation, it seems that this law resulted from its authors' awareness that the messianic expectations of the sect had not been fulfilled as had been predicted in the pesharim.[48]

In any case, even if there is no connection between the laws in 4Q375 and the fact that at first the sectarians identified the Kittim as the Seleucids and later as the Romans, there is still no doubt that this shift in identification must have posed a serious theological problem for the members of the Qumran sect.

It seems that the leaders of the Qumran sect stopped composing new pesharim before 31 B.C.E. This year was an especially turbulent one in the history of the Roman Empire in general, and of Judaea in particular. In this year Herod defeated the Nabateans in a battle near Philadelphia (Amman), a severe earthquake destroyed many settlements in the Land of Israel (including Qumran), Octavianus defeated Mark Antony in the battle of Actium and following this victory adopted the name Augustus, Mark Antony and Cleopatra VII committed suicide, and Herod executed Hyrcanus II, the son of Alexander Jannaeus.[49] There is no doubt that in the eyes of a group with such high messianic

47 For discussion of this text, see idem., "Moses-Pseudepigrapha at Qumran: 4Q375, 4Q376, and Similar Works," in *Archaeology and History in the Dead Sea Scrolls* (ed. L. H. Schiffman; JSPSup 8; Sheffield: Sheffield Academic Press, 1990) 221–56; G. Brin, *Studies in Biblical Law: From the Bible to the Dead Sea Scrolls* (Sheffield: JSOT Press, 1994) 128–64; A. Shemesh, "Law and Prophecy: A False Prophet and an Inciting Elder," in *Renewing Jewish Commitment: the Work and Thought of David Hartman* (2 vols.; ed. A. Sagi and Z. Zohar; Tel Aviv: Hakibbutz Hameuchad, 2001) 2.938–41 (Hebrew).

48 Gershon Brin, although not a historian but a biblical scholar, wrote that "the historical background of this law may be as follows: the prophet symbolizes one of the leaders of the sect … who was defined by the official leadership in Jerusalem as a false prophet" (Studies *in Biblical Law*, 163).

49 See *J.W.* 1.364–92; *Ant.* 15.108–201; W. W. Tran and M. P. Charlesworth, "The Actium Campaign," in *The Augustan Empire, 44 B.C.– A.D. 70, The Cambridge Ancient History* (12 vols.; ed.

expectations like the one residing at Qumran, these events would have been considered as sure signs that the Day of the Redemption was drawing near. The fact that we do not find any references to these events in the pesharim found at Qumran, testifies that at some point, before 31 B.C.E., the leaders of the Qumran sect stopped composing new pesharim. The *Pesher on Nahum* was composed after the conquest of Judaea by Pompey, so that one can date the decision to stop composing new pesharim to some time between 63 and 31 B.C.E. It may be that this very problem in identifying the Kittim was one of the reasons why no pesharim relating to the events that occurred after the mid-first century B.C.E. were found.[50] Since it is far more difficult to amend or explain away a written text, the leaders of the Qumran sect probably decided to restrict their activity to oral interpretations.

S. A. Cook, F. E. Adcock, and M. P. Charlesworth, Cambridge: Cambridge University Press, 1979) 10.100–11.

50 Gregory Doudna suggested that since the Qumran scrolls bear no reference to events later than the mid-first century B.C.E., it follows that the scrolls were already hidden in the caves by 40 B.C.E.; see G. L. Doudna, *4QPesher Nahum: A Critical Edition* (JSPsup, 55; Sheffield: Sheffield Academic Press, 2001) 683–705. For many reasons, including Radiocarbon tests, this hypothesis cannot be accepted.

Afterword

The subjective editorial stance which Josephus Flavius adopts in his historical writings on the Hasmonean state, and especially the details of the conflicts within the Hasmonean family, are profoundly disconcerting to the scholarly reader. As an author he seemed to take special pleasure in highlighting the dysfunctional infighting of the internally quarrelsome Hasmoneans.

Josephus wrote that John Hyrcanus despised his son Alexander Jannaeus from the moment of his birth, and sent him away from Jerusalem to grow up in the Galilee. The account goes on to stress that John Hyrcanus died without ever meeting his son Alexander Jannaeus (*Ant.* 13.321). Josephus describes another of John Hyrcanus' sons, Aristobulus who locked up his three brothers in handcuffs, and starved his mother to death (*J.W.* 1.71; *Ant.* 13.307–10). Further, Aristobulus went on to execute his brother Antigonus (*J.W.* 1.72–74; *Ant.* 13.307–10). In another account, Josephus also reports that Alexander Jannaeus had one of his brothers executed because of his reluctance to deal with state affairs (*J.W.* 1.85; *Ant.* 13.323). Another entry details how while Salamzion lay dying her son Aristobulus II tried to usurp the kingship (*J.W.* 1.117–19; *Ant.* 13.422–29). Josephus then elaborates on how the inner struggle between the sons of Alexander Jannaeus, Aristobulus II, and Hyrcanus II influenced Pompey to conquer Judaea (*Ant.* 14.77). A final horrifying example is the description of Mattathias Antigonus, the last Hasmonean ruler (40–37 B.C.E.), who, with his own teeth, ripped his uncle Hyrcanus II's ear in order to disqualify him from serving as High Priest (*J.W.* 1.270; *Ant.* 14.366).[1]

---

1   For the last episode, see H. Eshel, "An Allusion in the Parables of Enoch to the Acts

It is generally accepted that Josephus learned these tales from Nicolaus of Damascus, Herod's scribe, who was hostile to the Hasmoneans. It should therefore be assumed that Nicolaus intensified the accounts of the conflicts within the Hasmonean family in order to tarnish the image of the Hasmonean rulers and their dynasty. Since the only detailed accounts we have of the Hasmonean state are those written by Josephus, himself relying on Nicolaus, it is difficult to determine which details are reliable and which were fabricated by Nicolaus. One goal of this book has been to collect the historical allusions pertaining to the political history of the Hasmonean period as documented in the Dead Sea Scrolls in order to see if the details mentioned in Josephus' accounts can be verified.

This study began with a discussion of the events in Judaea and Jerusalem during the years 170-167 B.C.E., which led to the Hasmonean revolt. There are a considerable number of complementary accounts available about these turbulent events. They are documented in 1 Maccabees, 2 Maccabees, the Book of Daniel, and in the writings of Josephus. In one of the non-sectarian scrolls found in Cave 4 (4Q248), a composition which was probably one of the sources for the Book of Daniel is documented. This text relates Antiochus IV's journey to Jerusalem after his first invasion of Egypt but prior to his return from the second invasion to Egypt. It raises two possibilities: either Antiochus came to Jerusalem only once, a visit which took place between the two invasions, or he came to Jerusalem twice, once after his first invasion of Egypt and the second time after his second invasion. The main significance of 4Q248, however, lies in its description of the messianic expectations in Jerusalem in 168 B.C.E., during Antiochus IV's second campaign to Egypt. It is conceivable that one ought to situate the formation of the group later joined by the "Teacher of Righteousness" as being in the wake of these messianic expectations. In another scroll, 4Q390, there are harsh criticisms of the Hellenized priests who served in Jerusalem during the seventies and sixties of the second century B.C.E. This composition also includes complaints against the Hasmoneans, who had ruled Judaea since 152 B.C.E.

In chapter two we considered a variety of sources that lead to the identification of the political leader labeled in the scrolls as the "Wicked Priest" as Jonathan, the son of Mattathias, who served as High Priest between 152–143 B.C.E. Based on this hypothesis, I have concluded that both the "Teacher of

---

of Matthias Antigonus in 40 B.C.E.?" in *Enoch and the Messiah Son of Man: Revisiting the Book of Parables* (ed. G. Boccaccini; Grand Rapids and Cambridge: Eerdmans, 2007) 487–91.

Righteousness," the leader of the Qumran sect, and the "Man of the Lie" who was the leader of the Pharisees, were contemporaries of the "Wicked Priest" and lived in the mid-second century B.C.E. In chapter two I also discussed the possibility that the legal letter named MMT should be identified with the "Law and the Torah" mentioned in the *Pesher on Psalms* A and that the Qumran sectarians considered MMT to be an epistle which the "Teacher of Righteousness" had sent to the "Wicked Priest." Building on these points, I further suggested that the beginning of the "Wicked Priest's" time of service, before his arrogance and rebellion against God grew, is the period during which Jonathan, son of Mattathias, began his political activity while residing in Michmash, northeast of Jerusalem (1 Macc 9:73), or immediately after he was appointed as high priest in 152 B.C.E. The data presented in chapter two attests that the members of the sect believed that there was a chance that once Jonathan would be appointed high priest he would accept the strict priestly legal system. Jonathan, however, decided to adopt the Pharisaic Halakhah, which lead to the outbreak of the conflict between his own supporters and the "Teacher of Righteousness" and his followers. This struggle reached its peak when Jonathan tried to execute the "Teacher of Righteousness." Several pesharim state the sectarians' view that it was Jonathan's attempt to harm the "Teacher of Righteousness" that led to his own demise, when Tryphon captured and killed him, and chose to desecrate his corpse. Although it is difficult to determine when the "Teacher of Righteousness" died, I contend that his passing away caused a crisis among his followers. It was resolved by claiming that salvation would be delayed until all those who betrayed the "Teacher of Righteousness" would be dead.

I have not found any references in the scrolls that can be associated with the period of Simeon, son of Mattathias (143–134 B.C.E.), who seized power after his brother Jonathan was murdered. I did, however, find a reference to his son, John Hyrcanus. In chapter three I discussed a contemporizing exegesis of Josh 6:26 documented in two scrolls found at Qumran. This exegesis claims that Joshua's curse on the builder of Jericho was applied to John Hyrcanus who built his winter palace and the Hasmonean estate in Jericho, and on his two sons, Antigonus and Aristobulus, who died in 104 B.C.E. under what seemed to be unnatural circumstances. According to Josephus, Aristobulus killed Antigonus and died of an unspecified illness shortly after. Josephus relates that John Hyrcanus' followers awarded him the three crowns: priesthood, kingship, and prophecy. This contemporizing exegesis (or pesher) on Joshua's curse on the builder of Jericho is documented in the bottom paragraph of the four sections of 4QTest. The first paragraph quotes verses documenting God's promise to

183

send a true prophet to the people of Israel; the second quotes verses taken from Balaam's oracles, describing the ideal ruler; the third includes Moses' blessing of Levi, one which describes the ideal priest; and the last paragraph contains the pesher on Josh 6:26. I framed this section as a part of the Qumran sect's polemic against the followers of John Hyrcanus. In contrast to the followers of John Hyrcanus, the author of 4QTest denies that this Hasmonean ruler resembled the true prophet promised to the People of Israel in Sinai, and instead argued that he was neither the ideal prophet about which Balaam had prophesied, nor the ideal priest described in Moses' blessing. For this author, the definitive proof that John Hyrcanus' followers were wrong in regarding him as the ideal leader lay in the fulfillment of Joshua's curse of the builder of Jericho—the death of his two sons in a short period of time. In light of this reading, I believe that John Hyrcanus should be identified as the "Man of Belial" in the pesher on Josh 6:26. The author of this pesher alluded to the death of Antigonus and Aristobulus, the two sons of John Hyrcanus in 104 B.C.E. in order to anchor his pesher.

The *Pesher on Isaiah* A hinted to the events of 103–102 B.C.E., when Alexander Jannaeus was appointed king after the death of his two brothers as discussed in chapter four. According to Josephus, Alexander tried to conquer Acre immediately after his rise to the throne. The people of Acre turned for help to Ptolemy Lathyrus who was then the ruler of Cyprus. Ptolemy was not on good terms with his mother, Cleopatra III, and his brother, Alexander I, who jointly ruled Egypt. Deciding to take on Acre's cause, Ptolemy Lathyrus sailed from Cyprus to Shiqmona, south of Acre, conquered several cities in the Galilee, and defeated Alexander Jannaeus by the Jordan River. Inspired by that battle, he invaded Judaea and advanced towards Jerusalem. Fortunately for Alexander Jannaeus, Cleopatra III and her son, Alexander I, decided to intervene against their son and brother by landing at Acre. Ptolemy abruptly ended his campaign in Judaea, without conquering Jerusalem, and headed for Egypt. A similar sequence of events is described in a pesher on Isa 10:28–34 found in Cave 4 that has been fragmentarily preserved. The verses in Isaiah describe the approach to Jerusalem by the King of Assyria (Sennacherib) from the northeast. While he came near to his objective, he eventually failed to conquer Jerusalem. The *Pesher on Isaiah* A describes an enemy who came from the Vale of Acre, fought in Philistia, and reached the boundary of Jerusalem. I support Amusin's hypothesis which links Josephus' account of the events of 103 B.C.E. with this pesher.

In chapter five I discussed the *Prayer for the Welfare of King Jonathan*, which was composed by one of Alexander Jannaeus' supporters, and which also seems to be related to Judaea's invasion by Ptolemy Lathyrus. The prayer gives thanks to God for assisting King Jonathan on "the day of war," and was copied below a hymn which can be attributed variously to Hezekiah, King of Judaea, and to Isaiah, and supposedly composed during Sennacherib's siege on Jerusalem. Based on the pesher on Isaiah 10, I have suggested that the reason these two prayers were copied on the same scroll is that the authors of the pesharim associated Sennacherib's campaign to Jerusalem in 701 B.C.E. with Ptolemy Lathyrus' campaign to Judaea in 103 B.C.E. By reconciling these references, I believe that "the day of war" mentioned in the *Prayer for the Welfare of King Jonathan* is the day of Ptolemy's retreat from Judaea, when he turned away from Jerusalem to fight against Egypt.

Chapter six deals with Demetrius' invasion of Judaea in 88 B.C.E., and with Alexander Jannaeus' decision to execute the Pharisees who invited Demetrius to come to Judaea. The *Pesher on Nahum* mentions Demetrius by name, so it is widely agreed among Qumran scholars that Alexander Jannaeus should be identified with the "Lion of Wrath" mentioned in the *Pesher on Nahum*, a title which is also documented in the *Pesher on Hosea*. There are several clues indicating that the author of the *Pesher on Hosea* was also alluding to the events of 88 B.C.E., and that it was composed before the *Pesher on Nahum*. Following the publication of the *Temple Scroll*, Yadin proposed that Alexander Jannaeus was following the law written in it when he executed those who invited Demetrius to invade Judaea. As a result, several scholars who adopted Yadin's view assumed that the *Pesher on Nahum* does not criticize Alexander Jannaeus for his decision. Strangely enough, the *Pesher on Nahum* states that "regarding one hanged alive upon the tree it reads," yet fails to specify what ought to be read. However, the sentence seems to be an allusion to Deut 21:22–23, which describes that a corpse should not be left hanging overnight, since "the curse of God is hung." The author of the *Pesher on Nahum* decided not to quote the biblical verse, out of concern that his readers might misinterpret this phrase to mean that it is God who is cursed. It therefore seems that the author of the *Pesher on Nahum* accused Alexander Jannaeus of having left the corpses of those who invited Demetrius hung overnight. This assumption strengthens the view of scholars who assumed that the phrase "hung alive" refers to crucifixion. Crucifixion was a slow form of execution and usually the crucified were left on the cross for more than one day until they all died. Alexander Jannaeus probably believed that he was acting in accordance with the Law when he executed those who betrayed their people by delivering them into the hand of a "foreign nation." Yet while the author of the *Pesher on Nahum* would agree with him that those who invited Demetrius were deserving of capital punishment, he held that Alexander was wrong to crucify them and leave their corpses hung on the tree. According to the author of the *Pesher on Nahum*, following the law in Deuteronomy, Alexander Jannaeus should have buried those executed on the same day of their execution. Since he did not do so, the author noted that Alexander, under the epithet "Lion of Wrath," committed actions "which were never before done in Israel."

The Qumran scrolls provide some details on the history of Judaea after the death of Alexander Jannaeus. These are allusions to the events between 76 and 53 B.C.E., including those leading up to the conquest of Judaea by Pompey and the early years of Roman rule in Judaea. Chapter seven discusses texts relating to the famine in Judaea during the civil war between Aristobulus II and Hyrcanus II in 65 B.C.E., as well as texts mentioning Salamzion, Hyrcanus, and Aemilius (the Roman general whom Pompey appointed as the governor of Syria after the conquest of Judaea in 63 B.C.E.), as well as Potlais (who should probably be identified with Peitholaus, a Jewish officer who led a military unit of Jewish soldiers between 57 and 53 B.C.E. and is mentioned in Josephus' account). Most of these texts are so fragmentary that it is impossible to draw any substantial coherent historical data, but at the minimum it can be learned from them that on two different occasions Aemilius had his Jewish opponents executed.

Another scroll seems to allude to the murder of Pompey on the shore of Egypt in 48 B.C.E. Background for this event is not found in Josephus' account, but in other Roman historians who described how Pompey was murdered as he transferred from his ship to a boat which was supposed to take him to Pelusium. Following his murder, his assassins decapitated him and threw his body into the sea. A reference to this event apparently appears in a non-sectarian scroll, an apocryphal work based on the Book of Ezekiel (4Q386). It includes a prophecy that the wicked one who would scheme to oppress the People of Israel would be killed in Memphis. I suggest that the prophecy relates to the verses in Jer 46:13–16 which describe how Nebuchadnezzar failed in his attempt to conquer Egypt in 601 B.C.E.. These verses mention Memphis and including the following: "Why are your stalwarts swept away? They do not stand because the Lord thrust them down." The author of 4Q386 seems to have considered Jeremiah's prophecy to have been fulfilled (again) when the Son of Belial who conquered Judaea and annexed it to the Roman Empire, the man who desecrated the temple in Jerusalem, received his punishment when he was murdered and his body was washed up upon the shores of Egypt. The author apparently shared a similar view to the one expressed in the apocryphal *Psalms of Solomon*, which also describes how Pompey was punished when "His body was carried about on the waves in much shame, and there was no one to bury him."

In the last chapter I addressed the question of why there are no pesharim relating to the events in Judaea after the middle of the first century B.C.E. I tried to validate the hypothesis that this is due to the crisis of faith that the sectarian authors at Qumran faced, when they had originally identified the Kittim as the Seleucids and only later identified them as the Romans. This shift engendered a difficult theological problem for the authors who composed the pesharim, since they had claimed to have learned how to interpret prophecies from the "Teacher of Righteousness," who had been instructed by God Himself on how "to explain all the words of His servants the prophets." Therefore, it was very difficult for the authors of the pesharim to admit an erroneous identification of the enemy who was expected to torment the people of Israel at the End of Days. After the authors of the pesharim realized they were wrong about such a crucial issue, they apparently stopped writing down their pesharim. It may be that these authors continued to offer contemporizing interpretations of biblical verses, but restricted their activity to oral interpretations. The error of the identification of the Kittim may have also led to the legal ruling found in one of the scrolls according to which a prophet whose message of doom does not come to pass should be absolved if his community testifies that he is nevertheless righteous.

In this book I have tried to verify the hypothesis that the Qumran sectarians labeled Jonathan, the son of Mattathias, as the "Wicked Priest," his nephew John Hyrcanus as the "Man of Belial," and Alexander Jannaeus, the son of John Hyrcanus, as the "Lion of Wrath." On the following page is a genealogical chart of the Hasmonean dynasty with pertinent dates below those who were the leaders of the revolt and the Hasmonean state (all dates are B.C.E.):

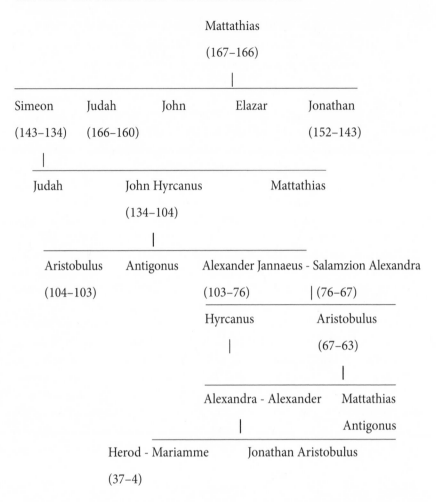

Mattathias

(167–166)

Simeon   Judah   John   Elazar   Jonathan

(143–134) (166–160)   (152–143)

Judah   John Hyrcanus   Mattathias

              (134–104)

Aristobulus   Antigonus   Alexander Jannaeus - Salamzion Alexandra

(104–103)   (103–76) | (76–67)

                           Hyrcanus   Aristobulus

                           | (67–63)

                           Alexandra - Alexander   Mattathias

                           | Antigonus

Herod - Mariamme   Jonathan Aristobulus

(37–4)

After the fall of Judas Maccabeus on the battlefield in 160 B.C.E., his brother Jonathan, son of Mattathias, became the leader of the rebels. In 152 B.C.E. he was appointed High Priest and ruled Judaea for a full decade, before being captured in Acre by Tryphon, who eventually had him executed in 143 B.C.E. John Hyrcanus became the ruler of Judaea after his father Simon, son of Mattathias, was assassinated in Jericho in 134 B.C.E. John Hyrcanus ruled Judaea for 31 years and died of natural causes in 104 B.C.E. His son, Alexander Jannaeus ruled Judaea for 28 years, between 103 and 76 B.C.E. The titles of the political figures mentioned in the pesharim such as the "Wicked Priest," "Man of Belial," and the "Lion of Wrath," refer to the three prominent figures in the history of the Hasmonean dynasty: the first Hasmonean High Priest, Jonathan (the "Wicked Priest"), and the two major rulers who ruled the Hasmonean state, John Hyrcanus ("Man of Belial") and his son Alexander Jannaeus ("Lion of Wrath").

The only Hasmonean who ruled for a considerable period and for whom I could not identify an epithet in the scrolls is Simeon, son of Mattathias. He was High Priest and ruler of Judaea for ten years, 143–134 B.C.E. It is possible that the reason that no sobriquet was found for him in the pesharim is due to their scarce number and their fragmentary state of preservation. There is no reason to assume that the sectarians of Qumran perceived Simeon any differently than they did his brother, son, and grandson.

The Dead Sea Scrolls have contributed immensely to the understanding of the Second Temple period. The Qumran scrolls have completely changed entire areas of study related to the religious history of the Second Temple period. The fields that have benefited from the discovery of the scrolls include textual criticism of the Hebrew Bible, ancient Jewish exegesis of the Bible, the study of the Apocrypha and Pseudepigrapha, the early history of Halakhah, the development of Jewish liturgy, and the linguistic study of Hebrew and Aramaic during the Second Temple period. In contrast, the contribution of the Dead Sea Scrolls towards the understanding of the political history of the Second Temple period is relatively marginal. Without Josephus' accounts, it would have been impossible to decipher the meaning of the historical allusions documented in the scrolls. When presented with allusions to events not documented by Josephus, such as the executions in the days of Marcus Aemilius Scaurus (discussed in chapter seven), it is practically impossible to understand their exact meaning. However, these allusions still bear significance, serving as evidence that some of the details provided by Josephus on the history of the Hasmonean state are in fact correct.

The events that took place in the mid-second century B.C.E. affected the course of all western history, as noted by Menahem Stern: "The Hasmonean revolt was in effect the only one of the many rebellions of the Jews under Graeco-Roman rule that ended in a Jewish victory, in the throwing-off the foreign yoke, and in the restoration of the independence of Judaea ... Those were the events that had saved the Jewish religion from extermination."[2] Based on the background of such dramatic events as the introduction of a statue of

2   See M. Stern, "The Hasmonean Revolt and Its Place in the History of Jewish Society and Religion," *Cahiers d'Histoire Mondiale* 11 (1968) 92–106.

Zeus into the Temple, the religious persecutions, the Hasmonean revolt, and Judaea's independence, messianic expectations rose high in different religious circles, encompassing large portions of the population living in Judaea. The moral crisis and the socio-economic gaps created in the Hasmonean state led to great disappointment, especially of the leadership. These developments are the background for the formation of a religious group which left Jerusalem and went to live in Qumran. Those who did so believed that they were living on the eve of the Day of God, and therefore renounced the quality of life they had enjoyed in Jerusalem and other towns of Judaea, settled in the desert, and shared their possessions while strictly observing the Law and learning the Torah. That decision is the reason the scrolls found in the Qumran caves were preserved. It is important, therefore, that we seek to understand their criticism of the Hasmonean rulers, and to try to extract from what remains of their writings any historical data that has been preserved.

Acknowledgments

We gratefully acknowledge permission granted by the publishers holding the rights to the copyrighted materials listed below to quote from their publications.

The Catholic Biblical Association of America, Washington DC
1502 words from pp. 13, 15–16, 18, 75–76, 88, 141,149, 163, 165, 195, 197 of
Maurya P. Horgan, *Pesharim: Qumran Interpretations of Biblical Books*,
© The Catholic Biblical Association of America, 1976.

Harvard University Press, Cambridge, Mass.
Reprinted by permission of the publishers and the Trustees of the Loeb Classical Library:
598 words from pp. 333–35, 43, 60–63, 74–75 of Josephus: II: The Jewish War, Loeb Classical Library, Vol. 210, translated by H. St. J. Thackeray, Cambridge, Mass.: Harvard University Press, © 1928, by the President and Fellows of Harvard College. The Loeb Classical Library ® is a registered trademark of the President and Fellows of Harvard College.
4443 words from pp. 343–47, 377–83, 385–87, 391–405, 413–19, 462–67, 486–91 of Josephus: VII: Jewish Antiquities, Loeb Classical Library, Vol. 365, translated by Ralph Marcus, Cambridge, Mass.: Harvard University Press, © 1943, by the President and Fellows of Harvard College.
The Loeb Classical Library ® is a registered trademark of the President and Fellows of Harvard College.

J.C.B. Mohr (Paul Siebeck), Tübingen

120 words from pp. 35–37, 41 of *The Princeton Dead Sea Scrolls Project: Hebrew, Aramaic, and Greek Texts with English translations,* edited by J.H. Charlesworth, vol. 1: *Rule of the Community and Related Documents,* © J.C.B. Mohr (Paul Siebeck), 1994.

753 words from pp. 13, 25–27, 29, 33–35, 37, 97 of *The Princeton Dead Sea Scrolls Project: Hebrew, Aramaic, and Greek Texts with English translations,* edited by J.H. Charlesworth, vol. 2: *Damascus Document, War Scroll, and Related Documents,* © J.C.B. Mohr (Paul Siebeck), 1995.

1692 words from pp. 13, 17, 19, 91, 93–95, 161–63, 169, 175–77, 179, 181–83 of *The Princeton Dead Sea Scrolls Project: Hebrew, Aramaic, and Greek Texts with English translations,* edited by J.H. Charlesworth, vol. 6b: *Pesharim, other Commentaries and Related Documents,* © J.C.B. Mohr (Paul Siebeck), 2002.

Oxford University Press, Oxford

260 words from pp. 256–58 of Yigael Yadin, *Scroll of the War of the Sons of Light against the Sons of Darkness,* © Oxford University Press, 1962.

352 words from p. 65 of *Discoveries in the Judaean Desert 4,* © Oxford University Press, 1993.

211 words from pp. 59, 63 of *Discoveries in the Judaean Desert 10,* © Oxford University Press, 1997.

235 words from pp. 419–23 of *Discoveries in the Judaean Desert 11,* © Oxford University Press, 2000.

218 words from pp. 78, 113–14 of *Discoveries in the Judaean Desert 19,* © Oxford University Press, 1998.

177 words from p. 280 of *Discoveries in the Judaean Desert 22,* © Oxford University Press, 2001.

604 words from pp. 238, 246, 386 of *Discoveries in the Judaean Desert 30,* © Oxford University Press, 2001.

489 words from pp. 189, 193, 239, 277–78, 283, 288, 410, 448 of *Discoveries in the Judaean Desert 36,* © Oxford University Press, 2000.

We also thank the institutions and photographers who hold the rights to the illustrations for permission to reproduce them. Full credit is given in the caption to each illustration.

INDEX OF ANCIENT NAMES

INDEX OF GEOGRAPHICAL NAMES

INDEX OF MODERN SCHOLARS